D1576971

The Prince
of Wales
(Highgate)
Quiz Book

The Prince of Wales (Highgate) Quiz Book

edited and compiled by

Marcus Berkmann

HODDER &
STOUGHTON

First published in Great Britain in 2006 by Hodder & Stoughton
A division of Hodder Headline

A Hodder & Stoughton Book

1

A CIP catalogue record for this title is available from the British Library

ISBN 978 0 340 93283 2
ISBN 0 340 93283 0

Typeset in Gill Sans by M Rules

Printed and bound by
Clays Ltd, St Ives plc

Hodder Headline's policy is to use papers that are natural, renewable
and recyclable products and made from wood grown in sustainable forests.
The logging and manufacturing processes are expected to conform to
the environmental regulations of the country of origin.

Hodder & Stoughton Ltd
A division of Hodder Headline
338 Euston Road
London NW1 3BH

CONTENTS

INTRODUCTION

Nobody really has a clue where or when the pub quiz came into being. Cricket has its Hambledon, rugby has its William Webb Ellis, but the origins of our little pastime are wholly mysterious. We can only imagine it. Picture a quiet pub, maybe thirty years ago, on a Tuesday evening, with after-work drinkers lingering and the more serious topers just arriving for their daily skinful. A man, an ordinary man, albeit one who knows the chemical symbol for potassium, idly fiddles with a microphone, which just happens to be plugged into an amplifier. And without knowing what he is doing or what he is letting himself in for, this man finds himself switching on the microphone, clearing his throat and saying, for reasons he cannot begin to understand, 'OK . . . round one, question one . . . and here's a nice easy one to start.' And people look at him strangely, and ask him whether he has pens and answer sheets. And after it's all over, and the winning team have collected their ten pounds fifty, everyone says, shall we do this again next week? Yes, let's. The pub quiz is born.

These days, of course, the pub quiz is big business. Well, not Microsoft exactly, but it certainly boosts takings for thousands of pubs every week on what used to be their quiet night. Drab rainy Sundays, Mondays and Tuesdays: these are the natural home of the pub quiz, competing only with vital Division 2 football matches and the odd karaoke evening for the drinker's attention. It's a modest entertainment but also a strangely addictive one. I know too many people who have wandered into the Prince of Wales in Highgate on a Tuesday evening and found themselves coming back week after week, year after year, drawn by who knows what. The camaraderie? The chance to win less money than they spend on crisps? It may be that our expectations of a pub quiz are so catastrophically low that when it turns out to be rather enjoyable we are taken by surprise. But if your mind is of a type that retains absurd pieces of trivial information, then a pub quiz was always where you were going to end up, whether you wanted to or not. Don't fight it; there's no point.

Everyone needs to play from time to time. 'All work and no play makes Jack a dull boy', as our parents used to say when they wanted us to go away and leave them alone. Adult life becomes so unforgiving, so weighed down with responsibility, that we are apt to forget our need to play, and show off, and behave like small children. This is where the pub quiz comes into its own. It provides hard-fought competition that manages to be both deadly serious and completely meaningless. It offers us opportunities to demonstrate obscure knowledge to our friends and gain their undying respect. We can also throw tantrums, argue with the questionmaster and drink lots of nice nourishing beer. If there's a better recipe for staying sane I don't know what it is.

My own quizzing history starts in the early 1990s in central London, at a pub called the Cock Tavern on Great Portland Street. The landlord, a weary Scotsman known to all as Billy Quiz, ran an early evening Monday quiz, which later experience told me was compiled mainly from quiz books, as it featured all the old favourites: phobias, currencies, American state capitals, flags of the world, 1960s hit singles, real names of long dead movie stars, the periodic table of elements. But I was instantly hooked. It probably helped that the rest of my team were comedy writers, who knew a vast amount (so we usually won) and were thoroughly bitter and twisted (and so very entertaining). Billy Quiz moved on in 1992 and the Cock Tavern quiz came to an end. We looked around for another central London quiz, but in vain, so I turned my attention instead to the pubs of north London, near where I lived. After brief reconnaissance my friends and I settled on an old man's pub in Highgate called the Wrestlers, whose continued existence we could only ascribe to accounting error. At the bar sat silent pensioners who could make a half of lager last as long as my childhood. A tape of Tom Petty and the Heartbreakers' *Full Moon Fever* played over and over again. Just about the only thing the pub had going for it, in fact, was Chris and Barry's quiz, which came to define Monday nights for us for the next year and a half.

Eventually, though, the Wrestlers too experienced regime change, and was refurbished to appeal to estate agents. This time we moved just up the road to the Prince of Wales, where we remain to this day. It's a strange little pub, small and modestly proportioned for the eighteenth-century travellers who once stopped there for a pint of Kronenbourg and a delicious Thai meal. In the summer it's an oven, and in the winter the two gas fires are switched on and it's an oven. The PA system – an old amplifier plugged into the wall – deafens those right next to the quizmaster's table and is inaudible round the corner twenty feet away. If there are more than seven teams there it's standing room only and the non-quizzing regulars moan and mutter under their beery breath. But for some reason we all love the pub and cherish its every eccentricity. Team members have come and gone, and I am still there and so is Chris, the quizmaster from the Wrestlers, who has become one of my closest friends. Each of us has been going to the Prince of Wales every week since late 1993. We both started setting quizzes there in 1997 and, between us, have been informally running the thing since 2002. You might as well try and escape from Alcatraz.

What makes the Prince of Wales unusual, and this book possible, is that the regulars set the quizzes there. Most pub quizzes are bought in from outside suppliers. They are often very good, having been carefully compiled and checked by professional questionsetters, but they tend to lack flavour. Prince of Wales quizzes can lack many things – consistency, fairness, questions about science – but they are always highly distinctive, reflecting as they do the knowledge and eccentricities of the men and women who set them. Over the years, I have to admit, this has produced some truly appalling quizzes. One occasional setter knew almost all there was to know about art history, and could not believe that everyone else did not know the same things. When team after team were scoring no points a round, he thought it was their fault rather than his own. Another occasional set a majority of questions on rugby league, science fiction and PhD-level physics, and then wondered why half the teams were leaving before the end. At times it has seemed that the quiz could not survive. It is, after all, a very small pub, with only eleven tables. With fifteen teams it's impossible to breathe. With three teams, tumbleweed blows through the bar and every cough seems like a reproach. One week there were just four teams and I remember feeling desperately sorry for the occasionals who were setting that day. Then they announced that they had a theme for every round, and the third round would be about – wait for it – Bulbs and Batteries. So boring were these ten questions that by the end of them I was laughing hysterically with relief that there were only four teams to hear them. To this day, dull questions are invariably greeted by murmurs of 'Bulbs and Batteries'. Those of us on the four teams who survived that round formed an unbreakable bond that day.

But just as the teams compete furiously every week to win

the quiz, so they compete when they are setting the quiz to set the best and most imaginative quiz. Standards have definitely risen. And as the reputation of the quiz has improved, so other good teams have fetched up and joined in. The astounding thing is how hard everyone works on their quizzes. None of them are being paid, unless you count the £15 of free drinks the quizmaster traditionally receives (it's so traditional that this amount has risen by not a single penny in fifteen years). Many of us have time-consuming jobs at which we toil for often abject sums of money, and yet we happily spend substantial chunks of our free time trying to think up questions that no one has thought up before. (If someone has thought them up before, we weren't there that evening.) Setting quiz questions, it turns out, is every bit as addictive as answering the damn things. Once your mind has started thinking along those lines, you realise that a part of you is now forever on the lookout for the killer question. You read newspapers and listen to Radio 4 in a different way, like a predator, ready to pounce on a stray fact. You even scour other quizzes, in newspapers and magazines, for questions you can enhance and shape to your own needs. Having a toe in both camps, I have come to realise that writing quiz questions is a little like writing jokes. It's a craft, which depends on precision and clarity, and at first glance it seems very limited in scope: how many possible quiz questions are there in the world? I remember, as a child, wondering how the supply of new jokes never seemed to end, and not realising until I was writing for a living that nearly all humour depended on apparently infinite variations on a relatively small number of themes. It's a matter of constantly renewing old ideas, of making the familiar fresh. So it is with quiz questions. If you are asked what school James Bond went to, you may not know the answer. Next time you are asked it, though, you may know the answer, and by the fourth time you will be writing down 'Eton' before they have finished reading out the question. How much more fun it would be to have the same fact teased out of you by a slightly more elliptic question. 'What do James Bond, Bertie Wooster and Captain Hook have in common?' You could throw David Cameron in there too if you want. (His parents certainly did.)

This may imply that a Prince of Wales audience is unusually tricky and demanding, and when the quiz is below par that's a perfect description of them. One of the hazards of trying to write as interesting a quiz as possible is that you make it too hard, and we have all done that at one point or another. 'Enjoyed the quiz,' people say afterwards, without obvious signs of pleasure. 'Very challenging.' Curiously the Prince of Wales Quiz has acquired a reputation for being the hardest in London, possibly even the hardest in the country. If that were true it wouldn't last a fortnight. Quizmasters would walk in fear of their lives. By contrast, no one complains when the quiz is too easy. Unless it's dull, and then you can hear the snuffles and wheezes of disappointment from all around. If you asked, for instance, what the seven wonders of the ancient world were (for a point each), a vast 9-tog duvet of boredom would envelop the pub. Similarly, which Hollywood film star was born Marion Morrison? What is the chemical symbol of potassium? They are not intrinsically bad questions, but they are like jokes we have heard far too many times. Not funny any more.

When I asked all the contributors to this book what they felt constituted a good or a bad question, they all answered in much the same way. The worst sort of question is one designed to show how clever the questionmaster is, which by implication is cleverer than anyone else in the room. If you ever forget that your primary role is to entertain, you are sunk. My rule of thumb is that, in a quiz of forty-five or so questions, I am allowed one or, at most, two that no one might know the answer to. Any more than that and I have cocked up. A string of questions that no one could possibly get right . . . well, that's essentially a waste of everyone's time. As it happens, at the heart of almost every terrible question, there is the kernel of a decent one. One I have never forgotten (and this was at least ten years ago, rage having no statute of limitations) was as follows: 'Marie Stopes, the birth control pioneer. What was the title of her only play?' Answer: *Our Ostriches*. Now, how are you going to know that? Only if you have been to a quiz and been asked such a stupid question before and never forgotten it because it made you so angry. Turn it round, though, and it's perfectly respectable. *Our Ostriches* (1923) was the only play written by which English birth-control pioneer and social reformer? Quite nice, because although you didn't know the fact before, you would still get the question right, and be pleased to have done. Sometimes I have been marking the answer sheets and everybody has got one right, and I have thought, too easy. Then I read the answer out and everybody cheers. So they had to think about it before finally working out the correct answer. That's a successful question.

A rotten question is one no one knows the answer to and no one wants to know the answer to. Good questions, on the other hand, come in many different forms, and I am hoping that you will find more of the latter than the former in the quizzes that follow. A word about the format. The essential structure of a Prince of Wales quiz has remained unchanged since antiquity. Entry fee is a pound per person, and teams can contain no more than six members. There are four rounds in the main quiz, of ten questions each. Generally it's two points per question, unless otherwise stated, but few questionmasters can resist the occasional multiple question (name the seven wonders of the ancient world), and these usually offer a point per answer. Most rounds are made up of a miscellany of questions, without any overarching theme. Occasionally a questionmaster does announce a theme for a round, and very occasionally there is an underlying one that he or she does not mention at all, and you have to find it out for yourselves. Between rounds two and three is the bonus round: this is unconnected to the main quiz, and usually consists of five questions and a numerical tie-breaker. The prize for this is a £10 beer voucher, another tradition that has remained unchanged across the decades, despite beer doubling in price in the meantime. The bonus round almost always has a theme, so assume it has unless told otherwise. After the four main rounds the scores are totted up and the top three teams win half of the money, a third of it and a sixth of it respectively. We keep wondering whether to raise the fee per person to £2 to bump up the pot a bit, but have yet to get round to it. Then it's time for the snowball . . . of which more later.

The quizzes that follow are the work of ten different setters, or teams of setters. This leaves out one or two of the regular setters, who may no longer be speaking to me, but I wanted everyone here to be represented by at least two quizzes, and also wanted a mix of ages, interests and experience. Chris and John (not the same Chris) have been coming to the quiz since 1990, while the Woans and Simon are recent recruits. If there is a second Prince of Wales (Highgate) Quiz Book, it will have a slightly different mix of questionsetters, and with a bit of luck, a few new questions. None of the quizzes printed here is exactly the same as the quiz that was read out in the pub. In editing them, I have removed a lot of the topical questions, many questions whose answers no longer apply, a few which were never correct in the first place, some dull ones and many repetitions. It is a curious thing that so many people can ask the same question about the chemical element that shares its name with a London theatre. Most surreally of all, there were so many questions about *Groundhog Day* that every time I read a new one, it felt like *Groundhog Day*. Even in the finished book, certain subjects crop up again and again: the 1966 football World Cup, Sir Isaac Newton, *Dad's Army*. As we are a London pub there were a lot of questions about London, but I have removed most of them to discourage readers who live elsewhere from burning this book in public. But for local colour I have kept a few Highgate questions. Highgate is of course a monied and very comfortable area of London, perched high above the rest of the city. Sting lives nearby, and Annie Lennox is regularly spotted around and about. Once, when I was reading out a question, it dawned on me that this was the single most bourgeois question I had ever encountered. For a point each, what are the four constituent parts of pesto sauce? Instantly all the teams started scribbling. But very few of the regulars in the Prince of Wales actually live in Highgate village: we all wander up from poorer, lower-lying districts, which at least means it's downhill all the way home. For this reason, and others, there are also slightly too many questions in the book about Dick Whittington.

What has taken a long time, far, far longer than I ever anticipated, was verifying the answers. You can get away with a lot in a pub quiz: by custom, the questionmaster is always right, even when he is wrong. In a book there is much less leeway. Many questions turned out to have been inspired by urban myths, and if you know they are not true, nothing is more annoying. At a high-powered literary quiz I went to a year or two back, the old fiction that the film comedian Will Hay discovered the planet Pluto was trotted out as verified fact. I had slightly too much to drink and ranted at length afterwards to the quiz organisers and anyone else who could not run away quickly enough. Wrong answers can push you that way. So we have checked and double-checked and triple-checked the answers in this book, and removed anything that whiffed of ambiguity. If you do find a howler, do not rupture anything: please tell us, because we want to know. Write to me c/o Hodder & Stoughton, and please cite two reliable sources, only one of which should be a newspaper or the internet. Some questionsetters, it has to be said, do not believe that either qualifies as a reliable source. Newspapers, in particular, have several ways of perpetuating factual errors. We don't see a huge number of celebrities at the Prince of Wales: once Ray Davies of the Kinks walked in as I was reading out question one, gave a look of horror, and raced out of the door as though he had left the oven on. Almost the only time anyone famous took part in the quiz, there were two of them: heartthrob actor Rufus Sewell and, on another team, by freak media coincidence, model/TV presenter Melanie Sykes. They were introduced, had a friendly chat, and that was that. But someone present called a gossip column and claimed that they had flirted, snogged and possibly even gone home with each other. This was printed and entered the cuttings files. Ever since, Sewell is routinely referred to in print as an ex-boyfriend of Sykes, and Sykes as an ex-girlfriend of Sewell. Because they sat on adjacent tables at a pub quiz. There's no smoke without fire, as Will Hay found out when he discovered Pluto.

Meanwhile, I hope you enjoy the book, and that some of these daft facts stick in your head as they are now sticking in mine, which is to say permanently, with some form of industrial adhesive. But I do have one important favour to ask. Please don't come to the pub. It's tiny. There is barely room for the people who are there already. You wouldn't enjoy it. It's really not that great. Honestly.

Marcus Berkmann, June 2006

QUIZ ONE
MARCUS (1)

Round One

1. 4-2-4 and 4-3-3 be damned. Where do football teams only ever line up 1-2-5-3?
2. What, during the First World War, was renamed 'liberty cabbage' in the UK and the US?
3. What is the longest nerve in the human body?
4. Quinine, aspirin and cinnamon. What do they all have in common?
5. What do cruciverbalists like doing?
6. Her dog was called Cliché. She named her pet parrot Onan, because he kept spilling his seed on the ground. Which American writer, who died in 1967?
7. The action of which 1952 western took place in virtually real time, starting at 10:40 in the morning and ending at five past midday?
8. What name is give to a valley formed by the subsidence of a block of the earth's crust between two or more parallel faults? Probably the most famous example runs through East Africa.
9. Eddie McCreadie was once a hard-tackling full-back for Chelsea and Scotland. Edie McCredie, along with Miss Hoolie, PC Plum and ridiculous posh Archie who lives in a pink castle, are characters in which CBeebies TV series?
10. What was Lady Chatterley's first name? What was Mr Darcy's first name (in *Pride And Prejudice*)? What was Mr Darcy's first name (in *Bridget Jones's Diary*)? What was Gulliver's first name? What was The Man With No Name's first name? A point for each.

Round Two

1. The 16th, 20th, 25th and 35th Presidents of the USA? What do they have in common?

2. Richard, Tamsin and Julie-Kate all went into the theatre, like their father and their mother before them. For a point each, who are or were their father and mother?

3. Matthew Thompson, a Jobcentre employee in Stockport, won a decision at an employment tribunal in March 2003 when it was deemed sexual discrimination for him to be forced to wear which item of clothing?

4. Which creature has species called Firebellied, Spadefoot and Midwife?

5. Five major Acts were passed in Britain – in 1729, 1736, 1743, 1747 and 1751 – to limit or even prevent the consumption of what?

6. Which cake was supposedly named in honour of the marriage in 1884 of a granddaughter of Queen Victoria to the German Prince Louis, son of the Grand Duke of Hess-Darmstadt?

7. Which Shakespeare play has the subtitle 'Or What You Will'?

8. Named after the first President Bush, which city in Texas is served by George Bush Intercontinental Airport? Clue: it's the city with the highest proportion of fat people in the world.

9. Lucian Freud's *Portrait Of Francis Bacon* (1952). Caravaggio's *Adoration Of The Shepherds With Saints Lawrence And Francis* (1609). Vermeer's *The Concert* (circa 1665-6). Cézanne's *Auvers-sur-Oise* (circa 1879-1882). Van Gogh's *Congregation Leaving The Reformed Church In Nuenen* (1884). What do all these paintings have in common?

10. A few Test cricketers – a very few – have played for two countries. In each case, you'll need to name both countries for the point. (i) Albert Trott; (ii) the Nawab of Pataudi Sr.; (iii) Kepler Wessels.

Bonus Round

Five questions about *Dad's Army*.

1. What was the name of Captain Mainwaring's arch-rival in the Eastgate platoon?

2. She was often mentioned but never seen. What was the name of Captain Mainwaring's wife?

3. Who worked at the Army & Navy stores before his retirement?

4. 'Don't tell him, Pike.' Who played the U-boat commander?

5. What was the highest rank Arthur Lowe actually achieved during World War II?

Tie-Break

In which year was soft toilet paper first sold in the UK? Harrods were the first to stock it, as you'd probably expect.

Round Three

1. In which European country is the slow lane of the motorway known as 'the lane of shame'?

2. The atmosphere of the planet Venus is composed almost entirely of carbon dioxide, while its thick cloud cover is composed of tiny droplets of which acid?

3. This French composer lived from 1866 to 1923. His works for piano include 'Flabby Preludes For A Dog' and 'Things Seen To The Right And Left, Without Spectacles'. His first work was entitled 'Opus 62'. What was his name?

4. The Olympic Games were held in honour of Zeus. In whose honour were the Pythian games held at Delphi? And for the second point, what was the four-year period between Pythian games called?

5. What name for a short haircut came from its popularity among the rowing teams of Harvard and Yale in the 1940s and 50s?

6. Immediately following the sudden death of John Smith in 1994, who took over as acting leader of the Labour Party?

7. In which English county are there places called Ham and Sandwich?

8. What significant, even climactic role did a man called Richard Brandon play in the life of Charles I?
9. If Thomas is a Tank Engine, what, equally alliteratively, are Bertie, Harold and Terence? A point for each.
10. Rainbow, Leaf, Summer, Libertad and River. What's the connection?

Round Four

1. 'Tasty, tasty, very very tasty. They're very tasty.' What were?
2. What was unique about Alan Shepard's golf shot on February 6th, 1971?
3. Which spring flower of the primula genus has a common name that is said to derive from a polite word for cattle dung?
4. Triskaidekaphobia is, famously, fear of the number 13. So what, accordingly, is paraskevidekatriaphobia?
5. Which breed of dog, which originated in China, is noted for its thick coat and distinctive blue-black tongue, and is reputed to be one of the stupidest dogs in existence?
6. Lord Byron was the first person to be commemorated in what way?
7. In Morse code which vowel is represented by a dot followed by a dash?
8. Which country referred to World War II as 'the Great Patriotic War'?
9. Solo, duet, trio and team are the events in which sport?
10. What was first used in 1792 and last used in 1977?

The answers to Quiz One begin on page 281

QUIZ TWO
CHRIS (1)

Chris Pollikett works in the truck rental industry and since 1992, with business partner Barry, has run a company that provides quizzes for pubs and clubs all over the country (www.inn-quizition.com). I met him when he was running the quiz at another pub in Highgate; when that ended, we scoured the postal district for another decent quiz and ended up at the Prince of Wales. He set his first one there on January 7th 1997 and has delivered more than forty since. Because of his enormous database of old questions he is the person I will ring if someone lets us down at the last minute. He once admitted, in his cups, that he can always hear an ambient hum of quiz questions at the back of his mind. We all nodded and agreed that we do too, now.

Chris's quizzes are perhaps the most populist in this book: the questions tend to be shorter, and more geared towards traditional quiz knowledge than some. This is mainly because he has been supplying questions for so long to so many people, but also because he believes quite passionately that the quizmaster's job 'is to find out what the audience knows, not to prove how clever he is'. His rule of thumb is that no team should get less than 40 per cent of the available points, but no one should get much above 80 per cent either. (Since formalised as 'the Pollikett Rule'.) He generally succeeds in this aim, and makes it look easy. I am always accusing of him of setting too many questions about World War II, so now he sets almost none, which was the required result.

Round One

1. Who designed the dress Madonna wore for her wedding to Guy Ritchie?
2. When Boris Johnson became an MP, which Tory grandee's seat did he take over?

3. In the Harry Potter novels of J.K. Rowling, what special talent is held by an Animagus?

4. A type of foodstuff, what can be either blanket or honeycomb?

5. Its effects have been likened to 'having your brains smashed out by a slice of lemon wrapped around a large gold brick'. What's the name of the cocktail invented by Zaphod Beeblebrox in *The Hitchhiker's Guide To The Galaxy*?

6. Which was the first film in which every credited member of the cast was nominated for an Oscar?

7. Which national leader punctuated an interview with the BBC's John Simpson, in 1998, with a long succession of not-quite-discreet farts?

8. Tony Greig, Allan Lamb, Robin and Chris Smith, Basil D'Oliveira: five England cricketers who were all born in South Africa. How many of them (you don't have to name them) played for England against South Africa?

9. The Hindenburg airship disaster, the Jasta Division of the Luftwaffe (slightly adjusted) and a building that stood at 96-98 St Mark's Place, New York City. Which famous rock band links these images?

10. Can you name the first six *Blue Peter* presenters? A point for each.

Round Two

1. What rare event held up the 1946 FA Cup Final?

2. What's the name of the slang language, much used among the gay community in the 1950s and 60s, that featured in *Round The Horne* on BBC Radio?

3. What is the connection between the corner shop in *Coronation Street* and that at 1, North Parade, Grantham, Lincs?

4. One from your childhood. Who lived in Bunkerton Castle?
5. What catastrophic error did the producers of *Top Of The Pops* make when Dexy's Midnight Runners appeared on their show in 1982, performing their song 'Jackie Wilson Said'?
6. Alluding to the colour of some of his fur, what name is sometimes given to a sexually mature male gorilla?
7. It started life as an insurance office. After the 1917 revolution it became a jail and later the offices of the KGB. What is this building in central Moscow called?
8. Who, at the age of seventy-seven in 1998, became the oldest person ever to go into space?
9. Charles II's wife was called Catherine of Braganza. The house of Braganza was the last line of monarchs in which European country?
10. What was the name of the nightclub Sharon Watts used to run in *EastEnders*?

Bonus Round

1. What was surrendered to Lieutenant-General Tomoyuki Yamashita on February 15th 1942?
2. The country once known as Tanganyika changed its name on gaining its independence, to Tanzania. With which island state did it merge to form the new country?
3. A kind of leather, developed in the 17th century, made of goat skin, with a unique surface finish and frequently reddish in colour, is often used for binding books. Where does it come from?
4. The legality of Mick Jagger and Jerry Hall's wedding has long been questioned, but where did it take place?
5. In which harbour was the liner *Queen Elizabeth* destroyed by fire in 1972?
6. Where else could we go?

Tie-Break

In the 2001 Census, how many people in the UK said that their religion was that of Jedi Knight?

Round Three

1. Which famous drinks company's name is derived from the medical condition it was originally intended to cure?
2. *Odds Against, Whip Hand* and *Come To Grief* – three novels published in 1965, 1979 and 1995 featuring the private investigator Sid Halley. Who wrote them?
3. In the annual ceremony known as swan-upping, the Worshipful Company of Dyers marks swans with a notch on one side of their bill, the Worshipful Company of Vintners marks them on both sides. How can swans owned by the Crown be identified?
4. He carried a trident as a weapon, but what form of defence was carried by the Roman gladiator called a 'retiarius'?
5. Under the Presidential Act of 1947, who is next in line for the US Presidency after the Vice-President?
6. In which sport did Mal Meninga captain Australia?
7. Scenes from which 1964 film were shot at Stoke Poges golf club in Buckinghamshire?
8. As the bass player in Buddy Holly's band, he could have been on the ill-fated plane on which Buddy died. Instead he gave up his seat to the Big Bopper. He had a long and successful solo career, before dying of slightly more natural causes in 2002. Who was he?
9. Which well-known name in the world of fashion is that of the man who was official tailor to Himmler's Waffen SS?
10. What were the six roles taken on by the members of the Village People? A point each.

Round Four

1. Which historic event took place on July 31st 1910 in Quebec harbour as the SS *Montrose* docked?

2. From 1936, the pre-decimalisation halfpenny had a picture of a sailing ship on the 'tails' side. Which ship?

3. You're playing cricket, and fielding in a helmet. You take it off and place it on the ground, whereupon the batsman plays a stroke and hits the helmet with the ball. How many runs have you given away?

4. Which communist revolutionary leader, after whom a city is named, trained in another city, London, as a pastry chef under the great Escoffier?

5. The Royal Standard that flies above Windsor when the Queen is in residence is divided into four quarters. The first and fourth have three lions on, the second has one lion. What's on the third?

6. 'We should be all right here, Stan. They haven't got the proper kit.' That was Billy Wright to Stan Mortensen at Wembley in 1953. What happened next?

7. What was the menu for the Owl and the Pussycat's wedding feast?

8. He was a Derbyshire farmer who became BBC Radio's *Brain Of Britain*. He then advertised Everest double glazing for years on TV, and latterly played Bill Insley in *The Archers*. What was his name?

9. To which adult and two children did Sir Edward Elgar dedicate his *Nursery Suite*, which he wrote in 1931? Two points for the full set.

10. What are the last seven words of each of the first three verses of what has become known as 'The Sailors' Hymn'?

Extra Tie-Break

In the 2001 Census, how many people in the UK said that their religion was Satanism?

The answers to Quiz Two begin on page 285

QUIZ THREE
DAVID (1)

David Burnage is a civil servant working for Jobcentreplus in central London and, at twenty-nine, one of the youngest regular quizsetters at the pub. He started coming to the Prince of Wales at the beginning of 2002, set his first quiz in July of the same year and has written twenty or so since. He doesn't really have a team of his own but is generally grabbed by whoever sees him first, for his knowledge of ancient radio and TV comedy is unrivalled. Recently, though, he seems to have become a semi-permanent member of the Ian Woan Memorial Team, in their long-standing and relentless campaign to stop coming fourth.

David's quizzes are among the most skilfully crafted in the pub: there are always at least half a dozen questions that leave a warm glow. He has an admitted weakness for the mindblowing piece of trivial knowledge, but unlike most writers can always turn it into a functional question. His favourite question of all time is his father's: Immediately prior to the birth of the present heir to the throne, who was heir to the throne? (Answer: Princess Elizabeth.) Each of his quizzes contains at least one question, usually skilfully masked, about his home town Bedford. David wishes to thank his parents Peter and Eileen for their encouragement and advice, his work colleagues for their forbearance and, by no means least, his friend, quiz tester, scorer, researcher and typist Bethen Thorpe.

Round One

1. Abdul Wahid Aziz won a bronze medal in weightlifting in 1960, and that remains, to date, the only Olympic medal won by which country?

2. For their radio show *Take It From Here*, Frank Muir and Denis Norden created a character who continually moaned about everything. The name of this character is now forever associated with anonymous writers of complaint letters. What is the name?

3. What is celebrated on February 2nd each year in the USA and Canada, and rather more famous to us now through a film of the 1990s?

4. Which breed of dog is the only one whose evidence is admissible in US courts?

5. In TV interviews given in 1991, what did David Icke claim to be the mystic and central colour of the universe?

6. Which is the only US state to have been a republic?

7. Cavity Sam celebrated his fortieth birthday in 2005. With which children's board game would you associate him?

8. Which sportsman insisted he was just making a friendly gesture when he signalled to Douglas Bunn in 1971?

9. How many days after Mussolini's death did Hitler kill himself?

10. Here are four final episodes of British TV situation comedies (excluding specials), and the years in which those episodes were first broadcast. For a point each, name the sitcoms.
   (i)   'Final Stretch' (1977);
   (ii) 'Summer Holiday' (1984);
   (iii) 'Anniversary' (1977);
   (iv) 'Things Aren't Simple Any More' (2000).

Round Two

1. Which sidekick rode a horse called Scout?

2. What precedent was established for London in Hyde Park in 1822 when Sir Richard Westmacott's statue of Achilles was first seen there?

3. The last territorial expansion of the British Empire took place in 1955 when a Royal Navy helicopter deposited troops on which North Atlantic territory?

4. He was a Fellow of the Royal Society of Astronomers, who discovered a white spot on Saturn; he was also one of Britain's first private pilots and gave flying lessons to Amy Johnson; but if he is known today it is as the star of a series of 1930s British film comedies including *The Ghost of St Michael's* and *Oh Mr Porter*. What was his name?

5. When Rolf Harris performed a version of 'Gentle On My Mind' on his TV show in 1969 he became the first person to give a public performance on which musical instrument?

6. Only three English counties are allowed to produce Stilton cheese. Which three (for a point each)?

7. On which 1960s LP cover can you read the words 'Welcome the Rolling Stones'?

8. What is the only creature that is capable of turning its stomach inside out?

9. Which major river is the only one to flow both north and south of the equator, as it crosses the equator twice?

10. Since World War II what have been the five most frequently performed operas at the Royal Opera House in London? A point for each.

Bonus Round

The following are all statements about actors in *The Magnificent Seven*. Which ones?

1. He was married for twenty-one years to the ex-wife of David McCallum.

2. Before he found fame as an actor, he was the producer of a live TV puppet show called *Life With Snarky Parker*. It was cancelled after one season.

3. While serving in the Marines, he saved the lives of five men, for which act of heroism he was chosen to be part of the Honor Guard protecting President Truman's yacht.
4. He made only a handful of films during the 1980s as he battled with crippling arthritis.
5. While on a shoot with Frank Sinatra in Hawaii, he saved Sinatra from drowning, which seemed to put a strain on their friendship.

Tie-Break

According to the IMdB (Internet Movie Database), how long does the film last (in minutes)?

Round Three

1. What Italian school of painting has had three distinct periods, the Early, the Roman and the Eclectic, yet, despite its name, has nothing to do with pasta?
2. Which component of English punctuation is also the name of a common British butterfly?
3. In the last twenty years ITV has televised both the Larkin and *My Uncle Silas* stories of H. E. Bates. In which counties were these stories set, for a point each?
4. When Carnegie Hall officially opened on May 5th 1891, which composer was its guest conductor?
5. While Elsie Mills, an employee of the Royal Society for the Prevention of Accidents, was having her lunch break one day in 1961, she saw an animal cross the road. This inspired her to found what?
6. The teeth of which animal were at one stage in history used by Native Americans as knife blades?

7. 'If you get in that car,' said Alec Guinness to a friend, 'you will be dead in a week.' The prophecy came true, but who did he say it to?
8. Which TV comedy sketch show was originally going to be called *Peter Sellers Is Dead*?
9. Which Italian city is served by Galileo Galilei airport?
10. Since Roger Bannister ran the first sub-four-minute mile, four British athletes have broken the world record for the mile. Who are they? (A point each.)

Round Four

1. Two people with the same name were father and son: the father was the detective in charge of the investigation into the murder of Charles Lindbergh's child, and the son came to prominence during the Gulf War of 1991. What is their shared name?
2. Wincanton is a town in Somerset. What is unusual about the city it is twinned with? And for a bonus point, name that city.
3. Complete this list from just over 40 years ago: Uruguay, Mexico, France, Argentina, Portugal and . . .
4. During his career he has played Dmitri Shostakovitch, Stanley Spencer, Nazi hunter Simon Wiesenthal and the 18th/19th-century actor Edmund Kean, but he is best known for having played another real-life role. Which famous actor?
5. When their song 'This Is Where I Came In' reached number 18 in April 2001, which British band became the first act to have Top Twenty hits in five separate decades?
6. As well as playing in seventy-eight Test matches, which legendary cricketer also played in the 1950 FA Cup Final?
7. The main square in Venice is named after which saint?
8. In which European country did women finally win the vote after a referendum held in 1971?

9. What connects the 1st, 3rd, 16th and 26th Presidents of the USA?

10. Which six countries are the only ones in the world whose names in English have only one syllable? A point each.

The answers to Quiz Three begin on page 289

QUIZ FOUR
PATRICK (1)

Patrick Routley is a barrister in his fifties who lives opposite the pub with his wife and daughter. Drawn inexorably into the weekly quizzing ritual, he joined our team full time in mid-2002 and was setting quizzes before the end of the year. He is a fearsome quizzer, with an extraordinary general knowledge that seems to have come about in the old-fashioned way, through education, curiosity and broad interests, allied to a mind like a steel trap. He and Chris are the main reasons our team often does well, although my neat writing has not gone unremarked upon.

Accordingly, Patrick's quizzes are some of the more challenging in this book. Uninterested in 'useless trivia', and recognising only with a sigh that popular culture has to exist, he is unashamedly elitist in his tastes. Knowledge of Greek and Latin are useful if you are doing his quizzes: poetry, classical music and English history are the mainstays. But behind the stern façade, he is as appreciative of a good question as anyone, and writes some absolute beauties himself. Each Patrick quiz contains at least one question about *Casablanca*, and his favourite question is the first one he ever thought of, which prompted him to compose his first quiz: In the film *To Have And Have Not*, whose voice do we hear when Lauren Bacall is singing? Answer: Andy Williams. Only recently has he found out that this may not actually be the right answer.

Round One

1. What kind of creature is a hippocampus?
2. Where in the body is the hippocampus?
3. Who wrote, 'We are all in the gutter, but some of us are looking at the stars'?
4. What feature of Japanese life is the Shinkansen?
5. In computer file-names, what do the letters 'pdf' stand for?

6. In whose Journal does the following entry appear for 19th November 1762: 'When we came upon Highgate Hill and had a view of London, I was all life and joy?'

7. What happened for thirty-four seconds during England's World Cup rugby match against Samoa in October 2003?

8. Which word means both 'a calculating machine' and 'the part of a column that supports the architrave'?

9. There are backbenchers and there is the front bench, but how many rows of benches are there on each side of the House of Commons (i.e. including back and front)?

10. Then felt I like some watcher of the skies
    When a new planet swims into his ken;
    Or like stout Cortez when with eagle eyes
    He star'd at the Pacific – and all his men
    Look'd at each other with a wild surmise –
    Silent, upon a peak in Darien.
    (i) Name the poem. (ii) Name the poet. (iii) Where will you see this poem quoted most weeks? (A point each.)

Round Two

1. The *Ghan* is the name of a train. Between which two towns, 1,851 miles apart, does it now run? (A point each.)

2. In March 1980 a ship called *Mi Amigo* sank off the British coast. What mainly illegal activity was this ship best known for?

3. A wide part of a canal where narrow boats can turn around is called what?

4. How many times was Dick Whittington Lord Mayor of London?

5. James Morris, the journalist, became Jan Morris, and Richard Raskind very nearly became the tennis player Renée Richards, but changed his mind at the last moment. Where?

6. 'They laughed when I said I was going to be a comedian. They're not laughing now.' Of whose inimitable humour is that an example?

7. One of the most famous images of the silent film era is of a man hanging off the hands of a clock. For two points, who was the man? And, for a bonus point, what was the film?

8. In measuring acidity or alkalinity, what does pH stand for?

9. What, among others, are St Aidan's, St Chad's, St Mary's and Hatfield?

10. Which song of the late Johnny Cash was going to be used to promote a proprietary haemorrhoids relief until his family objected?

Bonus Round

This beer round (first used in May 2004) celebrates an event that took place in May 1954.

1. Who was the timekeeper?
2. Where did it happen?
3. Who was the Australian rival who broke the record again 46 days later?
4. Who were the two pacemakers?
5. Who played Mr Lucas in *Are You Being Served?*

Tie-Break

Gunder Hägg of Sweden had previously held the record, having set it in 1945. In what time?

Round Three

1. What is the wife of (i) an Earl, and (ii) a Marquis? (A point for each.)
2. Which political leader, killed in a plane crash, was succeeded by his brother, an airline pilot?
3. The youngest and the oldest men ever to be elected US President were inaugurated on the same day exactly twenty years apart. Who were they, for a point each?
4. Truman Capote said he was 'about as sexy as a pissing toad'. Which rock star?
5. (i) How many fences are there on the Grand National course? (ii) How many times must the winning horse in the Grand National have jumped (if we assume it has finished the course)?
6. Sir John Anderson and Herbert Morrison, wartime Home Secretaries, both gave their names to types of air-raid shelter. What was the essential difference between an Anderson and a Morrison shelter?
7. A charity concert was held in Cape Town on behalf of AIDS charities in November 2003. It was called 46664. Why?
8. Someone asked the late Duke of Devonshire whether he belonged to Pratt's Club. What was the Duke's reply?
9. In which century was the doctrine of papal infallibility established?
10. Name the composers whose Requiem Masses were composed in the following years: (i) 1791; (ii) 1837; (iii) 1874; (iv) 1887–8; (v) 1961. A point for each.

Round Four

1. What was invented by Frederick Walton in 1860, using among other ingredients powdered cork, wood flour, resins, ground limestone and linseed oil?

2. Which British novelist has also written four crime novels, including *Putting The Boot In* and *Going To The Dogs*, under the pseudonym Dan Kavanagh? And for the second point, what is the family significance of that name?

3. Who are the only four successive kings of England to have had the same name?

4. What natural phenomenon is measured on a scale of which the first two points are 'growler' and 'bergy bit'?

5. 'Mr Salteena was an elderly man of forty-two' are the opening words of which novel, which also includes the line 'my life will be sour grapes and ashes without you'? Two points for the title, a bonus point for the author.

6. What is 210 by 297 millimetres?

7. What began with *The Man* in 1950 and ended with *The Score* in 2001?

8. Which children's author created the three Baudelaire siblings? 'Violet loved to invent; her brother Klaus loved to read; and their sister Sunny, she loved to bite.'

9. What did Admiral Sir George Rooke win for Britain in 1704?

10. 'You can tell a lot about a fellow's character by whether he picks out all of one colour or just grabs a handful.' That was Ronald Reagan talking about what?

The answers to Quiz Four begin on page 293

QUIZ FIVE
IAN WOAN
MEMORIAL TEAM

The Ian Woan Memorial Team is the usual alias adopted by Matt Odwell, Darrien Bold and Peter Hall, respectively a trainee biomedical scientist and two recent English graduates. They started coming to the quiz in September 2004 and set their first one a couple of months later. Three weeks or so before one of their quizzes they start writing down anything that could pass as a quiz question, and usually end up about fifteen short by the last weekend. Then they think of the answers they would like to include and try to write the questions afterwards, *Jeopardy*-style. If there is a surplus of material, Darrien vetoes anything he doesn't like, usually Peter's animal questions and Matt's periodic table trivia. They always ensure the following key topics are covered: the London Underground, Star Wars, the England cricket team and, crucially, Phil Collins. Their quizzes are among the most popular and enjoyable and they generally polish off the quizmasters' £15-worth of free drink earlier than anyone else.

And the team name? According to Darrien, 'Ian Woan was one of the most gifted English football players to never receive international honours, despite being one of the most talented left-footed midfielders to have plied his trade in the top flight. His career ended following brief spells at Shrewsbury Town and US side Syracuse Salty Dogs. He now presides over the Swindon Town Under-18s Centre of Excellence.' The Woans pride themselves on their in-depth knowledge of football, scientific jargon and 1980s soft rock. In the pub they are renowned for their uncanny ability to snatch fourth place from the jaws of victory.

Round One

1. The smallest measurable length is roughly 1.6×10^{-35} metres. How is it known?
2. 'Killing Me Softly With His Song' was a career-defining hit for Roberta Flack and, much later, for The Fugees. Who was it written about, and what was 'his song'?
3. Which Greater Manchester club holds the record for the biggest win in a FA Cup Final, after beating Derby County 6-0 in 1903?
4. In which film did John Malkovich play Dr Jekyll and Mr Hyde?
5. Gambia has a land border with only one other country. Which country?
6. Whom did William Blake describe as 'a true Poet, and of the Devil's party without knowing it'?
7. Which is the largest mammal to build a nest?
8. 'Who is the man that would risk his neck for his brother man?'
9. Which motorway links Bristol to the M4?
10. Five actors have played Anakin Skywalker. Name all five, for a point each.

Round Two

1. On May 25th 2001, at the age of sixty-four, Sherman Bull became the oldest man to do what?
2. Which band were responsible for the theme tune to the BBC's Formula One coverage? And for the second point, which band performs the theme tune to ITV's Formula One coverage?
3. The layout of which African city was based on the shape of the Union Flag?
4. Who was the first heavyweight boxing champion to regain his title?

5. Who became prima ballerina at the Maryinsky Theatre in 1906?

6. Who is the only winner of the Nobel Prize for Literature to have played first-class cricket? And for the second point, in which American TV series did the main character share his name?

7. The asteroid 2001DA42 is named after whom?

8. What term is given to the formation or use of words such as 'buzz', 'bang' and 'murmur' that imitate the sounds associated with the objects or actions they refer to? Bonus point if you spell it correctly.

9. Ted Maul, Austin Tassletine and Fur Q are three of many alter egos of which controversial TV satirist?

10. Between 1991 and 2005 there were six Home Secretaries. Name them, for a point each.

Bonus Round

1. Which film was promoted with the tagline 'As far back as I can remember, I've always wanted to be a gangster'?

2. Which daily newspaper switched to tabloid form in 1977 and was purchased by Richard Desmond in 2000?

3. The name of which game is derived from a word which in Italy and France refers to a black and white hooded cloak, once worn by priests?

4. Which band had hits in the 1960s with 'Walk Like A Man' and 'Big Girls Don't Cry'?

5. In the film *Spaceballs*, space adventurer Lone Star and his sidekick Barf make a deal with the King of Druidia to rescue Princess Vespa since they owe money to whom?

Tie-Break

American Melvin Hemker holds the record for growing a sunflower with the most heads. But how many heads did his sunflower have?

Round Three

1. Which American actor and singer complained to museum curators after finding his own photograph absent from a collection of memorabilia celebrating the fall of the Berlin Wall, claiming he was at least partly responsible for the destruction of the concrete divide?
2. The Mercalli scale measures the intensity of what?
3. Which poet's last words were, according to legend, 'I've had eighteen straight whiskies, I think that's the record'?
4. Which US state has the highest population, with more than 32 million inhabitants? And which US state has the lowest population, with only 509,000 inhabitants in 2004? A point for each.
5. What is the name given to the dot above the letter 'i'?
6. Constance, Countess Markiewicz was the first female MP elected in the United Kingdom. Of which politician party was she a member?
7. Since 1066 all but two monarchs have been crowned at Westminster Abbey? For a point each, who were they?
8. Who directed and starred in the Academy Award-nominated documentary *Super Size Me*, in which he ate nothing but McDonalds food for one month?
9. Which heavy metal guitar legend guested on Michael Jackson's 1983 hit 'Beat It'?
10. Which author said, 'An archaeologist is the best husband any woman can have. The older she gets, the more interested he is in her.'

Round Four

1. Which form of dance was derived from the Irish jig and Lancashire clog dancing, also being heavily influenced by African tribal beats?
2. Which two nations are Nordic but not Scandinavian? (A point for each.)
3. Months of the year that begin on a Sunday always have five Sundays, except February, of course. What other notable feature do they contain?
4. Before duetting with Phil Collins on the 1985 hit 'Easy Lover', Philip Bailey had achieved fame with which chart-topping group?
5. The first couplet of which famous song could be translated as 'It is death. It is death. It is life. It is life. This is the hairy man who caused the sun to shine again for me'?
6. George Bernard Shaw coined the word 'ghoti' to demonstrate the inconsistency of English spelling. Its pronunciation is the same as that of which common four-letter word?
7. From which country did Israel seize the Golan Heights during the Arab-Israeli war of 1967?
8. According to legend a 1951 mono recording of Beethoven's 9th Symphony, performed at the Bayreuther Festspiele, was later significant in the manufacture of which product?
9. Where would you find Niobe above her father Tantalus?
10. Between 1992-3 and 2004-5, eight captains have lifted the FA Premiership trophy. Name six of them, for a point each.

The answers to Quiz Five begin on page 296

QUIZ SIX
MARCUS (2)

Round One

1. Which American actor claimed in 2003 that his dyslexia, a problem he shared with his mother and three sisters, had been cured by Scientology?
2. There are four pairs of them in the human body, the palatine, the lingual, the tubal and the pharyngeal. Their primary function is to combat airborn infections entering the body. What are we talking about?
3. *Tikkabilla*, which determined viewers can find on CBeebies, is essentially an updated version of which classic children's TV show?
4. In which athletics event is the women's world record better than the men's?
5. An English river, a Scottish river, a Russian river: they all have the same name. What's that?
6. Which American woman was immortalised, in grey and black, sitting down at number 96 Cheyne Walk, London SW10?
7. Which England fast bowler of the 1990s made his debut in *The Beano* in May 2003, in a cartoon featuring the character Billy Whizz? It has to be said that his walk-on appearance was confined to a single word: 'Chortle'.
8. Who wear black because they are still mourning for Queen Mary II, who died in 1694?
9. At which educational establishment, in the 1950s and 1960s, was there blue murder, pure hell and a train robbery?
10. What relation was the first of these kings or queens to the second? A point for each.
    (i)   Ethelred the Unready and Edward the Confessor.
    (ii) Charles II and James II.
    (iii) William IV and Victoria.

Round Two

1. After being cast as the new James Bond, Daniel Craig admitted that he was afraid of guns. This is not unprecedented. Which other actor who played James Bond also had a morbid fear of firearms?

2. Which 17th/18th-century English scientist's only recorded speech in his period as a Member of Parliament was a request for a window to be opened? Clue: he is also believed to have invented the catflap.

3. Where would you see the letters BCE, ECB, EZB, EKT and EKP?

4. Which Australian marsupial has three species, the Common, the Southern Hairy-nosed and the Northern Hairy-nosed?

5. Who painted the Rokeby Venus, now in the National Gallery in London, which was badly damaged by a suffragette in 1914?

6. In geometry, what value do complementary angles add up to? And what value do conjugate angles add up to? A point for each of these.

7. On October 1347 a fleet from the Orient landed in north-east Sicily. What of great significance did they bring with them?

8. One of Heinz's lesser known but most venerable tinned products is something called London Grill. It has baked beans, pork sausages and what two other meaty ingredients, for a point each?

9. What did the Canadian poet and novelist Elizabeth Smart do by Grand Central Station, according to the title of her best known book?

10. Who is the actor Samuel West's mother? Who is the actor Toby Stephens's mother? Who is the actor Rachael Stirling's mother? A point for each.

Bonus Round

Each of the following five film directors has won the Best Director Oscar twice. For each director, I'll give you two dates: these are the years in which he won. All you have to do is name the two films he won for. (In each case, the year is the one in which the film came out, not the following year when the awards were handed out.) You'll need to get the films in the right order to get the points.

1. Robert Wise: 1961 (with Jerome Robbins) and 1965.
2. Oliver Stone: 1986 and 1989.
3. Fred Zinnemann: 1953 and 1966.
4. Milos Forman: 1975 and 1984.
5. Steven Spielberg: 1993 and 1998.

Tie-Break

Six US Presidents had previously been generals. Four had been teachers. How many had been lawyers?

Round Three

1. First class 62 per cent, second class 41 per cent, third class 25 per cent, crew 23 per cent. What am I talking about?
2. The chocolate chip cookie, the dishwasher, the disposable nappy, the windscreen wiper, the coffee maker, dipped headlights and suspension bridge piles. What did the inventors of these things have in common?
3. The beggar at the gate of the rich man's house is the only character in any of Jesus's parables to be given a proper name. What name?

4. With an audience of nearly 106 million, the highest rated individual programme in American television history was the last episode of which long-running comedy series, shown in 1983?

5. Which 1978 UK hit single ended with the producer/co-writer of the song saying the words 'Oh, those Russians'?

6. What term is used to denote a number that cannot be expressed as an exact fraction? For example, the square root of 2, or of 3, or of 5, or pi.

7. In Greek mythology who was the handsome young man loved by the moon goddess Selene, by whom he supposedly had fifty daughters?

8. The Pope's New Castle, Windmill, Between Two Seas and Roasted Slope – what are they?

9. What word links the fluid portion of the blood in which corpuscles and cells are suspended, and ionised gas?

10. Which Test cricket-playing countries have the following first-class clubs? Three points in all.

    (i)   Northern Districts, Central Districts, Otago, Canterbury.

    (ii) Eastern Province, Easterns, Griqualand West, Gauteng.

    (iii) Nondescripts, Air Force, Colts, Sebastianites.

Round Four

1. In EastEnders, who ran over Tiffany? And who ran over Jamie Mitchell? A point for each.

2. Forget truncheons. According to Ian Arundale, Assistant Chief Constable of West Mercia police, speaking in 2004, the ideal weapon for police officers to use would be what, derived from a famous TV programme?

3. Acetylsalicylic acid is better known as what?

4. Which group of three islands was originally named 'Las Tortugas' after the turtles found there, but now share their name with a reptile of the alligator family?
5. In Act 3, Scene 3 of *The Winter's Tale*, how does Antigonus leave the stage?
6. What new name was given to the Chinese gooseberry by farmers from New Zealand when they started exporting it to the USA in the 1960s?
7. What was the name of the most famous horse sired by Quorum out of Mared?
8. This word was on all decimal coins when they were introduced in 1971, and was removed from all decimal coins in 1982. What word?
9. On which date does the big ship sail on the alley-alley-o?
10. Which chat show host once asked George Best, 'Did you ever think, if you hadn't done all that running around playing football, you might not have been so thirsty?'

The answers to Quiz Six begin on page 300

QUIZ SEVEN
DAVID (2)

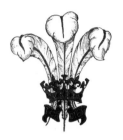

Round One

1. What subject did Margaret Thatcher originally study at Oxford in 1944?
2. Crabeater, Ross and Northern Fur are all species of which animal?
3. *Carry On* veteran Jim Dale performs what task in the USA, which in this country is carried out by Stephen Fry?
4. Which boxer, world champion for seven years, is the only man who can claim to have fought Mohammed Ali, Mike Tyson and Evander Holyfeld in title contests?
5. Which 20th-century novel was set 'in the year of our Ford 632'?
6. If you suffer from anosmia what have you lost?
7. What do you need to have done in order to be allowed to join the sporting charity The Primary Club?
8. In Germany she is Fräulein Ming, in France they call her Mademoiselle Rose. What do we call her?
9. Which children's comic was named after the son of Andy Capp?
10. Who were the youngest members of the following groups? A point for each. (i) The Beatles; (ii) Monty Python; (iii) The England 1966 World Cup team.

Round Two

1. What was the second song David Bowie performed in his solo set for Live Aid?
2. Which reporter searched for *Red Rackham's Treasure*, *King Ottokar's Sceptre* and *The Blue Lotus*?
3. What disease, known by inhabitants of the East Indies as 'the lameness', was first described by Dutch physicist Nicolas Tulp in 1652?

4. Napoleon liked to relax with one before battle, Nixon was seen with one on stage at the Grand Ole Opry, Abbie Hoffman was cited for contempt of Congress for using one in 1968, and Figaro relieved tension with one in Beaumarchais' play *The Marriage of Figaro*. What?

5. How was William Joyce better known during World War II?

6. In *The Mikado* what is the name of the youngest sister in the care of Lord High Executioner Ko-Ko?

7. Which band released albums in the 1980s called *Infected*, *Soul Mining* and *Mindbomb*?

8. What was the original name for a wall or other boundary marker that is set in a ditch so as not to interrupt the landscape? It's a feature particularly of 18th-century landscape gardening.

9. What was the name of the secret society which led a revolt of the Kikuyu people of Kenya in 1952?

10. Which character in a hugely successful TV series for young children, no longer being made, was played by Nikki Smedley?

Bonus Round

1. Which TV sitcom character married her boss Clive Dempster in 1988, after years of lusting after her previous boss?

2. In the radio version of *Hancock's Half Hour*, what was the surname of Tony Hancock's secretary, played by Hattie Jacques?

3. When a bunch of the boys were whooping it up at the Malamute saloon, who got shot?

4. In the Jeeves and Wooster short story 'The Great Sermon Handicap', what is the name of the vicar who preaches at Boustred Parva, Glos? First name and surname are required.

5. Described by Dr Johnson as 'much inhabited by writers of small histories, dictionaries and temporary poems', and situated near Moorfields, which London street was renamed Milton Street in 1830?

Tie-Break

Back to Cluedo. How many possible outcomes are there in a standard game of Cluedo?

Round Three

1. What did cabinet minister Hugh Dalton inadvertendly leak to the press in 1947, for which deed he subsequently resigned?
2. Only two American states end in the letter T. What are they, for a point each?
3. According to a 16th-century law what colour must all Venetian gondolas be painted?
4. What is the connection between someone mentioned in a 1968 Simon & Garfunkel hit and someone mentioned in a 1974 Elton John hit?
5. The Hindu god Hanuman and the Egyptian god Thoth both take the form of which type of creature?
6. Which are the only two American states that end with a Y and the only one that ends with a G? Three points in all.
7. Which man-made material was first marketed in the USA in 1950 as Dacron?
8. It has places called New York and Miami Beach, and one of its best known towns has the same name as an American state capital. Which English county?
9. Which former West Indian cricketer became, in 1969, the first black life peer?

10. Bill Owen played Compo for twenty-eight years in *Last Of The Summer Wine*. During that time four different characters completed the main trio with Compo and Norman Clegg. Name them for a point each.

Round Four

1. Where did America lose land in 1949?
2. Who was Britain's first Christian martyr?
3. In which month do the Queen and Prince Philip celebrate their wedding anniversary?
4. Princess Aurora and Prince Philip are characters in which Disney animated film?
5. Brian Blessed commentated on which sport when it was shown on British TV for the first time in the late 1980s?
6. Which game was reputedly invented by the French mathematician Blaise Pascal as a by-product of his experiments with perpetual motion?
7. In which 1980s US crime series did Sheena Easton appear as the love interest?
8. What incident did Richard Widmark and Sidney Poitier find themselves in in the 1965 film of the same name?
9. What is the only city found on two continents?
10. Of the four US Presidents who were assassinated, who took the longest to die?

The answers to Quiz Seven begin on page 304

QUIZ EIGHT
TOM, ALI & PETE (1)

Tom Bannatyne is forty-four and an evil financial speculator, who in 1984 represented Queens' College Cambridge in *University Challenge* (won one, lost one). 'The core of our team has always been made up of parents from our children's school. It started with Rebecca and me, and Pete and his wife Sarah, and after a year or so we were joined by Ali and Madeleine.' Pete Smith is forty-five and a post-production/special effects compositor for films and commercials, whose work commitments regularly made him late, hence their team name 'Where's Pete?' Green-fingered genius Ali Goodyear, thirty-two, is a mine of information on all aspects of top-class sport and a master of the exotic tie-break question ('What is the longest time a chicken has survived after having its head cut off?'). He cannot believe that a pint of Kronenbourg costs more than £3.

Their quizzes, of which they produce about three a year, are always perfectly judged, a solid mix of the straightforward and the wildly opinionated and quirky. Pete no longer comes to the quiz, having moved with Sarah and kids to Kent in 2004. He recently went to a quiz in aid of a dog charity in his village hall and got food poisoning from the buffet. But Tom and Ali carry on, occasionally producing one of their unbelievably wriggly music rounds, in which identity of artist and title of song are always just beyond the reach of memory. Even more cruelly, they usually ask who is number one, and no one ever knows.

Round One

1. What was the name of the possibly inebriated driver of the car that crashed in 1997 in Paris, killing Princess Diana, Dodi Fayed and himself?
2. The name of which oriental place translates into English as 'fragrant harbour'?
3. The addition of which vegetable turns a simple dish of poached eggs into Eggs Florentine?
4. Lite, Dry, Dark, Lady, Raspberry, Private Reserve and Tartar Control are all varieties of which drink?
5. Which famous person of the first half of the last century once entered a Charlie Chaplin lookalike contest in San Francisco and came third?
6. If three dice are stacked on top of each other and a 3 is showing on top, what is the total of the hidden spots?
7. What is the official language of the principality of Andorra?
8. What is the most common name of the large dog that sometimes lives with Tom and Jerry?
9. In which decade was Diet Coke introduced?
10. What were the forenames of the following classical composers? A point for each. (i) Sibelius; (ii) Ravel; (iii) Rodrigo; (iv) Fauré (v) Haydn; (vi) Mussorgsky.

Round Two

1. Which Olympic swimming medallist became better known as both Flash Gordon and Buck Rogers?
2. Whose maiden speech to the House of Lords in 1992 included the words 'I will at all times try to live up to the reputation of your lordships' House as expressed so eloquently by the Scottish bard: "Princes and Lords are but the breath of Kings. An honest man is the noblest work of God."'?

3. What is the name of the American Football team based in St Louis?

4. In the musical *Grease*, Danny Zuko's gang are the T-Birds. Which gang are their arch-rivals, especially when it comes to racing cars?

5. Which footballer won an FA Cup Winner's medal with Wimbledon in 1988, joined Liverpool for £3.5m in 1994, won three England caps before finishing his career with Tottenham and finally Ipswich Town, and is often listed in newspaper selections of the worst eleven ever to have played for England?

6. The African song 'Mbube' was originally a big hit in what is now Swaziland, but English lyrics were not added until 1961, when it became a US number one hit for The Tokens. Since then it has reached the UK charts three times, the last in 1982 when it reached number one here too. It also features in one of the West End's most successful current musicals. What does the Zulu word mbube mean?

7. Which 1988 film has the rather sketchy synopsis 'A physically perfect, but innocent man goes in search of his brother, who is a short small-time crook'?

8. Which record label's first release, and therefore first huge moneyspinner, was Mike Oldfield's *Tubular Bells*?

9. What is the name of the small uninhabited island in the middle of the Niagara Falls, named after the animals who used to roam freely there?

10. From which 1969 hit, taken from a controversial stage musical, do the following lyrics come: 'When the Moon is in the Seventh House, and Jupiter aligns with Mars, then peace will guide the planets, and love will steer the stars'?

Bonus Round

1. Which playwright wrote *Caesar And Cleopatra* and *Man And Superman*?
2. The names of the teddy bears in the appalling Australian children's programme *Bananas In Pyjamas* were Amy, Morgan and what?
3. In the John Lennon song 'Imagine', what line follows 'No need for greed or hunger'?
4. Which cocktail was invented by the barman Mr McGarry in 1921, and is often, not entirely accurately, regarded as interchangeable with the Mimosa?
5. What form of audience participation reputedly made its first appearance at a professional sporting event in October 1981, during an American League Championship Series baseball game between the Oakland Athletics and the New York Yankees?

Tie-Break

To the nearest 100,000, how many Americans believe they have been abducted by aliens?

Round Three

1. In 1955 the pathologist Thomas Harvey completed a post mortem on a seventy-six-year-old man who had died of natural causes in New Jersey, and took the dead man's brain home as a souvenir. Whose brain was it?
2. Raphael Ravenscroft, author of *The Complete Saxophone Player*, played on the Pink Floyd album *The Final Cut* and, more famously, on which 1978 hit single?

3. Which American cinema action hero offered a $1 million bounty for the capture or killing of Osama bin Laden and Abu Musab Al-Zarqawi?

4. The characters Jooji Uiizurii, Nebiru Rongubotomu, Shiriusu Burakku and Arubasu Danburudoa appear in the Japanese version of which book or books?

5. In the 16th century, the French and the English called it the Italian disease. The French also called it the English disease, and the Italians and English called it the French disease. The Dutch called it the Spanish disease, and the Poles and the Russians called it each other's disease. The Arabs called it the disease of the Christians. What disease?

6. The village of Crogedene, mentioned in the Domesday Book, is now better known as the birthplace of the model Kate Moss. What is the village called today?

7. Of what item of clothing was it said by *Modern Girl* magazine in 1957, 'it is hardly necessary to waste words over it, since it is inconceivable that any girl with tact and decency would ever wear such a thing'?

8. Which legendary British comedian lent his voice to the character of Space Navigator Brad Newman in the 1966 feature film *Thunderbirds Are Go*, and also sang the theme tune to the slightly ropey sitcom *You Rang, M'Lord*?

9. When the Romans landed on the coast of Kent in 43 AD, how can we be sure that they did not set foot on what is now the Royal St George's Golf Club, home of, most recently, the 2003 Open Championship?

10. Excluding the words 'The Book of . . .', 'First Book of . . .' and similar refinements, there are, according to the 1611 Authorised Version of the Bible, four books of the Old Testament that have more than ten letters in their name. For a point each, what are they?

Round Four

1. How many different men have walked on the moon?
2. In Elton John and Bernie Taupin's song, 'So goodbye yellow brick road, where the dogs of society howl. You can't plant me in your penthouse, I'm going back to my plough. Back to . . .' what else?
3. Which Kent town is or was home to the politician Benjamin Disraeli, the novelist William Golding and the actor Tom Baker, as well as one of only two football clubs ever to leave the Football League in mid-season?
4. The shortest is 117 and the longest is 119. There are 150 of them. What?
5. Which sometimes controversial Italian-born composer was appointed court composer to the Holy Roman Emperor Joseph II at the age of twenty-four, wrote more than forty operas (including *Falstaff* in the early 1790s), and was given a state funeral when he died in 1825 at the age of seventy-four?
6. What today is the NatWest Bank, now part of the Royal Bank of Scotland group, was formed by the merger in 1968 of which two banks?
7. What are the generally accepted terms for the two basic forms of physical pain, one being sharp, severe and usually short-lived, the other being continuous and persistent? (A point each.)
8. Shares listed on the New York Stock Exchange all have unique 'ticker symbols'. What is the three-letter symbol for the stock of Anheuser-Busch, the world's largest brewing company?
9. Name the two grape varieties used to form the base of most blends of claret (for a point each). For a bonus point, name any one of the other three that are typically used to round out the wine.

10. Eight English football clubs in the Premiership or the Nationwide League (in the 2005/6 season) have the same number of letters in the first word of their name as they do in the last word of their name. For a point each, name six of them.

The answers to Quiz Eight begin on page 309

QUIZ NINE
CHRIS (2)

Round One

1. What, in 1997, went from two sessions of fifteen minutes a week to one of thirty minutes a week?
2. The Biblical strongman Samson used what as a weapon to slay 1,000 Philistines?
3. In which country would you find the Fjordland National Park?
4. In 1938, Sweden were awarded a walkover in the first round of the football World Cup. Who should they have been playing?
5. What was a member of the Waffen SS required to have tattooed on the underside of his left arm, about twenty centimetres up from the elbow?
6. It was founded in Vienna in 1923, but in which city now are the headquarters of Interpol?
7. Who played the actress Dorothy Michaels in a memorable 1982 film?
8. At the time of his appearance at the 1988 Winter Olympics, what trade was followed by Eddie 'the Eagle' Edwards?
9. Which English king is buried in St Stephen's Abbey in Caen in France?
10. Which two characters were involved in the first interracial kiss screened on US national television? A point for each.

Round Two

1. 'Ah, isn't that nice. The wife of the Cambridge President is kissing the cox of the Oxford crew.' Who said this to a huge TV audience after the Boat Race in 1977?
2. Which London landmark was opened in 1873, burnt down 16 days later, and was named after the then Princess of Wales when rebuilt?

3. Which UK city's underground system runs in a circle that has just 15 stations?
4. Which prominent senior educationalist was originally called Armon Tanzarian before he changed his name?
5. Which band that had a number of hits in the late 1970s and early 1980s (including two number ones) took its name from some characters in Woody Guthrie's semi-autobiographical novel *Bound For Glory*?
6. At the age of forty-four, the sprinter Merlene Ottey competed in her seventh Olympic Games at Athens in 2004. Which country was she running for?
7. What did Elvis Presley, Henry Cooper and Mark Thatcher have in common?
8. Which one word can mean a container, to plunder, a dismissal and a drink?
9. The film director George Lucas once owned a dog whose name he gave to one of the more enduring characters he has been associated with. What was the dog called?
10. 'What a drag it is getting old' is the first line of which great 1960s rock song?

Bonus Round

1. 'A fixed point such that the distances of a point on a conic section from it and from the directrix have a constant ratio.' This is the mathematical definition of what?
2. Which ITV regional company produced *Jewel In the Crown*, *Brideshead Revisisted*, *Crown Court* and *The Krypton Factor*?
3. In which town in the Dolomites should the Winter Olympics of 1944 have taken place? (They eventually went there in 1956.)

4. What does the BBC's weather database define as 'a westerly breeze with warm weather, supposed to prevail at the time of the summer solstice'?
5. Which letter was used in medieval Rome to represent the number 160?

Tie-Break

How many Popes have been assassinated?

Round Three

1. Young children often suffer from bone fractures that do not break completely, but rather bend and split on one side. What name is given to this kind of fracture?
2. The road along the seafront at Nice, in France, was built at the expense of English visitors as a token of gratitude for the hospitality they had received. What is it called?
3. In the Arabian Nights, what kind of bird was so vast and strong it could lift an elephant?
4. Which fashion designer is married to the playwright David Hare?
5. In the House of Commons on March 2nd 1978, Michael Foot said of Norman Tebbit: 'It is not necessary that every time he rises he should give his famous imitation of . . .' what?
6. In philately it's the white space between stamps on a sheet. In building it's something else. What?
7. Which road had the postcode L43 6TZ?
8. Which creature had 'jaws that bite' and 'claws that catch'?
9. Lord Olivier was the first actor to be raised to the peerage. But who was the first actor to be knighted?
10. Jute, jam and journalism: the three best known industries of which Scottish city?

Round Four

1. Who famously sank a German World War I ship called the *Louisa*?

2. In America in 1994 it was the Questra, in France in 1998 the Tricolore and in Japan and South Korea in 2002 it was the Fevernova. What was?

3. Who was the first member of Take That to have a solo number 1 hit?

4. The British National Ice Skating Association is based, appropriately, in Torvill and Dean's home town. Where?

5. You need to get permission from DEFRA to do this, and it can only be done off the coast of Newhaven or The Needles on the Isle of Wight. What can?

6. On what date every year is the feast day of the first Christian martyr?

7. In 1959 the winner of the Men's Singles at Wimbledon was one Alex Olmedo. He is the only person of his nationality to win tennis's premier event. What nationality?

8. Which John Steinbeck novel is based, more or less, on the story of Cain and Abel?

9. For Eurythmics it was 'A Stranger'. For the Troggs it was 'All Around'. What was it for Pat Benatar?

10. The road outside the Savoy Hotel is the last place in Britain where you drive on the right. Its associated theatre was the first public building in the world to benefit from which innovation when it opened in 1881?

The answers to Quiz Nine begin on page 314

QUIZ TEN
PATRICK (2)

Round One

1. Created by Davros, what was the most famous export of the planet Skaro?

2. New Zealander Chris Cairns broke the world record for the highest number of sixes in a Test career when he hit his 86th at Lords against England in May 2004. Who had previously held the record?

3. Alec Guinness played Professor Marcus in the original. Who played the equivalent character Professor Dorr in the 2004 remake? And what was the name of the film?

4. Describe the work of art entitled *The Physical Impossibility of Death in the Mind of Someone Living*. And for the second point, name the artist.

5. The first woman to be executed by the US government was Mary Surratt, who was hanged in 1865. What was her crime?

6. Who was the Roman god of boundaries? His name survives as a current English word, albeit with a different meaning.

7. Which Shakespeare character uttered the following words?
The soldier's pole is fall'n; young boys and girls
Are level now with men; the odds is gone
And there is nothing left remarkable
Beneath the visiting moon.
And for the second point, why?

8. What is the name of the logical proposition *entia non sunt multiplicanda praeter necessitatem*, meaning that no more facts should be assumed than are necessary?

9. In France it is a musette or a cornemuse, in Germany a Dudelsack, in Italy a zampogna and in Spain a gaita gallega. What is it in English?

10. What five sports (not necessarily the precise events) make up the modern pentathlon? A point for each.

Round Two

A round with a Cornish theme.

1. Describe the Cornish flag.
2. What is the name of the Cornish independence party?
3. What was created in 1932 by Rowena Cade?
4. What is the characteristic feature of 'star gazy' or 'starry gazy' pie?
5. Which road goes to Land's End? And for a bonus point, in which London borough is the other end of this road?
6. At Land's End is a famous and much photographed signpost. 874 miles to where, for one point, and 3,147 to where, for another point?
7. Born in Penzance in 1778, he discovered among other things potassium, sodium, calcium and barium. Faraday was his assistant. Who was he?
8. Which two Cornish projects do you associate with the name Tim Smit, for a point each?
9. In which Cornish town might you witness the Furry Dance each May?
10. Which poet with Highgate connections wrote about, and is buried at, St Enodoc's church near Rock?

Bonus Round

1. Who composed the orchestral works Liverpool Oratorio (1991) and Standing Stone (1997)?
2. Who said, 'Life is too short to stuff a mushroom'?
3. Who won the Turner Prize in 1999, beating Tracey Emin's notorious bed into second place, with a video called *Deadpan*, an imitation, or homage to, a famous scene by Buster Keaton?
4. Who gave a lift to Betty Burke in 1746?
5. Name the sweet yellow herbal liqueur which forms an essential ingredient of the Harvey Wallbanger cocktail?

Tie-Break

How many days elapsed between the mutiny on the Bounty and the storming of the Bastille?

Round Three

1. Upon which everyday object might you see the words 'Standing on the Shoulders of Giants'? And for the second point, whose words are they?

2. Which London sports ground hosted both the first FA Cup in 1872 and the first England vs Ireland rugby union match in 1875?

3. What is the better known name of the artist Arthur George Carrick?

4. Founded in the 18th century, and named after a native American chief who had befriended William Penn, this social club later became synonymous with intrigue and corruption in the Democratic party in New York. What was its name?

5. Richard Wagner in 1883 and Robert Browning in 1889 died in different buildings on the same watery thoroughfare. Which?

6. The Italian firm of Piaggio makes a small van called 'ape', which is the Italian for bee. It also makes another vehicle, whose name is the Italian for wasp. What is it?

7. In 2005 the A52 trunk road between Nottingham and Derby acquired a new name, linked with both places. What is it?

8. Who was born in Bombay in 1865 and named after a lake in Staffordshire?

9. What product was originally advertised with the slogan 'For your throat's sake ...'?

10. To whom is attributed the saying, 'Show me a sane man and I shall cure him for you'?

Round Four

1. Which country are the current Olympic rugby union champions?
2. Which of Henry VIII's wives is buried beside him?
3. Only one X-rated film has won the Oscar for Best Picture. Name it.
4. Cayenne is a kind of chili pepper. It's also a capital city. Of which country?
5. The famous tree inside the boundary at Canterbury cricket ground was blown down in a gale in early 2005. What kind of tree was it?
6. In World War I, what were known as 'Big Willy' and 'Little Willy'?
7. Where on the human body would you find the philtrum?
8. What traditional Hindu custom was banned by the British in 1829?
9. What is the fishier name for a sky full of cirrocumulus or smaller altocumulus clouds?
10. The US Presidential retreat has been called Camp David since 1953. (i) After whom was it named? (ii) What was it called before then? A point for each.

The answers to Quiz Ten begin on page 318

QUIZ ELEVEN
WOANS (2)

Round One

1. What did Jim Davidson, Paul Daniels and Frank Bruno all threaten to do in 1997?
2. In the 2003 TV drama chronicling the life of Henry VIII, which of his wives was played by Helena Bonham-Carter?
3. On June 7th 1989, Denmark became the first country to legalise what?
4. What is the offspring of a female tiger and a male lion called?
5. Five male tennis players have won all four grand slam trophies (Wimbledon, US Open, French Open and Australian Open). But who is the only one to have won each title on a different surface?
6. A 2005 survey from Planet Rock radio to find the ultimate rock supergroup polled over 3,500 fans on the matter. The first-placed drummer, bassist, guitarist and vocalist were all members of the same band. Which band?
7. Which London district, which was the setting for a popular and long-running TV comedy series, has a name derived from the Old English for 'homestead by a peak or a hill'?
8. What children's toy was first unveiled in 1959 by a French motor mechanic named Arthur Granjean? He called it 'The Magic Screen'.
9. After the death of Sir John Betjeman, Ted Hughes was appointed Poet Laureate in 1984. Who had earlier declined the post?
10. The following slogans or catchphrases were used on television commercials, but for which brands or products? Five points in all.
  (i) 'A newspaper, not a snoozepaper.'
  (ii) 'Because life's complicated enough.'
  (iii) 'The appliance of science.'
  (iv) 'It's too orangey for crows.'
  (v) 'Papa! Nicole!'

Round Two

1. In 1986 Christa McAuliffe became the first schoolteacher ever to do what?
2. Which two actors jointly hold the record for the most Academy Award nominations without ever taking home an Oscar? A point each.
3. The layout of which city is shaped like an aeroplane, although the designer Lucio Costa had wanted it shaped like a butterfly?
4. Who was the first Labour Prime Minister to serve for a full parliamentary term?
5. Who is the only current US golfer who has won two major tournaments but never represented his country in the Ryder Cup?
6. In which 19th-century novel is Gateshead Hall the childhood home of the title character?
7. Which singer/songwriter once appeared on *Top Of The Pops* with a pot of paint and a paintbrush on top of his piano, not long after his wife had left him for a painter/decorator?
8. First shown on British TV in 1985, which Spanish-produced cartoon was based on the work of Alexander Dumas and is now regarded as something of a minor classic?
9. Which Warwickshire town, subject of a work by Sir Walter Scott, is home to Queen Elizabeth I's favourite castle?
10. The following are nicknames for Italian football teams. But which ones? A point for each. (i) Rossineri. (ii) La Vecchia Signora. (iii) Viola. (iv) Nerazzurri. (v) Azzurri.

Bonus Round

There is a link, and it's a wriggly one.

1. Who was Formula One world champion in 1981, 1983 and 1987?

2. Created a life peer in 1995, who presented the BBC television series *The Human Body*, *The Secret Life Of Twins* and *Superhuman*?

3. On July 2nd 2005, two Live 8 concerts took place in Great Britain. One was at Hyde Park, but where was the other held?

4. Who in the year 2000 became the first ever boxer to be knighted?

5. In 1999 which singer was arrested at Heathrow Airport for allegedly trying to frisk a security guard, just after he had tried to frisk her?

Tie-Break

When George Washington became President of the US in 1789, what was the life expectancy at birth for American men?

Round Three

1. Which actor's real name is Andrés Arturo García Menéndez?

2. Which British ruler lived the longest, finally passing away at the age of eighty-five?

3. Who released a self-titled album in 1997 after its original title, *Impossible Princess*, was scrapped as a mark of respect to Princess Diana?

4. This is a three-part question. If Kevin Pietersen is 626, who was (i) 24, (ii) 474, and (iii) 600?

5. When Mitsubishi launched their Pajero car it was renamed the Montero in Spanish-speaking countries. Why was this?

6. In 2005, which author poked fun at J.K. Rowling's confession that she didn't realise she was writing fantasy novels, saying, 'I would have thought that the wizards, witches, trolls, unicorns, hidden worlds . . . would have given her a clue.'?

7. Ján Ludwik Hoch was Labour MP for Buckingham between 1964 and 1970. He died in 1991. By what name was he better known?

8. In 2003 Ilich Ramirez Sánchez published a collection of writings from his prison cell. By what nickname is he better known? And for a bonus point, how did he come by this nickname?

9. Which physicist attempted to illustrate the incompleteness of the theory of quantum mechanics by proposing a theoretical experiment which involved putting a live cat in a sealed box?

10. Name the following pop duos. A point for each.
   (i) Siobhan Fahey and Marcella Detroit;
   (ii) Roland Orzabal and Curt Smith;
   (iii) Paul Humphreys and Andy McCluskey;
   (iv) Bill Medley and Bobby Hatfield;
   (v) David Peacock and Charles Hodges.

Round Four

1. Which popular American television drama originally had the working titles *Family Guy* and *Made In Jersey* before the producers settled on the name by which it is known today?

2. According to German lawyer Ralf Hocker, what act synonymous with his countrymen is not legally binding?

3. Which British writer, who died in November 1963, wrote a draft of the screenplay for Disney's animated *Alice In Wonderland*?

4. Which London institution was originally constructed above the ancient Temple of Mithras, the Roman god of contracts?

5. At the 1996 Brit Awards, Pulp frontman Jarvis Cocker was arrested on suspicion of assault after invading the stage during a performance by Michael Jackson. But which comedian, a qualified solicitor, accompanied him to the police station to represent him?

6. In order to calculate distances from London, what is generally treated as the capital's central point?

7. What is the Torino Scale used to measure?

8. What name links a town in Maryland, a star of the American TV show *Saturday Night Live* and a 15th/16th-century English war ballad?

9. Stephen Fry appeared as Lord Melchett in *Blackadder II* and as General Melchett in *Blackadder Goes Forth*. As whom did he star in *Blackadder the Third*?

10. Who fell for Ann Darrow in 1933?

The answers to Quiz Eleven begin on page 322

QUIZ TWELVE
RUSSELL & TARA (1)

Russell Taylor is a writer and journalist, best known as half of the team that produces the 'Alex' cartoon in the *Daily Telegraph*. Tara Spring is a freelance TV and radio producer who once worked on *Celebrity Fit Club*, but has since atoned in marriage to Mo and the birth of baby son Cosmo. They set their first Prince of Wales quiz on June 17th 1997, and these days do two or three a year.

It is fair to say that their quizzes polarise the regulars. Those who like a straightforward quiz, with lots of regurgitation of facts, and no fuss and nonsense, can find Russell and Tara's quizzes too rich for their tastes. But those of us who genuinely relish the craft of question-writing look forward to their quizzes all year. Russell in particular has a stern, almost puritanical approach to quiz-setting, refusing ever to purloin questions from quiz books and setting himself only the highest of quality thresholds. For copyright reasons this book sadly cannot reproduce their many and splendid picture rounds, and for practical reasons the same is true of their music rounds, which are usually performed by their friend Harry on an electronic keyboard. But what remains certainly captures the flavour of their quizzes. Russell's degree in Russian frequently manifests itself in questions on a Slavic theme, and he never fails to include a question on the Beatles. Tara's questions, by contrast, often have a Tottenham Hotspur theme: her favourite ever question involves David Ginola and some very rude words indeed.

Round One

1. Who in 1945 came out of an elevator carrying a violin case, in 1947 got off a train carrying a cello and in 1951 got on a train with a double bass?

2. Paneer is an ingredient in Indian cuisine. It is the only form of this common foodstuff, of which varieties are found all over the world, to be made in India. What type of foodstuff is it?
3. Which US Army Private was assigned the serial number 53310761?
4. Who are or were: (i) Mr Wint and Mr Kidd; (ii) Mr Statler and Mr Waldorf; (iii) Mr Cohen and Mr Greenfield?
5. In 1971, what screen relation was Glenda Jackson to Keith Michell?
6. Which word (or rather, sound) can mean the following things, each spelt in a different way: an author, a prop, a brand of deodorant and a brand of microphone?
7. They were born in Italy and Devon in 1943 and 1942 respectively but would probably not be so well known today if they had called themselves by their surnames, Proesch and Passmore. Who are they?
8. What do or did the following pop groups have in common: Oasis, Radiohead, All Saints and Crowded House?
9. The Duke of York, later George VI, competed in which sporting tournament in 1926?
10. Dick Whittington was Mayor of London four times but only elected three times. (The first time he took over when the previous incumbent died.) Each time he was elected there was a different king on the throne. A point for each king.

Round Two

1. Who was the first female in space?
2. Which international celebrity and sex symbol is the daughter of the late Earl of Abingdon, was once engaged to the Earl of Farringdon and has been credited with the discovery of 16 archaeological sites of international significance? She is 5 feet 9 inches tall, was born in Wimbledon, is an Aquarius and her blood group is AB-negative.

3. Two hundred years ago Pitt the Younger introduced taxes on, among other things, hair powder, clocks, dogs, female servants and racehorses, all to fund the war with Napoleon. Which other tax, which still exists today, did he also introduce?

4. Fuddy Heffernan is a Muswell Hill-based cabaret artist whose act is a tribute to an internationally famous pop singer who was born at 507 Archway Road in 1945. Who?

5. In Duke Ellington's signature tune he advises us to 'Take The A-Train'. Where, according to the Duke and, indeed, the New York subway map, does the A-Train go?

6. What is the zoological connection between these men: Ronald Reagan, Clint Eastwood, Eric Cantona?

7. Which real-life character appears in all the following works of fiction: *The Negotiator* by Frederick Forsyth, *XPD* by Len Deighton, *Titmuss Regained* by John Mortimer and *The Child In Time* by Ian McEwan?

8. Which saint was martyred by the Romans on the eve of Lupercalia, a pagan festival of youth, love and fertility?

9. Which modern sport was effectively invented by a Greek soldier called Pheidippides in 490 BC?

10. The following fictional characters are all known by their surnames. What were their first names? A point for each.
(i) Rambo; (ii) Magnum; (iii) Quatermass; (iv) Mr Magoo; (v) Dr Jekyll; (vi) Dr van Helsing.

Bonus Round

What is the opening line of the famous poems to which these are the closing lines?

1. And then my heart with pleasure fills,
And dances with the daffodils.

2. For he on honey-dew hath fed,
   And drunk the milk of paradise.
3. The red-breast whistles from a garden-croft;
   And gathering swallows twitter in the skies.
4. And I will come again, my love,
   Tho' it were ten thousand mile.
5. By sea-girls wreathed with seaweed red and brown
   Till human voices wake us, and we drown.

Tie-Break

The largest earthworm ever found was uncovered in South Africa. In feet and inches, what did it measure, from tip to tail?

Round Three

1. What is the connection between financier George Soros, artist Yoko Ono and the former Argentinian President Carlos Menem?
2. The title of which classic American cop show celebrates an event that took place in 1959?
3. In a classical concert who is the only musician who will sit with his/her back to the conductor?
4. Which is the only colour which is shared by the names of characters in *Reservoir Dogs*, *Captain Scarlet* and the board game Cluedo?
5. The Chair of Language and Communication at Oxford University was endowed in 1993. Who is it named after?
6. The Frenchwoman Agnès Sorel, who lived from 1421 to 1450, during the reign of Charles VII, was the first to be officially recognised as what?
7. Which contemporary American author's name means 'I have seen woe' in Russian?

8. Which is the only Beatles UK number one hit on which none of the Beatles played an instrument? (NB This is a record released by the Beatles under their own name, not a cover version by another artist.)

9. In the Bible there were five cities of the plain: Admah, Zeboiim, Zoar . . . and what were the other two, for a point each?

10. According to the preamble to the original radio series, what was Superman faster than? What was he more powerful than? And what remarkable athletic feat was he able to perform? A point for each.

Round Four

1. 'It's amazing what you can do with an E in A-level Art, a twisted imagination and a chainsaw.' Who said that?

2. If three o'clock is six, and six o'clock is three, and nine o'clock is eleven, what is twelve o'clock?

3. A famous woman disappeared between August 21st 1911 and December 12th 1913. Who was she?

4. The name of the writer of *Birds Of The West Indies*, which was first published in 1936, has become better known since it was borrowed for the name of a fictional character in a series of novels. Who was this once obscure ornithologist?

5. Which spiritual leader's name translates as 'Ocean of Wisdom'?

6. Tony Blair was the first British Prime Minister to have gone to public school since whom?

7. Peter Cook and Dudley Moore made some very rude records under the alter egos of Derek and Clive. Which was Derek and which was Clive?

8. If Shakespeare's plays were listed in alphabetical order of title, which play comes first and which comes last, for a point each? (Disregard definite and indefinite articles.)

9. Which West End musical role was played in the 1960s by both Davy Jones of the Monkees and Phil Collins?

10. What did Pink Floyd sing about once, Liza Minnelli sing about twice and Abba sing about three times?

The answers to Quiz Twelve begin on page 327

QUIZ THIRTEEN
MARCUS (3)

Round One

1. Of the many technologies seen in Star Trek, which is the only one that scientists agree is absolutely impossible?

2. In which British city would you find a football club on opposite sides of Stanley Park and a cathedral at each end of Hope Street?

3. In 1281 the Mongol army of Kublai Khan launched an invasion of Japan. Its fleet was wrecked by a massive typhoon, and the troops that did manage to land were easily dealt with by the Japanese. The Japanese named the typhoon after their expression for 'divine wind', and that name later came to be used in another context. What was that name?

4. (i) Which famous cinematic car had the number plate GEN 11?
   (ii) Which famous TV character had a car with a number plate 248 RPA?

5. Who in Macbeth is revealed to have been 'from his mother's womb untimely ripp'd'?

6. What is the only animal that has four knees?

7. How many matches must a player in the men's singles at Wimbledon win in order to win the title?

8. A sesquicentennial anniversary celebrates how many years?

9. The forces of which two countries fought a battle at New Orleans in 1815, as news had not reached them of a peace treaty that had been signed at Ghent in Belgium two weeks earlier?

10. For a point each, what are the most northerly, easterly, southerly and westerly capital cities in South America?

Round Two

1. What number connects basketball player Michael Jordan at the Chicago Bulls, David Beckham at Real Madrid, the chemical element vanadium and the number of camels once offered by an Arab for the actress Diana Dors?

2. It was founded in 1379 as St Mary's College of Winchester in Oxford, but there was already a St Mary's College in Oxford, so it has been known ever since as what?

3. The tops of the towers of the Humber Bridge are 36 millimetres further apart than their feet. For what reason?

4. What did John Hinckley do to try and gain the attention of Jodie Foster?

5. Which now familiar verb was actually coined in 1966 by the TV show *Mission Impossible*?

6. Alberta Martin, a sharecropper's daughter from Alabama, died aged ninety-seven in May 2004. She was the last person alive to have been married to a veteran of which war?

7. To which clan did the Scottish freebooter and folk hero Rob Roy belong?

8. Name the following pairs of film director brothers. A point for each pair.
   (i) The Coen brothers; (ii) The Farrelly brothers; (iii) The Wachowski brothers.

9. Is more sunlight hitting the earth's surface than forty years ago? Or less? Or is it about the same?

10. The cruiser USS *Phoenix* survived the Japanese attack on Pearl Harbor; indeed she sustained no casualties at all. Accordingly, for some years afterwards, she enjoyed a reputation as the luckiest ship in the US Navy. Under what name did she end her life?

Bonus Round

This round is entitled Celebrity Death Match. For each question you get two celebrities. All you have to do is identify which one was younger when they died. For instance: Paula Yates or Michael Hutchence? Answer: Michael Hutchence, who died at the age of thirty-seven, while Paula Yates died at forty-one.

1. Tommy Cooper or Eric Morecambe?
2. Sir Bobby Moore or St Thomas More?
3. Battle of the loincloths. Mahatma Gandhi or Johnny Weissmuller?
4. Food fight. Karen Carpenter, who starved herself to death, or Mama Cass Elliott, who ate herself to death?
5. Sid Vicious or Red Rum?

Tie-Break

What is the median age of the British population? That is, exactly half the population is younger than this age, exactly half is older. In years, months and days, please.

Round Three

1. Who was declared a traitor in 1538, a mere 368 years after his death?
2. Which artist, who died in 1954, was cut off without a penny because his family thought he had no talent and was wasting his time? For a while he had to be supported by his wife's millinery shop in Paris.

3. The largest, deepest and oldest freshwater lake in the world is in southern Siberia, and contains roughly 20 per cent of all the fresh water in the world. What is its name?

4. On which Caribbean island were V.S. Naipaul, Trevor McDonald and Brian Lara all born?

5. Abba famously had nine number ones in the UK, but only one in the US. Which song?

6. The first was Bald. The second was Fat. The third was Simple. The fourth was Fair. The fifth was Wise. The sixth was Foolish. Who or what am I talking about?

7. (i) What is the correct name for someone who hails from Sardinia? (ii) And which word can mean someone deaf to persuasion or rational argument, and is also a term for an irrational quantity in algebra?

8. Which Welsh county came into being in 1974 when Montgomeryshire, Radnorshire and the greater part of Breconshire were amalgamated?

9. In the human body, which organ in the upper part of the abdomen is responsible for filtering out ageing or imperfect red blood cells and other debris from the bloodstream?

10. Which five-times-married Hollywood actor, who also won a screenplay Oscar in 1996, suffers from aviophobia (fear of flying), chronic cutlery anxiety (particularly silverware), fear of antiques (particularly French and English antique furniture), fear of clowns, pathological hatred of Komodo dragons (which he would like to see obliterated), and possibly uniquely, a fear of Disraeli's hairstyle (because of a film he saw as a child)?

Round Four

1. The names of three Commonwealth countries start with the letter C. For a point each, what are they?
2. Dennis Tito in April 2001, Mark Shuttleworth in 2002 and Gregory Olsen in 2005. Where did they go on holiday?
3. (i) Who wrote *The Descent Of Man*? (ii) Who wrote *The Ascent of Man*?
4. The union flag appears in the top left corner of the flag of which US state?
5. Men with the surnames Reed, Newley, Kass, Holm and most recently Gibson have all performed which important role in public life?
6. If you were running the 400 metres hurdles, how many hurdles would you have to clear?
7. Who stood, without success, for the Greater Manchester constituency of Stretford and Urmston in the 2001 general election under the slogan 'For A Bigger and Betta Future', promising free breast implants, more nudist beaches and a ban on parking tickets?
8. What would native Americans do with a calumet?
9. Which fashion chain came into being in 1964 as a small shop in a Peter Robinson store in Sheffield, where it could be found up a flight of stairs?
10. Ian and Janette Tough: how were they better known during the 1970s and 1980s?

The answers to Quiz Thirteen begin on page 331

QUIZ FOURTEEN
TOM, ALI & PETE (2)

Round One

1. In the children's TV series *Bagpuss*, what was the name of the little girl who owned Bagpuss?
2. The artists Caravaggio and Michelangelo shared which Christian name?
3. Other than on a Sunday, and provided you spot him within the city walls after dark, it is legal in York to shoot a Scotsman with what weapon?
4. What, by area, is the smallest country in the European Union?
5. Pat Simmons, who died in October 2005, received £500 for winning a competition which led to her voice being known to millions between 1963 and 1985. She received dozens of marriage proposals, but never married. For what is she remembered?
6. After the death of Prince Rainier of Monaco, who is now Europe's longest-reigning monarch?
7. French rivers. Somme is 80. Loire is 42. Dordogne is 24. What is 69, and for a bonus point, why?
8. In the BBC children's programme *The Story Makers*, what is the surname of the characters whose first names are Milton, Rossetti, Byron and Shelley?
9. What is the minimum age at which it is legal to operate a petrol pump?
10. In Dad's Army, what were the Christian names of Captain Mainwaring, Sergeant Wilson, Lance Corporal Jones and Privates Frazer, Walker, Godfrey and Pike? A point for each.

Round Two

1. Who was the South African President who began the dismantling of apartheid in the late 1980s, leading to the freeing of Nelson Mandela?

2. Which word, now meaning an easy victory over weak or virtually non-existent opposition, takes its name from a contest popular in America in the 19th century, in which couples competed, strolling arm in arm, with an edible prize being awarded to the most graceful and stylish team?

3. Since November 2001, at what address would you find Ashwin, Madhuri, Sushila and Sanjeev?

4. In Britain they were extinct by the 13th century. Attempts to reintroduce them into the wild in the 17th century were wholly unsuccessful. But since farming of these animals started in the UK in the early 1980s, several have escaped captivity and there are now at least five breeding populations in England. Which animal?

5. A 13th-century piece of furniture in Winchester suggests there were 25 of them. A classic comedy film of 1975 suggests there were six, mainly for budgetary reasons. Other historical sources suggest anywhere between 12 and 1,600. What?

6. Which television gameshow, which originally ran in the UK from 1971 to 1983, was once reprimanded by the Independent Television Authority for 'gloating too much over the high value of its prizes'?

7. With the present Pope calling himself Benedict XVI, his name has moved up to second equal in the chart of most popular Papal names. For one point, what is Benedict now second equal with? And for the second point, which Pope's name is still way out in front?

8. What colour was the infamous, slightly stained dress worn by Monica Lewinsky during at least one of her appointments with Bill Clinton?

9. The autobiography *From Rags to Richie* tells the life story of whom: the cricket commentator Richie Benaud, the actor and entertainer Shane Richie, the former Deep Purple guitarist Richie Blackmore, or the former member of the boyband 5ive and sometime reality show star Richie Neville?

10. Who or what are the Linton Ploughman, the Teviot Bridge, the Circassian Circle and the Duke of Perth?

Bonus Round

1. What is the name of a province and an archipelago of the Philippines, and of a sea surrounding them? It takes its name from the word 'sug', meaning water current.

2. Who won an Olympic rowing gold medal in 1924, and in 1946 published a book that originally sold for 25 cents, but would go on to be the second biggest selling book of the next fifty years, after the Bible?

3. Which dramatist and writer of short stories, in a letter to Alexander Tikhonov, wrote, 'All I wanted was to say honestly to people: "Have a look at yourselves and see how bad and dreary your lives are!"' – in which task he might be said to have succeeded?

4. Which Canadian snooker player, born in 1958, was famous for his swashbuckling style and white suits (with matching shoes)?

5. You have 206 of them in your body. What?

Tie-Break

According to the World Nuclear Association, how many nuclear reactors were in operation worldwide in May 2004?

Round Three

1. When William Herschel discovered this planet, he wanted to name it 'George' after the reigning monarch. When he was overruled, it was given which name, which it still bears today?
2. The rivers Valency and Jordan, and Paradise stream, all flow through which Cornish village?
3. Which Irish singer and one-time punk, famous for dental problems, was rather implausibly educated for a time at the august public school of Westminster?
4. On the red, white and blue London Underground sign, what colour is the word 'UNDERGROUND'?
5. Nikolai Ivanovich Yezhov, head of the Russian secret police the NKVD in the mid-1930s, shared his nickname with which soft fruit and popular modern-day gadget?
6. The actress Lucy Davis, who played the receptionist Dawn in *The Office*, is the daughter of which British comedian, star of *All About Me*, a rather less distinguished sitcom?
7. Which Caribbean island takes its name from one of its national plants, the Bearded Fig Tree?
8. The term 'Paralympics' is a contraction of which two-word phrase?
9. Which Christian name is shared by a legendary soul singer of the 1960s, and the son of the rock star Bryan Ferry, who was arrested in 2004 when protesting against the abolition of fox hunting?
10. What are the names of the three bones in the middle ear? Either Latin or English names are acceptable. Three points in all.

Round Four

1. Michael Jackson was quite badly burned while making a TV advertisement in 1984. For what product?

2. Who, in the mid-1890s, originally failed his entrance exams to enter college in Zurich, and later published his most famous works while employed as a technical examiner (3rd class) in the Swiss patent office at Bern, having been passed over for promotion until he had 'fully mastered machine technology'?

3. What word can mean either a cylindrical or barrel-shaped cheese whose height exceeds its diameter, or a small bed on wheels that can be stored underneath another bed?

4. What name connects militant pigs, New Scotland Yard, the TV game show *Give Us A Clue* and the spotty teenage character in the sadly missed TV soap *Eldorado*?

5. Sir Isaac Newton moved permanently from Cambridge to London in 1696 to become Warden of which organisation?

6. In September 2003 an environmentally-friendly power plant was opened in Australia, fuelled by which overpriced constituent of many hotel minibars?

7. In which US state would you find the town of Amarillo?

8. Holland and Germany in 1971, Sweden in 1973, the UK in 1974 and Switzerland in 1975 were the first European countries to have what?

9. In which Olympic event is there a minimum age requirement of seven years?

10. The following six names include four genuine characters from Charles Dickens novels. One point for identifying each of the two phoney ones.
Captain Brastrap, Serjeant Buzfuz, Luke Honeythunder, Dick Swiveller, Mrs Todgers, Reverend Worthywinkle.

The answers to Quiz Fourteen begin on page 334

QUIZ FIFTEEN
DAVID (3)

Round One

1. 'He is not a great man,' said Herbert Asquith, 'he is a great poster.' Who?
2. In human anatomy, genioglossus, hyoglossus, styloglossus and chrondoglossus are all muscles that act to move what?
3. In their English spelling, only two countries in the world begin with the letter A but don't end with the letter A. Which two, for a point each?
4. What substitution was made for the first time in the history of the football World Cup in the 1994 game between Bulgaria and Mexico?
5. When Marion Crane steals $40,000 from her boss she chooses the wrong place to hide away. Where is that?
6. Parliament Street is, by all accounts, the world's narrowest street, reaching 122 cm (4 feet) at its widest. In which English cathedral city can you find it?
7. The country residence of Styles is the setting for both the first and the last cases featuring which fictional detective?
8. Which Oscar-winning actor turned down the role of Del Boy in *Only Fools And Horses*, but made several subsequent appearances as the character DCI Roy 'the Slag' Slater?
9. By what flighty nickname was Robert Stroud better known?
10. The following are Royal Houses still ruling. Which countries, for a point each?
    (i) Orange-Nassau; (ii) Bourbon; (iii) Bernadotte; (iv) Chakri.

Round Two

1. 'Dear Liz' starts a telegram supposedly sent in the 1970s, suggesting to the Queen that if she wanted to know a real man, she should get in touch. Who, according to legend, sent it?

2. Which two European countries have both Atlantic and Mediterranean coastlines? A point for each.

3. What name links the character played by George Innes in *The Italian Job*, three novels by Catherine Cookson, the subject of a song published in 1902, and *Never Mind The Buzzcocks*?

4. David Gest's marriage to Liza Minnelli, Larry Fortensky's to Elizabeth Taylor, Uri and Hannah Geller's renewal of wedding vows. What or who is the connection between these events?

5. A cameo in the 1987 children's series *Supergran* was the last ever screen appearance for which Carry On veteran?

6. At the age of fifteen she married Edward, Lord Borough, who died in 1529. Then she married John Neville, Lord Latimer, who died in 1542. After three years of marriage her third husband died aged fifty-five in 1547. Who was she?

7. The oldest complete flag known to exist in the US is the flag of which town in Massachusetts?

8. Which non-British bird is the only bird with nostrils at the end of its bill? It is almost blind, and uses its sense of smell to find food.

9. Performances of which Shakespeare play were banned in this country between 1788 and 1820?

10. Who wrote *The Curious Incident of the Dog in the Night-time*? From which developmental disorder does the narrator suffer? Which other fictional character first remarked on the curious incident? In which story? A point for each of these.

Bonus Round

1. Who said, 'To the unwashed public Joan Collins is a star, but to those who know her she is a commodity who will gladly sell her own bowel movement'?

2. Which one-time resident of 10 Downing Street co-wrote a biography of the opera singer Joan Sutherland?
3. Which British racing driver won four consecutive Belgian Grands Prix in the 1960s?
4. Which transport minister introduced the breathalyser and began the campaign for compulsory wearing of seatbelts but never learned to drive?
5. Who, in 1998 and 2000, has twice been runner-up in the BBC Sports Personality of the Year award; was nominated in 1993 as Greatest Midlander of All Time but lost out to Reginald Mitchell, the inventor of the Supermarine Spitfire; and in 2004 took part in the BBC dancing competition, *Strictly Come Dancing*, coming second?
6. And the familial link?

Tie-Break

For how many years did Anthony Blunt hold the post of Surveyor of the King's (or Queen's) Pictures?

Round Three

1. Uniquely, what crime is considered an instantly sackable offence for a BBC employee?
2. It sounds as though it comes from Northamptonshire, but has actually been manufactured in Windsor since 1930. You would find it in most hotels. What?
3. When the first example of this creature was seen in the British Museum, the curators thought it was a fake, and tried to pull its beak off. What creature?
4. Roy Figgis, Archie Glover and Norman Binns were the principal characters in which ITV sitcom?

5. What was the first major film in which the two lead actresses both had surnames beginning with Z?

6. Which painting had the original title of 'Landscape: Noon'?

7. Only two countries in the world are not only landlocked, but are surrounded by countries that are landlocked. Name them both for a point.

8. Which Hollywood duo made their final appearance together, after almost a decade apart, in the film *The Barkleys Of Broadway*? A point for each.

9. Which physicist and astronomer received an official apology from the Catholic Church in 1992?

10. 'Snooker Loopy', the 1986 'hit' by popular duo Chas and Dave, featured memorable contributions by five snooker players. Name them, for a point each.

Round Four

1. In the 19th century a scientist spilt some battery acid on his clothing and so needed his assistant. This was the prelude to the world's first what?

2. Postage stamps bearing the inscription 'Magyar Posta' come from which European country?

3. Who was murdered by an example of the species *passer domesticus*?

4. Why was nobody allowed to drive in Sweden for five hours on Sunday September 3rd 1967?

5. In the early days of *Blankety Blank* who used to tie Terry Wogan's microphone in a knot?

6. Terry Waite was special envoy to which Archbishop of Canterbury when he was taken hostage in Lebanon?

7. What is the oldest (and possibly also the smallest) republic in the world?

8. For the past seventy years you should be able to read the phrase 'a Bronx cheer' on every genuine what?

9. In the Just William stories, what was William's dog called?

10. Despite the fact that his American nurse was in attendance at his deathbed, Einstein's last words are unknown. Why?

The answers to Quiz Fifteen begin on page 338

QUIZ SIXTEEN
SIMON (1)

Simon O'Hagan is an assistant editor at the *Independent*, and for the past five years has compiled the *Independent on Sunday*'s Quiz of the Year. 'I'd wanted to do the Prince of Wales quiz for years. Finally I got a team together and we had a date for our debut – September 11 2001. I'm not sure what others felt that afternoon, but I know I nearly cried off. Then I thought, what would be the point of that? We finished runners-up and had a great time. We are four middle-aged blokes and two women in their twenties. This, of course, is for purely demographic reasons. Oh yes. We have an excellent record at the quiz but we've never actually won it. We're very often runners-up. Maybe we lack bottle. We blow leads. We need a session with a sports psychologist.'

Simon first set the quiz in 2003 and now does a couple a year. His are, perhaps appropriately, the most journalistic quizzes we encounter – pithy, sharp-witted, usually very topical – and even more appropriately he writes a lot of his questions at the last minute. (Half of one round was scrawled on a sheet of paper in the cab on the way to the pub.) Among his favourites are the one about where the post ended up that was intended for the Ascension Islands, and the order of the Beatles on the *Abbey Road* cover. 'A question like that really gets people going – which is what a good quiz night should be all about.'

Round One

1. Which 20th-century poet claimed that there was nothing he could do about the decline in his output, describing it as 'a bit like going bald'?

2. As you may know, Elvis Presley's middle name was Aron. And as you also may know, Elvis had a stillborn twin brother who was given the first name Jesse. What you may or may not know is that Jesse's middle name rhymed with Aron. What was it?

3. Which celebrated and extremely tall French film director, born in 1908, played top-class rugby for the Racing Club de France?
4. Who is the only man to captain a World Cup-winning football team and later to manage one too?
5. Which European city claims to be the setting for 128 operas, more than anywhere else in the world?
6. The first was Vic Oliver, a comedian, in 1942, and there have been around two and a half thousand more since. What?
7. Going by the shortest route, only one Canadian state separates Alaska from the other 48 mainland US states. Which one?
8. This religious sect was founded in Dublin in the late 1820s but sounds as though it should have come from somewhere else. It has no ordained priesthood and its 'exclusive' branch disdains contact with outsiders. What is the name of the sect?
9. This ductile, malleable, silver-white metallic element, with atomic number 46, is also the name of a famous theatre in the West End of London. What is it?
10. Astronomers at Johns Hopkins University announced in January 2002 that they had determined the colour of the universe. Two months later they changed their minds, and announced it was a different colour altogether. A point for each colour.

Round Two

1. Which London Underground station has the same name as a station on the Paris Metro? Clue: It's on the Circle Line.
2. *Goodbye To All That* was, as we know, the title of Robert Graves's autobiography. It was also the title used for the autobiography of a former member of Neil Kinnock's Shadow Cabinet, who lost to John Smith in the 1992 Labour Party leadership election. Who was he?

3. In 2001 a boxing match was contested between the daughters of which two former world heavyweight champions, for a point each? And for a third point, which one won?

4. Which two countries are linked by the Oresund Bridge? A point each.

5. The decisive battle in the first English Civil War, in which the Royalists were defeated by the New Model Army under Sir Thomas Fairfax, was named after the Northamptonshire village near where it was fought. Which village?

6. Which notorious figure from 1950s Britain is buried in an unmarked grave in Amersham?

7. In the men's version of this sport there are ten players on each side. In the women's version there are twelve players on each side and they play on a slightly bigger pitch. Which sport?

8. Which is the only mainland European country that is in the same time zone as the United Kingdom?

9. Name the site in Wiltshire that is home to the Defence Science and Technology Laboratory, a highly secretive UK government facility for military bio-chemical research.

10. Which 1960s rock legend was shot in the leg in January 2004 after he chased two men who had mugged his girlfriend in New Orleans?

Bonus Round

Name the year. Two points if you are spot on; one point if you are a year out.

1. In which year was the X certificate replaced by the 18 certificate in British cinemas?

2. Which year did the Queen describe as her 'annus horribilis'?

3. In which year was the first sponsored League Cup final? An extra point for naming the sponsor.

4. In which year did the first commercial Eurostar trains run?

5. In which year was Nelson Mandela released from prison?

Tie-Break

Asked in a 2002 survey which was Britain's highest mountain, what percentage of respondents answered 'Mount Everest'?

Round Three

1. In 1969 the leading French film director François Truffaut lost a few admirers when he said that there was 'a certain incompatibility between the terms "cinema" and . . .' He then named a country. Which country?

2. The Colossus of Rhodes, one of the seven wonders of the ancient world, was a huge bronze statue of which Greek god?

3. The death of the Mayor of the East Riding village of Wetwang was front page news when it happened in June 2005. What was his name?

4. What were soldiers in the British army first allowed to wear in 1902?

5. This word, originally Italian, describes a structure sited to take advantage of a fine view. It is also the name of an area of Kent close to the outskirts of London. What is the word?

6. Who died in Spandau Prison in Berlin in 1987, after decades of being addressed only as 'Prisoner Number Seven'?

7. The three points of the so-called Bermuda Triangle, where ships and planes were forever disappearing in unusual circumstances, are Bermuda itself and which two other places? A point for each.

8. *The Lemon Table* was the title of a 2004 collection of short stories by Julian Barnes, mainly on the theme of ageing, and was so called because in Chinese folklore the lemon is a symbol of what?

9. Which Midlands team have reached the FA Cup Final most times without ever having won the trophy?

10. The cover of the Beatles album *Abbey Road*. Very famous. The four Beatles are shown crossing the zebra crossing outside the St John's Wood studios. From left to right, in what order are they walking?

Round Four

1. Born in Hungary in 1847, he emigrated to America and made his name as a newspaper publisher. He is now generally credited with creating the format for the modern newspaper. Who was he?

2. He was a French scholastic philosopher who worked on logic and theology, and she was one of his pupils. Their romantic liaison caused a medieval scandal. Who were they?

3. This term dates from 1920s America and originates from the practice of concealing illegal flasks of alcohol about one's person. What is the term?

4. Which rock guitar legend was born left-handed and taught himself to play a right-handed guitar upside down?

5. Which two European Union capital cities are only 60 kilometres apart by road?

6. Up to what percentage of a pint of beer can legally be froth? Two points if you are spot on, one point if you are a percentage point out.

7. Four acts have reached number 1 in the UK with versions of 'Unchained Melody'. A point for each.

8. Which is the largest country by area in Africa?

9. In 2000 this prominent British woman was made an honorary citizen of Volgograd in Russia but died before she could visit. Who was she?

10. When Neil and Christine Hamilton went on a charity edition of *Who Wants To Be A Millionaire?*, how much did they win?

The answers to Quiz Sixteen begin on page 342

QUIZ SEVENTEEN
CHRIS (3)

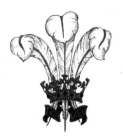

Round One

1. From where did the 1980s band T'Pau get their name?
2. Which bird was associated with the Greek goddess Athene?
3. You visit a doctor and are subjected to an Ishihara test. What are you being tested for?
4. In which fictional town might you find the characters Willy Nilly the postman, twice-widowed Mrs Ogmore-Pritchard, nostalgic Captain Cat, and Organ Morgan, who cries out 'Help!' in his sleep?
5. Possibly the best known shortstop in baseball history was born on the Daisy Hill Puppy Farm and made his public debut in October 1950. His name?
6. James Galway, the so-called Man with the Golden Flute, was a member of which orchestra between 1969 and 1975?
7. It was built in the 12th century, rebuilt twice in the 17th century and twice more in the 18th, and finally demolished in 1902. What stands now on the site of the old Newgate Prison?
8. Which major religious leader won the Nobel Peace Prize in 1989?
9. In which sport did Pakistan's Jahangir Khan remain unbeaten for five years eight months from 1981, winning 555 consecutive matches?
10. Which 1965 film, in which he didn't appear, took its title from a line Warren Beatty used to use on his girlfriends at the time?

Round Two

1. In US comic books, when a youth named Billy Batson said 'Shazam', who or what did he become?

2. Which record company, a significant name in blues and rock 'n' roll, had its headquarters at 2120 South Michigan Avenue, Chicago?

3. They are bred in Argentina, and are the smallest of their kind in the world. What kind of creature is a falabella?

4. Jenners department store became part of the House of Fraser group in March 2005. In which city might you find it?

5. Which British athlete was helped over the line by his father after his injury in the Barcelona Olympics?

6. A fillet of beef, covered in paté and mushrooms, wrapped in puff pastry and baked in an oven. What's the name of this dish?

7. In 1366, in the Belgian town of Leuven, a brewery called The Horn was established. It still exists, but under what other name?

8. On an Ordnance Survey map, what is represented by a red triangle?

9. In the Harry Potter novels of J.K. Rowling, Harry can understand the language of snakes. This makes him what special type of wizard?

10. What, according to Peter Cook's E.L. Wisty, prevented him from being a judge?

Bonus Round

1. Who was the leader of the Labour Party from 1980 to 1983?

2. How does the name of the terrorist group Al-Qaeda translate into English?

3. Who played Harry in *When Harry Met Sally*?

4. As in the dish 'chilli con carne', what is the translation of the word 'carne'?

5. What was Kenny Rogers' first solo number one single in the UK?

6. The link?

Tie-Break

How many different versions of the Beatles' song 'Yesterday' were recorded by other artists in the song's first seven years?

Round Three

1. What name does Fireman Sam give his engine?
2. The doyenne of war correspondents, she was married for five years in the 1940s to Ernest Hemingway. What was her name?
3. How can you identify a teddy bear made by the German firm of Steiff?
4. What word is used in Inuit for a polar bear?
5. John Connelly, Terry Paine, Jimmy Greaves and Ian Callaghan. What particularly connects these four footballers?
6. 'A bribe to make a housekeeper think she's a householder.' That's the American writer Thornton Wilder describing what?
7. What is the national treasure of the Middle-Eastern country of Lugash?
8. Who, in the early 1920s, united a number of trade unions to form the Transport and General Workers' Union?
9. David van Day and Thereze Bazar had a few hits in the early 1980s under what name?
10. Who is the most famous man ever to have managed a branch of Swallow's Bank?

Round Four

1. The musical *Chicago* won the Best Picture Oscar for 2002. What was the last musical to win the same award? Bonus point for the year. (Remember, it's the year in which the film came out, not the following year when the awards are handed out.)

2. Which measurement is the greater: the height of Mount Everest, or the depth of the Marianas Trench, the deepest point in any ocean?
3. The band, The Corrs. What's the brother's name?
4. Which pottery manufacturer was Charles Darwin's most famous grandfather?
5. 'It's a good thing to follow The First Rule of Holes: if you are in one, stop digging.' Useful advice for any politician from the former MP for Leeds East. Who is he?
6. What is the name of the super-hero played by Ardal O'Hanlon (and since 2006, by James Dreyfus) in the BBC1 sitcom *My Hero*?
7. Which creatures form the main part of the diet of ladybirds?
8. *Losing My Virginity* is the title of whose autobiography?
9. What is the name of the Jack Russell terrier that accompanies TV chef Rick Stein on his travels around Britain?
10. Apparently she had never heard of Bob Geldof, and spent all day during the recording of the Band Aid 20 single calling him 'Mr Gandalf'. Who is this?

The answers to Quiz Seventeen begin on page 346

QUIZ EIGHTEEN:
RUSSELL & TARA (2)

Round One

1. What is the name shared by the heroes of the films *If . . .* and *Taxi Driver*, which is also the name of a Scottish band?
2. Which fruit, native to Pacific South America, was once known as a 'love apple' in the US because some people believed it had aphrodisiac qualities?
3. Mrs Dupree was last seen driving to the end of town wearing her golden gown in strict defiance of the orders of her three-year-old son. What was his full name?
4. In the Bible, who slaughtered a quarter of the world's population?
5. Audie Murphy was America's most decorated soldier in World War II. Who played him in the 1955 Hollywood biopic *To Hell And Back*?
6. A question on games. It is known as a 'runner' (Laufer) in German, a 'fool' (fou) in French, and an 'elephant' (slon) in Russian. What is it known as in English?
7. What colour is the upholstery in (i) the House of Commons, and (ii) the House of Lords? A point for each.
8. As well as being the co-founder of the motor company, the Hon. Charles Stewart Rolls in his death in 1910 achieved what other distinction?
9. How many individuals are mentioned in the titles of novels by Dickens? (Individuals either mentioned by name and referred to more indirectly. We just need a number for the points.)
10. Twenty years ago it was possible to take the Trans-Siberian Express from Sverdlovsk to Gorki. Today it isn't. Why not?

Round Two

1. Who came fourth for Spain in the Eurovision Song contest in 1970, singing a song called 'Gwendolyne'?

2. The four most renowned World War I poets were Rupert Brooke, Siegfried Sassoon, Wilfred Owen and Isaac Rosenberg. Which one didn't die in the War?

3. Who is the only ambassador who doesn't have to work in a foreign country?

4. These are three famous stars of a long-running radio, TV and cinema series. One was called after a metal, the name of the second means 'fool' in Spanish, and he in turn always referred to the third character by a name that translates as 'trusty scout'. A point for each.

5. In 1903 Earl Russell queued all night to get the first ever what?

6. In which country is the bridge over the river Kwai?

7. What is the connection between Jean Paul Marat, the 18th-century French revolutionary, Jim Morrison of The Doors, and Claude François the French pop singer?

8. Who was the object of the narrator's affections in John Betjeman's poem 'A Subaltern's Love Song'?

9. Which former night club pianist has been musical director to Marlene Dietrich, collaborated with Elvis Costello and performed on stage with Noel Gallagher?

10. Name the four Shakespeare plays that begin and end with the same letter. A point each. (Note: regnal numbers do not count as words, so *Henry V* and *Henry VIII* are not valid answers. And ignore subtitles like 'Prince of Denmark'.)

Bonus Round

1. Which famous three-sided structure located on a triangular island block at 23rd Street, Broadway and 5th Avenue was one of New York's first skyscrapers and is now a National Historic Landmark?

2. In *Alice in Wonderland*, what was advertised as 'in this style 10/6'?

3. What word goes with friend, lord and war?

4. Which one-hit-wonder band charted in February 1977 with 'They Shoot Horses, Don't They'?

5. If James Joyce was a man, what was Dylan Thomas?

6. What item of clothing is missing?

Tie-Break

According to a 2002 poll in *Maxim* magazine, what percentage of women would rather date someone who liked cats than someone who didn't?

Round Three

1. The name of Christian Ludwig is known today for a series of musical works which were dedicated to him, but which he never bothered to have performed. Of which German state was he Margrave?

2. Petit gris and Bourgogne are varieties of which foodstuff?

3. In the late 1960s, the Beatles set up their own record company and called it Apple. The idea for the name and logo came about after Paul McCartney bought a painting by which artist?

4. At whose funeral in 1928 were the pallbearers Rudyard Kipling, J.M. Barrie, John Galsworthy, George Bernard Shaw, Edmund Gosse and A.E. Housman?

5. What was called 'Goddess Mother of the World' until 1865 when it was renamed prosaically after a local surveyor?

6. What is the link between the following films: *Home Alone, Die Hard, It's A Wonderful Life*?

7. Who was the author of the following Victorian novels: *Beatrice, The Autobiography of a Flea, The Yellow Room* and *The Whippingham Papers*? We're just looking for one name.

8. Talking of fleas, the most commonly found flea on cats is the cat flea (*ctenocephalides felis*). What is the common name of the flea that is most frequently found on dogs?

9. John Huston's 1962 film *The Misfits* was the last screen appearance of two Hollywood legends. Which two, for a point each?

10. What word links these years: 1666, 1851, 1963?

Round Four

1. Two European countries have names that translate as East Land (or East Realm). Which two, for a point each?

2. Which European cinematic genre was invented in 1964 in a German/Spanish/Italian co-production?

3. Three eminent British composers died in 1934. A point for each.

4. Which Canadian province consists of an island and a length of coastline, both of which have a breed of dog named after them?

5. Five alphabets: English, Greek, Arabic, Russian and Hebrew. For a point each, which of these five has the most letters, and which has the fewest letters?

6. What modern word derives from the practice of Popes having to claim that their illegitimate sons were actually their nephews in order to recognise them?

7. In World War II how many enemy aircraft did a fighter pilot need to shoot down to qualify as an ace?

8. Which quasi-military organisation, founded in London in 1865, has the motto 'Blood and Fire'?

9. Who said, 'You can't imagine the extra work I had when I was a God'?

10. Munroe, Garrett, Duncan, Munroe, Welles, Rogers. Who were they?

The answers to Quiz Eighteen begin on page 346

QUIZ NINETEEN
PATRICK (3)

Round One

1. The first episode of *Doctor Who* was shown the day after what international event?
2. Who is sixth in line to the throne?
3. Lord Snowdon in 1950, Colin Moynihan in 1977 and Hugh Laurie in 1980: what did they all do in those years?
4. What links Singapore with London Zoo?
5. Which prominent American politician's Christian name is a misreading of an Italian musical term meaning 'with sweetness'?
6. What is the correct word for (i) a player on the flute, and (ii) a player on the lute?
7. When Queen Victoria died which of her grandsons was by her side?
8. The Princess Royal unveiled a new war memorial in Park Lane In London in November 2004. A memorial to whom or what?
9. What links Old Etonians, Old Carthusians and Clapham Rovers?
10. (i) Who was appointed Clerk of Works to King Richard II in 1389? (ii) Who was appointed Latin Secretary to Oliver Cromwell's Council of State in 1649? (iii) Who was appointed secretary to the Admiralty in 1672?

Round Two

Each question in this round is a list of four items. Note that they are not necessarily the only four in the group. But in each case the question is: what do they have in common?

1. The sun, the new, the hidden, the stranger.
2. James, Margaret, John, Anthony.

3. Max von Sydow, Robert Powell, Willem Dafoe, James Caviezel.
4. Lady Cabstanleigh, Dr Smart-Allick of Narkover School, Captain de Courcy Foulenough and Dr Strabismus (Whom God Preserve) of Utrecht.
5. Flowery, Reddish-coloured, Snowy, Mountainous.
6. Tatiana Romanova, Anya Amasova, Pola Ivanova, Natalya Semyonova.
7. Cardiff (1905), Leicester (1919), Sunderland (1992), Preston (2002).
8. King David, Alexander the Great, Julius Caesar, Charlemagne.
9. John Bunyan, Oscar Wilde, Adolf Hitler, Jeffrey Archer.
10. Jason, Darren, Marlon, Mark.

Bonus Round

1. Which English composer, who died in 1972 at the age of ninety-six, composed thirty-two symphonies, the first of which is subtitled 'The Gothic'?
2. Name the character played by Ardal O'Hanlon in Father Ted.
3. Why did actor Neil Morrissey buy a pub called Brown's Hotel in Laugharne, west Wales, in 2004?
4. In which city could you see a memorial portrait of Sir John Hawkwood by Paolo Uccello?
5. In the Bible, who was the father of the apostles James and John?

Tie-Break

In which year were one-way streets first established in London?

Round Three

1. Who took over as the narrator of *The Magic Roundabout*, nine years after the death of Eric Thompson?
2. In 1816 a French ship was wrecked off the west coast of Africa. The fate of the survivors of the wreck was the subject of a famous painting. For a point each, name the ship, and name the artist.
3. Charlotte Brew in 1977 was the first woman to do what?
4. Who is the only US President to have been granted a patent?
5. In a famous novel, and more recently in a musical, how was Anne Catherick better known?
6. The top line of a French typewriter keyboard differs from ours by two letters. What is it?
7. What motoring first was achieved by a Mr Beene on March 16th 1935?
8. As they stand, which is higher, the London Eye or the Wembley Arch?
9. Whose was the first face seen on Channel 4 when it started broadcasting in 1982?
10. What do the following intials stand for: FRS, FRCS, FRICS? A point each.

Round Four

1. Where was the *Titanic* built?
2. What are Baskerville, Caslon, Garamond and Bembo?
3. Thomas Bruce, born in 1766, was HM Ambassador to Constantinople between 1799 and 1803, and is mainly remembered now for a controversial bit of archaeology. How is he better known?
4. In January 1943 a conference between Churchill and F.D. Roosevelt was held in which African town?

5. A stock market crash in 1883 provoked whom to give up stockbroking and paint full-time?
6. Who was married successively to Louis VII of France and Henry II of England?
7. To an organist, what is a cipher?
8. 'Who's your fat friend?' asked Beau Brummell. Which king did the fat friend become?
9. Which US state has a border with only one other?
10. What, very precisely, have the following in common: St Thomas More, Mozart, Emile Zola, Gandhi, General Patten and T.E. Lawrence?

The answers to Quiz Nineteen begin on page 355

QUIZ TWENTY
WOANS (3)

Round One

1. In February 2005, who became the youngest ever Dame Commander of the Order of the British Empire at the age of twenty-eight?

2. Which coffee shop franchise shares its name with a character in Herman Melville's novel *Moby Dick*?

3. Which band have had more hit singles than any other in UK chart history, scoring more than sixty chart successes since their debut in 1968?

4. Who replaced his uncle as President of the Football Association in 2005? And for a bonus point, which football team does he support?

5. Which brewery, founded by J.C. Jacobsen in 1847, originally used a swastika as one of its logos?

6. In September 1978, Janet Parker, a photographer for the University of Birmingham Medical School, was the last person in the world to die from what?

7. Who was the first black footballer to play for England? And who was the first black footballer to captain England? A point for each.

8. The 12 certificate was introduced to British cinemas in 1989. Which film, the first in a long-running series, was the first to be given this rating?

9. In 1995 King Abdullah II of Jordan appeared as an extra in his favourite science fiction TV show. What was it?

10. After the England cricket team's success in the 2005 Ashes series, those who took part received many accolades and plaudits. For a point each, who were the beneficiaries of the following:

(i) The freedom of Sheffield;

(ii) Appointed honorary vice-president of Bristol City FC;

(iii) A seat in the Newcastle United directors' box for life;

(iv) British citizenship;

(v) Signed a sponsorship deal with Heinz?

Round Two

1. In April 2003, eighty-six-year-old great-grandfather Alexander Muat became the oldest person in the country to receive what?

2. Who won the 1991 Best Actor award at the Oscars despite being on screen for only a fraction over 16 minutes?

3. Which island was discovered by the Portuguese in 1511, was captured by the British in 1810, became a republic in 1992 but remains a member of the Commonwealth?

4. The P.G. Wodehouse character Roderick Spode and the Elvis Costello song 'Less Than Zero' were both inspired by which politician, who in 1918 became the youngest member of the House of Commons to take his seat, stood for election for the last time in 1966, and died in December 1980?

5. Which is the only song with a palindromic title recorded by a group with a palindromic name to hit the UK top ten?

6. What are the following fears of: (i) pluviophobia; (ii) papaphobia; (iii) dutchphobia?

7. In October 2000, footballer 'Sir' Les Ferdinand admitted to being part of a gang responsible for the 1983 vandalism of what?

8. Who published her debut novel *Swan* and released her debut album *Baby Woman* in 1995?

9. What are the alcohol-by-volume contents for the following drinks: (i) Smirnoff Red vodka; (ii) Jameson; (iii) Lambrini?

10. Many writers die leaving a work unfinished. For a point each, then, which writers were working on the following novels when the Grim Reaper intervened:

(i) *The Salmon Of Doubt*;

(ii) *The Double Tongue*;

(iii) *The Mystery of Edwin Drood*;

(iv) *The Last Tycoon*.

Bonus Round

1. In August 2005 the ashes of which writer were blown into the sky from a cannon in Aspen, Colorado?

2. Which online retailer was originally going to be called Cadabra, until someone pointed out that the name sounded too much like 'cadaver', as in corpse?

3. When Great Britain rugby league captain Andy Farrell switched codes to rugby union in 2005, which club did he sign for?

4. What is the biggest selling bottled 'Indian' beer in the UK?

5. According to William of Malmesbury, the tribute of 300 of these animals, payable yearly by the King of Wales to Edgar the Peaceful (who ruled from 959 to 975), ceased after the third year because 'he could find no more'. But some were to be found in England until the 15th century and in Ireland and Scotland until the 18th century. Which animal?

Tie-Break

In 1988 the largest game of musical chairs of all time took place in Singapore. How many people took part?

Round Three

1. Which biblical character's name means 'the one who draws' in Hebrew and 'the child' or 'the offspring' in Egyptian?
2. In 2005, which country threatened to sue comedian Sacha Baron Cohen for portraying them as 'a country populated by drunks who enjoy cow-punching'?
3. Who is the only United States citizen ever to be offered a position as a foreign head of state?
4. Who said, 'It's like a dagger to my heart to think a Scouser would rob me,' after her home was burgled in August 2003?
5. Who, on November 30th 2005, became the sole owner of a number of London theatres, including the Palladium, the Theatre Royal and the Gielgud Theatre?
6. The radioactive element Americium 241 is occasionally found in what kind of household object?
7. Which charitable organisation was founded in 1866 and has benefited fashion designer Bruce Oldfield and actor Neil Morrissey, among others?
8. Martin Scorsese's 1997 film *Kundun* was a biopic of whom?
9. Who, with Tony Thompson, replaced the late John Bonham on drums for Led Zeppelin's performance at the 1985 Live Aid concert?
10. The following all won the 1966 football World Cup with England, but which club sides were they playing for at the time? A point for each.
   (i) Jack Charlton; (ii) Gordon Banks; (iii) Alan Ball; (iv) Nobby Stiles; (v) George Cohen.

Round Four

1. Which members of the Royal Family acted as team captains in the 1987 special edition of *It's A Knockout*? Two points for all four.

2. Which king was the only grandson of William the Conqueror to take the throne?

3. Which village in the Peak District is reputedly the highest in England at 1518 feet above sea level? As an isolated community it formerly enjoyed a reputation as a hotbed of illicit activity, including cockfighting and counterfeiting.

4. Which video game character has shifted over 184 million units, making it by far the bestselling video game franchise ever? And for the second point, who played this character in the 1993 film?

5. Who was the first black Member of Parliament to become a Cabinet Minister?

6. Which Indian cricketer broke the record for the highest number of one-day international appearances at the end of 2005 when he represented his country for the 357th time?

7. Why was Mandy Alwood all over our front pages in August 1996?

8. In the human body, what are the more common names for (i) the axilla, and (ii) the hallux?

9. The George Gershwin songs 'Nice Work If You Can Get It' and 'Someone To Watch Over Me' come from which 1990s portmanteau musical?

10. In Britain, putting the word 'Regis' after a place name indicates a close connection with the king or queen of the time. There are eight such places in the UK. Name four of them for a point each.

The answers to Quiz Twenty begin on page 359

QUIZ TWENTY-ONE
MARCUS (4)

Round One

1. In which EU country is it legally possible, if still highly unusual, to marry a dead person?
2. The three primary colours of light are red, green and blue. What are the three primary colours of paints or pigments?
3. According to Pliny the Elder, the ancient Greeks thought that this animal's parents were a camel and a leopard, and so named it a 'camelopard'. What do we call it?
4. Tony Blair had no previous Cabinet experience when he became Prime Minister in 1997. Who was the last man before him to become Prime Minister without previous Cabinet experience?
5. The inner core of the earth is chiefly composed of which metal?
6. Who wrote 'Baby Love', 'Where Did Our Love Go' and 'Stop! In The Name of Love' for the Supremes, 'I Can't Help Myself' and 'Reach Out I'll Be There' for the Four Tops, 'How Sweet It is' for Marvin Gaye and 'This Old Heart Of Mine' for the Isley Brothers, among many others?
7. What did the ancient Greeks call the region that now covers modern Lebanon and the coastal plains of Syria?
8. Football. In a 1987 Freight Rovers trophy tie between Aldershot and Fulham, there were a record 28 . . . what?
9. Which two rivers meet at Tewkesbury in Gloucestershire? A point for each.

10. Second novels. A point for each of these.

(i)   Zadie Smith's first novel was *White Teeth*. Her second, published in 2002, was what?

(ii) Evelyn Waugh's first novel was *Decline And Fall*. His second, published in 1930, was what?

(iii) Alex Garland's first novel was *The Beach*. His second, published in 1998, was what?

(iv) Charles Dickens's first novel was *The Pickwick Papers*. His second, published in 1838, was what?

Round Two

1. Who most famously rode the horses Salvador, O'Malley, Mattie Brown and Farmer's Boy?

2. Who won the Best Actress Oscar for 1969?

3. This illegitimate son of the 1st Duke of Northumberland lived between 1765 and 1829 and devoted himself to chemistry and mineralogy. But in a fit of pique at the Royal Society's rejection of a paper by him in 1826, he bequeathed £105,000 to found an institution in America 'for the increase and diffusion of knowledge among men'. What was his surname?

4. In the animated version Pongo always had 72 spots, Perdita had 68 spots and each pup had an even 32. According to one source that made 6,469,952 spots in the completed film. Who created these characters?

5. London history. By the eleventh century, according to Peter Ackroyd, this area just beyond the city walls was a recognised venue for the sale of horses, sheep and cattle, so well known for drunkenness, rowdiness and violence that it had already earned the nickname 'Ruffians' Hall'. How do we know this area today?

6. Who took 5 for 19 in his only Test match in 1889 and later appeared in *Lord Fauntleroy* and *Wee Willie Winkie*?

7. This religious leader was born in Sharon, Vermont, and received his first 'call' as a prophet in 1820. Three years later an angel told him of a hidden gospel on golden plates, and on the night of September 22nd 1827, the sacred records were delivered into his hands. In 1830 he founded the Church of the Latter-Day Saints. What was this man's name?

8. Who directed the films *The Tall Guy* and *Bean*, and had a top 5 hit single in 1987 with 'Rockin' Around The Christmas Tree', a duet with Kim Wilde?

9. One of the two stars of this early 1970s American TV series committed suicide after the end of the first season, and was replaced for season two by the man who had previously done the voice-over on the opening credits. What was the series?

10. What was the name of the lead guitarist of this band?

Bonus Round

Football World Cup finals. We give you the result, you supply the year.

1. Uruguay 2 Brazil 1.
2. Argentina 3 Holland 1 (after extra time).
3. Brazil 3 Czechoslovakia 1.
4. West Germany 1 Argentina 0.
5. Italy 4 Hungary 2.

Tie-Break

My old friend Terence is a management consultant, who lives in London. Not long ago he had to visit a client in Stratford-upon-Avon. He needed to arrive there by 9:15 a.m. and felt like going by train. So he rang National Rail Enquiries and asked them what train he would need to catch. The helpful man on the other end of the line consulted his timetables and told Terence that there was indeed a service from Marylebone that arrived in Stratford at 9:17 a.m. What time would Terence have to be in Marylebone in order to catch this service? Note: this was a service, not a single train. Terence would have to change at least once.

Round Three

1. Three American Presidents, John Adams, Thomas Jefferson and James Monroe, all died on the same date, and Calvin Coolidge was born on that date as well. Which?
2. 9.4607 x 10^{15} metres. How is that more frequently referred to?
3. The New Testament, the Beatitudes. 'Blessed are the pure in heart: for they shall . . .' what?
4. Josef Stalin took his name from the Russian word for 'steel'. His foreign minister, and later deputy prime minister, Vyacheslav Molotov, took his name from a word for which implement?
5. (i) Do any centipedes have a hundred or more legs? (i) Do any millipedes have a thousand or more legs? A point for each correct answer.
6. Smersh, Spectre, Thrush, Uncle: which is the odd one out and why?

7. In the early 13th century the mathematician Leonardo de Pisa, also known as Fibonacci, travelled to North Africa and brought back the Hindu-Arabic number system (1, 2, 3 ,4 . . .) we use today. He also brought back a numerical concept unknown to the ancient Greeks, but one without which modern civilisation simply couldn't have come into existence. What was it?

8. What two first names are shared by the 19th-century painter of *Chaucer Reciting His Poetry* and *The Last of England* and his grandson, the author of the novel *The Good Soldier*?

9. The smallest margin of victory in a horse race is a short head. What is anything over 30 lengths called?

10. Roy and Silo live in New York's Central Park Zoo. They cohabit, they are affectionate in public, have been inseparable for years, and have even displayed an urge to procreate, having once tried to hatch a rock. They are both male, and the first observed gay examples of which bird?

Round Four

1. After the nationalisation of the railways in 1947, what did the Fat Director become?

2. In March 1969 David Quayle and Richard Block opened their first shop on Portswood Road, Southampton. What did they call it?

3. 'It wasn't a donkey jacket at all. It was a perfectly respectable green coat. The Queen Mother said she liked it very much.' Whose words on the eve of his 90th birthday in 2003?

4. What is the nearest European capital city to London?

5. Which month made Don McLean shiver?

6. Which British Prime Minister was reputedly one sixteenth Iroquois, of the American Indian Confederation?

7. Which moon of Jupiter is the largest satellite in the Solar System?

8. 'The Dead of Jericho', 'The Silent World of Nicholas Quinn' and 'Service of All The Dead' were the first three episodes of which TV series?

9. Who went in search of the Great Pink Sea Snail?

10. A Liverpudlian called Mark Roberts has done what at the Superbowl, Royal Ascot, Wimbledon and the Tour de France? He is the only known person to have done this at all four events.

The answers to Quiz Twenty-One begin on page 363

QUIZ TWENTY-TWO
TOM, ALI & PETE (3)

Round One

1. Crocodile dung. A mixture of acacia bark, honey and dates. Carrot seeds, and a drink made from dried beaver testicles. These have all been used in the past, by various cultures, for what purpose?

2. In the last century, only three people resigned their membership of the Privy Council. Two of them had the same first name, and the third's first name, if abbreviated, sounded the same as the first two. Who were they?

3. Which sporting goods company was founded by the Humphreys brothers in Cheshire in 1920?

4. The word 'ombudsman', meaning an official appointed to address complaints by individuals against public authorities, has its origins in which European language?

5. If Lord Lucan were to reappear tomorrow, why could he not make a speech in the House of Lords explaining where he has been all this time?

6. The slogan 'pile it high and sell it cheap' was an early catchphrase of which prominent high street retailer?

7. Which Sheffield-born seventy-seven-year-old, easily recognised by his pink face, blue-and-black hat and black-and-white striped top, has stated repeatedly that he has no plans to retire?

8. What, in London, has at various times served as a zoo, an observatory, a mint and a prison?

9. What is the common Japanese abbreviation of a longer phrase meaning 'the digits must remain single'?

10. Who are the only three footballers who have scored more goals for England than Michael Owen? A point for each.

Round Two

1. In March 2005 twenty-five-year-old Johnson Beharry became the first new owner in nearly twenty-three years of what?

2. What name is shared by a suspension bridge, a modern Roman Catholic cathedral and a city that styles itself 'the Norwegian capital of Texas'? And for a bonus point, which popular children's TV character has this surname?

3. Which film, made for only $300,000 and released in 1978, went on to become the highest-grossing independent film ever made (at the time)?

4. (i) The Corkscrew, at Alton Towers, was the world's first what?
   (ii) Oblivion, at Alton Towers, was the world's first what? A point for each.

5. What was the name of the first *Blue Peter* dog?

6. In the years after 1660, under a set of laws known as 'the Bloody Code', what was the maximum sentence for stealing from a shipwreck, impersonating a Chelsea Pensioner or cutting down a young tree?

7. Which foodstuff and educational aid was reintroduced by its manufacturers Heinz in 2005 after a fifteen-year absence?

8. Homer Simpson shares his middle name with which perching bird of the crow family? And for the second point, what forename is shared by his boss Mr Burns and Scotty from *Star Trek*?

9. What comes next in this sequence: six-bagger, five-bagger, four-bagger, turkey, double . . . ?

10. Which long-running play is set in a small hotel in snowbound rural Berkshire, and was originally titled *Three Blind Mice*?

Bonus Round

1. In which New York borough is John F. Kennedy airport?
2. The song or nursery rhyme 'Pop Goes the Weasel' celebrates which profession?
3. *Corvus frugilegus*, which literally translates as 'fruit-picking crow', is the Latin name for which bird?
4. Auckland Castle is the official residence of whom?
5. Cambridge has one, founded in 1441. London has one, founded in 1829. Oxford does not have one. What?
6. Which one is missing?

Tie-Break

What, according to a calculation by the mathematician Bertram Felgenhauer, is the number of possible valid solutions to a standard 9×9 Sudoku grid?

Round Three

1. The Austrian-born chemist and writer Carl Djerassi, later dubbed 'the father of free love', participated in the invention of what in 1951?
2. 'Of course it's fantastic to have bands formed in garages, but there is a market for other types of music. I mean, think of all the great bands from the past who didn't write their own music, like the Beatles. Well, actually, the Beatles did write their own music, didn't they? But loads of others.' Which former pop band member and now pouting solo artist said this in 2005?
3. Which is the largest island in the Mediterranean? And the second largest? And the third largest? A point for each, but only if you get them in the right order.

4. In *Only Fools And Horses*, Rodney Trotter shares his middle name with which premiership football club?

5. Several people have won *Time* magazine's 'Person of the Year' award on more than one occasion, but only three non-Americans have done so. The years were: (i) 1939 and 1942; (ii) 1940 and 1949, and (iii) 1987 and 1989. Who were those double winners, for a point each?

6. In the *Indiana Jones* films, what is Indiana's real first name?

7. The name of which composer, who died in 1856 at the age of forty-six, is an anagram of 'Brahms nocturne'?

8. Which characters make up the Fantastic Four in the classic comic strip and recent film? A point for each.

9. Roman Abramovitch famously owns Chelsea Football Club, but there is one part of it he does not in fact own. Which part?

10. The following are children of celebrity mums. For a point each, name the mums.
(i) Apple and Moses; (ii) Dylan and Carys; (iii) Lila; (iv) Harvey and Junior; (v) Finlay, Rafferty, Iris and Rudy.

Round Four

1. Which word, meaning to cancel or annul, is also the term for failing to follow suit in a card game when able to do so?

2. The screenwriter Paul Schrader wrote the scripts for *Taxi Driver* and *The Last Temptation of Christ*, and co-wrote *Raging Bull*. He also supplied the original script for a 1977 film, but refused a credit after the director Steven Spielberg made huge changes to it. Which film?

3. Which Olympic athletics event was reinstated in 1960 after a 32-year break, which had been caused by the distressed state of some of the competitors after the final in 1928?

4. There are eighty-eight keys on a standard piano. How many are white and how many are black?

5. 'Heartbreaker' by Dionne Warwick, 'Islands in the Stream' by Kenny Rogers and Dolly Parton, 'Chain Reaction' by Diana Ross. What's the connection?

6. Who said, after losing a libel case, 'If this is justice, I'm a banana'?

7. Springfield is the home of the Simpsons, and it's also the real-life capital of which US state?

8. Footballers' salaries are often described as equivalent to the GDP of a small country. What does GDP stand for?

9. In 1929 a new soft drink was introduced under the name 'Bib-Label Lithiated Lemon-Lime Soda'. It's still popular today, but under what name?

10. The following TV series were spin-offs from other shows. Name the original show, for a point each. (i) *Tucker's Luck*; (ii) *Robin's Nest*; (iii) *Laverne and Shirley*; (iv) *George and Mildred*; (v) *Mork and Mindy*.

The answers to Quiz Twenty-Two begin on page 367

QUIZ TWENTY-THREE
RUSSELL & TARA (3)

Round One

1. What three rivers make Manhattan an island?
2. Shrove Tuesday is so called because it is the day on which people were traditionally 'shriven'. What does 'shriven' mean?
3. What community would you find in between Whitechapel Road and Old Kent Road, Marlborough Street and Bow Street, and Bond Street and Oxford Street?
4. Marie Curie became the first woman to win a Nobel prize when she won the award for Physics in 1903. What was remarkable about the next two female recipients of Nobel Prizes for science? They were both for Chemistry, and awarded in 1911 and 1935.
5. What, collectively, are The Lass That Loved a Sailor, The Slave of Duty, The King of Barataria and The Town of Titipu?
6. London postcodes are derived from points of the compass (N, SW etc.). But two points of the compass are unrepresented: NE and S. Which two British cities have these postcodes instead?
7. Four countries on the South American continent don't have Spanish as their official language. For a point each, which four? Clue: all four have a different language.
8. What is the catering connection between film director Anthony Minghella, rocker Francis Rossi, actress Daniela Nardini and singer/songwriter Chris Rea?
9. Which great musician's middle name literally means 'Love God'?
10. Of British Prime Ministers who held office in the 20th century: did more of them have moustaches or beards, were more clean-shaven, or did we have the same number of each? In other words was it a victory for the Hairies, a victory for the Smoothies, or a draw? Two points for the result, and an extra three points for the exact score.

Round Two

1. How many replies did Sting get to his message in a bottle?
2. Which national airline's name means 'Towards the sky'?
3. According to a much-loved song, what might you do on the Pont St-Benezet in the south of France?
4. The spire of St Bride's church in London EC4 provided the inspiration for what culinary innovation?
5. Which of the following was NOT killed by a tree: James Dean, Jackson Pollock, Albert Camus or Marc Bolan?
6. Which best-selling book, first published in 1972 and billed as a 'gourmet guide', was originally divided into three sections called 'Starters: the Basic Ingredients', 'Main Courses Which Everyone Needs' and 'Sauces and Pickles for Special Occasions'?
7. Hungarian Horntail, Common Welsh Green, Swedish Short Snout and Chinese Fireball are all breeds of what type of animal?
8. He was secretary of state twice and First Lord of the Admiralty three times and is the British Earl whose name remains the most commonly used throughout the world. Who was he?
9. Which onetime world leader wrote a trilogy of novels called *Small World*, *Resurrection* and *Virgin Soil*, which won a hatful of literary awards?
10. Manifest, Bittersweet, Bohemian, Unchained. Which pilot is missing?

Bonus Round

The answers are the names of goalkeepers who played for England.

1. He represented England 61 times and in his club career played for Liverpool and Tottenham, among others. His son Stephen is also a professional footballer.
2. He was born in 1966 and capped 23 times for England between 1992 and 2003.
3. His father had been a goalkeeper at Ipswich Town. He played twice for England, made 373 appearances for Manchester United between 1978 and 1987, and now lives in South Africa.
4. He was born in 1942, played once for England and 535 times for Manchester United for whom he also scored two goals, both from the penalty spot.
5. What are the two missing places?

Tie-Break

The record for unsupported book balancing goes to John Evans of Sheffield. In 1998 he balanced how many identical books on his head?

Round Three

1. Which classic film is this? The first words spoken are 'Here you are, sir, Main Level D', and they occur 21 minutes 35 seconds into the film.
2. In around 330 BC the Greek writer Archestratos wrote the first ever book in a genre which these days is rather fashionable. What sort of book was it?

3. Alexander the Great told his soldiers to remove them and Peter the Great levied a tax on them. What? And for a bonus point, what would you be if you were frightened of them?

4. Edgar Allen Poe, Chairman Mao, Doris Day, Harold Wilson, Edward Heath, Sir Walter Raleigh, Bob Dylan, Matt Busby and the Queen. All mentioned where?

5. What can be estimated by the formula $\sqrt{(3x/2)}$, where x is height above sea level in feet?

6. Louis XIV, Louis XV and Louis XVI were consecutive French monarchs of the Bourbon dynasty. What relation was Louis XVI to Louis XIV?

7. Which Italian dish literally means 'pick me up' and was apparently a favourite of Venetian courtesans who might have needed picking up (in both senses)?

8. In the Paris Olympiad of 1900 Leon de Lunden of Belgium won the gold medal in the only event in Olympic history which involved the deliberate killing of animals. What was the discipline?

9. The actor Derek Royle, who died in 1990 at the age of sixty-one, was probably best known while alive for playing a dead person on TV in 1979. In which series?

10. In 1993 the US Post Office issued what soon became its most profitable ever stamp, featuring a famous singer. Who was the singer, and for the second point, why did so many people using the stamp deliberately misaddress their envelopes?

Round Four

1. Who said of what in 1953, 'we done the bugger'?

2. What is the connection between two men, one of whom in 1971 wrote the song 'Diamonds Are Forever', and the other in the same year scored a record 180 points for the British Lions in New Zealand?

3. What was located on the island of Isla Nublar?

4. 31 HCH never caught on. Nor did 33 HST, 34 DDE or 37 RMN. What were the missing three that did? (You will need all three for the two points.)

5. In Sergio Leone's film, which character gets killed in the three-way duel at the end: the Good, the Bad, or the Ugly? And for the second point, who played him?

6. 'I'm sitting in the railway station, / Got a ticket for my destination.' The first lines of 'Homeward Bound'. Which northern English town did Paul Simon feel this overwhelming desire to leave?

7. The city of Ta-Tu, modern day Beijing, was founded in 1267 by the first Emperor of the Yuan dynasty, who much later was the subject of a well known poem. His name?

8. Which semiautonomous state is more than fifty times larger than the country it is part of?

9. If you were to buy them separately in different European countries you might get *Luces del Norte*, *La Lama Sottile* and *Das Bernstein Teleskop*. What are they collectively?

10. Eight kings named Edward and eight named Henry have ruled England. But which ruled collectively for longest, the Edwards or the Henrys?

The answers to Quiz Twenty-Three begin on page 371

QUIZ TWENTY-FOUR
CHRIS & JOHN (1)

Chris Millington, an IT consultant, and John Osmond, an ex-civil servant, normally make up a team of two. They were contemporaries at Oxford in the 1970s and started coming to the Prince of Wales in around 1990 when they both found themselves living in north London. They set their first quiz in 1995 and have since set around 30 more. They are the longest-serving regulars at the Prince of Wales quiz, and can remember the pub when it was . . . well . . . very much the same as it is now, in fact.

Their quizzes probably set the benchmark for what is now deemed acceptable. They try and ensure a mix of topics, avoid an age bias, eschew obscurity for its own sake, leave telltale clues in their questions. If they are represented in this book by only two quizzes, it is because the older ones are long since lost on dead computers, and they don't set as many quizzes as they used to: usually only one a year. But they retain the important knack of making familiar material fresh, as in this, one of their favourites: 'Whose reappearance, three years after his obituary appeared on the front page of the Times in 1891, was greeted with relief at the time and appreciated by subsequent generations?' Answer: Sherlock Holmes. They also wrote my all-time favourite question (quiz 2, round 2, question 3). Chris spotted it on a plaque when taking his daughter round the ship. It was in the quiz the following week. Whoever said you don't learn anything from quizzes don't know nothing.

Round One

1. It was nearly 140 years old and in 1968, the City of London decided to sell it for $2.46 million to Robert P. McCulloch, founder of Lake Havasu City, Arizona. On October 10th 1971, it was officially dedicated before a crowd of 50,000 in a lavish ceremony. What is it?

2. When released in Poland, the title of a 1979 blockbuster film underwent a startling title change. In English, it translated to *The Eighth Passenger of the Nostromo*. Which film?

3. What causes a 'fulgurite', which is sand melted into a glass-like state?

4. Which of these landmasses extends furthest south: Australia, New Zealand, South America or South Africa?

5. A lot of words referring to scientific study end in -ology. But what are (i) oology and (ii) otology?

6. In New World wines this grape is known as Shiraz. How is it known in the Rhone valley?

7. Probably the most famous Volkswagen Beetle in the world has the registration letters LMW 281F. Where would you find it?

8. Who, when asked his reason for not drinking water, said, 'Fish fuck in it'?

9. How are Bella, Fizz, Milo and Jake known collectively?

10. In a 2002 study of surnames in England and Wales, it was found that a pool of just 500 surnames accounted for 80 per cent of the population. What's more, the five most common names had remained unchanged, in the same order, since 1985. Can you name these five surnames? One point each and an extra point for the correct order.

Round Two

1. If Eugene Cernan was the last, who was the first?
2. What, for the first time in living memory, happened on February 18th 1979 in Saharan southern Algeria, causing traffic to stop for a while?
3. If you were in Coppergate in York, or Fishergate in Preston, or Kirkgate in Bradford, or Marketgate in Lancaster, or Milburngate in Durham, or Queensgate in Peterborough or even Wellgate in Dundee, what would you be most likely to be doing?
4. In Chaucer's *Canterbury Tales*, what do the dyer, the weaver, the tapestry-maker, the haberdasher and the carpenter have in common, other than being pilgrims?
5. 'A little learning is a dang'rous thing'; 'Fools rush in where angels fear to tread'; 'Hope springs eternal in the human breast'; and 'To err is human, to forgive, divine'. An impressive list of poetic lines and epigrams, all written by the same author. By whom?
6. Edward Oxford tried in 1840, then came John Francis in 1842, followed by John William Bean in the same year, William Hamilton in 1849, Robert Pate in 1850, Arthur O'Connor in 1872 and, finally, Roderick Maclean in 1882, but he, like all the rest, failed. What did they all try to do?
7. If a *coup d'état* is a sudden and violent change of government, what kind of *coup* is (i) an action that puts an end to something, and (ii) love at first sight or a sudden and amazing event? A point for each.
8. A memorial fountain in honour of the 7th Earl of Shaftesbury, and actually intended to depict the Angel of Christian Charity, is better known as what?

9. 'Who's there?' is the first line of which Shakespeare play?

10. What do the following have in common: Leonardo da Vinci, Michelangelo, Sir Isaac Newton, Jimi Hendrix and Paul McCartney?

Bonus Round

To celebrate its 25th anniversary in March 2004, the Plain English Campaign published a survey recording its members' most hated words and phrases used in everyday conversational English. Among them, but not in the top five, were such gems as 'it's not rocket science', 'going forward', 'I hear what you are saying', 'basically', 'absolutely' and 'let's touch base'. Can you name the top five words or phrases? (Clue: there are four phrases and one word in the top five.)

Tie-Break

What percentage of snake species are venomous?

Round Three

1. Which apparently fictitious cardmember name has for many years appeared on illustrations of the American Express card in their advertisements? It's possible that he is related to a famous poet, but not probable.

2. In equestrian three-day eventing, what are the three disciplines horse and rider are tested in over that period? A point for each.

3. Members of which religion might worship in a gurdwara?

4. It's December 3rd 1966 and we are aboard HMS *Tiger* off Gibraltar. Which two Prime Ministers are on board and what are they discussing? Three points in all.

5. It's September 11th 1978 and a BBC World Service correspondent is walking over Waterloo Bridge. What happens next?

6. In sport what French word, meaning literally 'fishing out again', applies to a stage in a tournament when previously eliminated contestants compete again?

7. Where on your body would you find a lunula?

8. What name was given to Britain in *1984*?

9. Which flower is sometimes called the lent lily?

10. How many horses have won the Derby twice?

Round Four

1. What inscription on the Victoria Cross explains what it is awarded for? And for a bonus point, what specifically are all Victoria crosses made from?

2. What was the name of the less-than-scrupulous press photographer, played by Walter Santesso, in Fellini's *La Dolce Vita*?

3. *Talpa europea*, *bufo bufo* and *arvicola amphibius* are the Latin names for the three main characters of which book?

4. Which boxer, after a famous defeat in 1926, explained to his wife, 'Honey, I forgot to duck'?

5. Which military unit has its headquarters at Aubagne, near Marseilles?

6. Cassata is what kind of food?

7. According to a popular American rhyme, based on an infamous 1892 murder, who 'took an axe/And gave her mother forty whacks'?

8. What is the largest National Park in England?

9. Which literary characters regularly pitted their wits against the following Scotland Yard policemen: (i) Inspector Lestrade; (ii) Inspector Japp; (iii) Inspector Teal? A point for each.

10. Christopher Columbus made four trips to the Americas between 1492 and 1502. How many times did he land in what is now the USA?

The answers to Quiz Twenty-Four begin on page 376

QUIZ TWENTY-FIVE
DAVID (4)

Round One

1. Which former international cricketer's initials were MCC?
2. If the answer is 'sling him in the longboat till he's sober', what is the question?
3. The impact of the BBC TV drama *Cathy Come Home* was so intense it led to the founding of which charity?
4. Which actor died in 2000, just over half a century after he had had a stroke, fallen off a weir, been shot, drowned, poisoned and involved in two explosions and an aircrash?
5. The American actor Thurl Ravenscroft was the voice of which advertising cartoon character, from its first appearance in 1952 until his death in 2005, aged ninety-one?
6. In summer 1995, at the height of Britpop, the Blur vs Oasis battle was in all the papers. What were the two singles released by these bands on the same day in a much hyped battle?
7. For what reason was sports fan Günter Parche arrested on April 30th, 1993?
8. A mathematician who won the 1994 Nobel Prize in Economics for his contribution to game theory, a British painter who specialised in the depiction of flowers, and the architect and designer of Marble Arch and the Haymarket theatre. What full name do they all share?
9. YES, NO and GOODBYE are the only words found on what?
10. Complete these three comedy exchanges:
    (i)   'I came here in all good faith to help my country. I don't mind giving a reasonable amount, but a pint?'
    (ii) 'Me? You started it.' 'We did not start it.'
    (iii) 'I don't know, Mr Wentworth just told me to come in here and say that there was trouble at the mill, that's all.'

Round Two

1. The 1969 and 1989 Ryder Cups were both tied. The only people involved in both events were the rival captains in the 1989 match. Name them, for a point each.

2. *Lord Malquist and Mr Moon* is the title of the only novel by which British playwright?

3. When Baron von Richthofen and his successor Wilhelm Reinhard were both killed in quick succession, who became the leader of Richthofen's 'flying circus', the 11th Chasing Squadron?

4. At the end of the 19th century, British soldiers who had finished a tour of India were usually holed up at a military camp 100 miles north-east of Bombay, sometimes for months, and it drove many of them barmy. A slang form of the camp's name quickly passed into common usage. What was it?

5. Englishman James Blades did it and Bombardier Billy Wells mimed to it and the result is familiar to all film fans. What is it?

6. It spoke a language based on Japanese grammar with a polyglot of Hebrew, Chinese and Thai, and was the toy of the year in 1998. What?

7. In 1941 which Hollywood star mailed his Best Actor Oscar to his parents' hardware store in Indiana, Pennsylvania, where it stayed for twenty-five years?

8. In 2004 which symbol became the first to be added to the Morse Code since World War I?

9. Which comedy film of 2004 has reported healthy DVD sales, which isn't bad after *The Times* devoted the whole of page three to it, under the headline 'Is this the worst British film of all time?'

10. In 1994 he appeared in a film whose title contained just two letters. Just under a decade later he started hosting a TV show, the title of which was the same two letters reversed. Who is he?

Bonus Round

Here are the second lines of ten limericks written by Edward Lear. In each case, name the place (mentioned in the first line) that the subject of the limerick comes from. (There was a young man from . . .)

1. Whose head was infested with beads.
2. Whose soup was excessively cool.
3. Who stood on one leg to read Homer.
4. Who frequented the top of a tree.
5. Who embellished his nose with a ring.
6. Whom several small children did pester.
7. Who danced at the end of a bough.
8. Whose food was roast spiders and chutney.
9. Who rushed down the crater of Etna.
10. Whose face was distorted with anger.

Tie-Break

How many different species of mosquito are there in Florida?

Round Three

1. Who is Dawn French married to?
2. What was Dawn French's previous occupation?

3. Which singer, who, despite the ennobling of her husband, declines to call herself Lady Dankworth, is the only person to have received Grammy nominations in the jazz, classical and popular music awards?

4. What is the name of the Highland dance based on a song written by Sir Henry Rowley Bishop in the 1820s, which was devised for two groups of three people, and which is still played in graduation week at several prominent military academies?

5. Led by John Sebastian, which American band was formed in 1965 and had hits with 'You Didn't Have To Be So Nice', 'Darling Be Home Soon' and 'Do You Believe In Magic'?

6. In November 1990, whose 1824 work *The Lock* was sold at Sotheby's for £10.78 million, the then-record price for a British painting?

7. Which rock 'n' roll performer who died in 2000 aged seventy said, 'When I die for Christ's sake don't bury me; I've leapt out of so many goddamn caskets in my career, I don't think I'll stay there'?

8. Which role links Omar Sharif and Hans Matheson?

9. Who was elected President of the NUS in 1969, became Shadow Education Secretary in 1987, moving on to Shadow Environment Secretary in 1992, and was executed in 1381 for his involvement in the Peasants' Revolt?

10. In which state capital was America's first ever gas station situated?

Round Four

1. In 1953 Constance Spry and Rosemary Hume created which cold dish so that the general public did not have to spend hours over a hot meal on the day Elizabeth II was crowned?

2. A titled woman by the name of Anna Maria in the early 1800s is believed to have introduced the concept of afternoon tea. What was her title?

3. In 1893 Tottenham Hotspur were accused of professionalism and almost had to surrender their amateur status after they agreed to buy what for one of their players?

4. Clothing, March 1949. Petrol, May 1950. Meat, July 1954. What am I talking about?

5. Which controversial figure declined to give video evidence in his trial in early 2005 because his toenails had grown too long?

6. (i) Why is Len Hutton's dismissal vs. South Africa at the Oval in 1951 unique in Test history? (ii) Five years later, the man who appealed for Hutton's dismissal, South African wicketkeeper Russell Endean became the first man to be dismissed in what way? A point for each.

7. Where specifically in Staffordshire would you find places called Ug Land, Merrie England and Gloomy Wood?

8. Bill Masen wakes up in hospital to find that, after an unusual meteor shower, he is the only person who can still see. This is the opening scenario of which classic work of British science fiction?

9. By removing the first two letters of which US state do you get the name of another?

10. In September 2005, the *Mirror* reported that a Frank Sinatra impersonator had been arrested for speeding. What was the name of the policeman who arrested him?

The answers to Quiz Twenty-Five begin on page 379

QUIZ TWENTY-SIX
SIMON (2)

Round One

1. Which south-east Asian country has nine royal families, each of whose heads takes it in turn to be King?

2. Reigning from 1952 to 1956, who is the only world heavyweight boxing champion to retire undefeated and without any draws?

3. What is the official residence of the Lord Mayor of London?

4. Which is the only Shakespeare play in which the name of an animal appears in the title?

5. Sir Ben Kingsley got in trouble in early 2006 for insisting on being referred to by his title. He wasn't entirely without support, though. Another actor knight revealed that he refuses to open post that does not include the 'Sir' in front of his name on the envelope. Which actor?

6. With four separate periods in office, spanning twenty-six years, who has been British Prime Minister the most times?

7. In which English cities would you find the following theatres: (i) the Royal Exchange; (ii) the Northcott; (iii) the Yvonne Arnaud? A point for each.

8. One was named after his propensity for chasing women. One was named after the musical instrument he played. One was named after a type of aircraft. What was the name of the fourth member of this quartet?

9. This is the name given to a blue-ish flamelike electrical discharge that sometimes occurs above ships' masts and other pointed objects. It's also the title of a 1985 film starring Demi Moore and Rob Lowe. What is it?

10. Christmas 2004. The Royal Mail managed to send all the post intended for Ascension Island to another destination entirely. Which destination?

Round Two

1. In 1986, which Hollywood actor – slightly better known now than he was then – was arrested in Macao on a charge of attempted murder before breaking out of jail and escaping the country by jetfoil?

2. Which war ended in 1648 with the signing of the Treaty of Westphalia?

3. These birds were introduced to the Chilterns in 1989, where they now form the densest population of its type in Europe. What type of bird are we talking about?

4. In the mid-19th century a young man who would go on to become a celebrated author was working as a cub pilot on a Mississippi steamboat. The leadsman would call out to warn him of the depth of the water. When he wanted him to 'allow twelve feet', what two words would the leadsman shout?

5. www.hop-ski-jump is the website address of which popular Lake District attraction?

6. In 1982 this well-known television presenter and keen amateur yachtsman set sail with his wife for the West Indies. They ran into trouble and were forced to detour to Majorca, where the presenter built his own house, and they have lived there ever since. Who is he?

7. For fifteen years, from 1986 to 2001, the Russians operated a manned space station. What was it called?

8. Which England batsman got the highest individual score in the 2005 Ashes series?

9. The record number of visitors ever drawn to an art exhibition in the UK was in 1999 at the Royal Academy. Whose work was on show?

10. Which Hollywood actress said in August 2005 that she would 'rather die' than feed her daughter instant soup?

Bonus Round

Here are eight Desert Island Disc castaways, and eight luxuries. Match the castaway to the luxury.

1. Jeremy Clarkson.
2. George Clooney.
3. Billy Connolly.
4. Robin Cook.
5. Nick Hornby.
6. Jan Morris.
7. Graham Norton.
8. Gordon Ramsay.

Luxuries: A mirror; a hot water bottle; a banjo; a fresh vanilla pod; an iPod; an anchored yacht; a jet ski; a chess computer.

Tie-Break

Table tennis. In a 1936 Swaythling Cup match, Alex Ehrlich of Poland and Paneth Farcas of Rumania recorded the longest rally in table-tennis history. How long did it last?

Round Three

1. Mime artist Marcel Marceau's most famous creation is a white-faced character called what?
2. What publication was launched in October 1966 with a gig at The Round House that featured the fledgling Pink Floyd?
3. Duncan Jones is a thirty-something commercials director who made an impact in February 2006 with a raunchy ad for French Connection. He is also the son of which major rock star?

4. In 1930 Clyde Tombaugh, a twenty-four-year-old who had grown up on a farm in Kansas, discovered what?
5. In January 2006 which former tennis player, a one-time Wimbledon men's singles finalist and world no. 4, was sentenced to a two-year jail sentence in Florida for violating probation after being convicted of theft?
6. One of the shortest ever Oscar-winning performances was given by a British actress and won her the Best Supporting Actress award in 1998. It lasted less than eight minutes. Name the actress and the movie, for a point each.
7. What is the name of the device used for measuring radioactivity by detecting and counting ionising particles?
8. Originally a French word, it described a projecting part of a rampart, connected by two flanks to the main fortification. It's now more commonly used to describe a person or an institution who upholds a principle or an attitude. What is the word?
9. Under legislation introduced in 1994, what is the maximum number of hours that larger stores such as supermarkets are allowed to open for on Sundays?
10. US state capitals. One point for each of the following: California, Florida, New York and Texas. And for an extra point, Augusta is the capital of which US state?

Round Four

1. In 2006 Ronnie Barker became only the third comedian to be honoured with a memorial service in Westminster Abbey. Of the previous two, the first was a woman in 1980, the second was a man in 1994. Who were they?
2. Who, until very recently, was believed to be the subject of the so-called Grafton portrait?

3. This country is sometimes referred to as the Switzerland of Central America. It has the region's longest history of political stability, its soundest economy, and its highest standard of living. Which country is it?

4. Who has installed twenty-four bathrooms in his mansion on the banks of Lake Washington, just outside Seattle?

5. Labour's general election slogan in 2005 was the subject of a complaint by the Plain English Society because of its bad grammar. What was the slogan?

6. Which Hollywood star completed the takeover of Australian rugby league club South Sydney in March 2006?

7. Which male pop star tore off which female pop star's leather bustier to expose a breast and cause outrage during TV coverage of the 2004 Super Bowl? A point for each.

8. Fidel Castro has ruled Cuba since 1959. What was the surname of the dictator he overthrew?

9. On air since 1953, what is the longest-running programme still shown on British television?

10. Which celebrated TV character is 900 years old and has two hearts?

The answers to Quiz Twenty-Six begin on page 383

QUIZ TWENTY-SEVEN
A.J. & CEILI (1)

Andrew 'A.J.' Leonard and Ceili Williams are old friends of each other's from university and of mine from the cricket team I run in my spare time. (A.J. is a slightly slower bowler than he used to be and a good late-order hitter, while Ceili's long-time partner Howard is our dashing number three batsman.) I somehow persuaded them to come to the quiz in 1998, even though Ceili lives on the other side of London. She was a regular until giving birth to Ciara in late 2003. A.J. still comes most weeks. They have been the science bedrock of the team: Ceili is a patent agent and A.J. is a biomedical research scientist in obs. and gynae. Each has more degrees than is entirely decent.

Perhaps surprisingly, then, the quizzes they set are not dominated by science questions, although a few creep in from time to time. A.J. believes a quiz should cover broad areas of knowledge, although he adds, possibly dangerously, that 'it can have an element of educating people about things I feel are important.' But he says he does try to limit that aspect of his megalomania. According to Ceili, 'most questions are usually done in a corner of the pub, surrounded on all sides by reference books, on the Sunday or Monday night before the quiz.' Not that you would ever know from the finished result, which is never less than thought-provoking. Although without either of them on our side, we tend to do rather poorly on the science questions.

Round One

1. What number comes next in this sequence: $1/4$, $1/2$, 1, 3, 6, 12, 24?
2. What artistic style had its origins in the Exposition Internationale des Arts Décoratifs et Industriels Modernes in Paris in 1925?

3. Which Asian country has a capital city whose name translates as 'Red Hero'?
4. In which northern town was the synod held in AD 664, at which it was decided that England would follow the Roman rather than the Celtic form of Christianity?
5. Which Corsican word meaning 'thicket' or 'dense scrub' came to be applied to the French Resistance during World War II?
6. In *Friends*, what was the title of Phoebe's best known song and, for the second point, what was the name of her identical twin sister?
7. How many engines does a VC-10 have?
8. In which decade did the following all occur: the February Revolution took place in France, Turner painted *Rain, Steam and Speed*, Dumas wrote *The Three Musketeers*, ether was first used as an anaesthetic and the British occupied Hong Kong?
9. Which Mercury award-winning artist was born Niomi McLean-Daley, the eldest of eleven children?
10. In an ancient Siamese custom, the monarch bestowed a sacred albino on one of his subjects, who would then be ruined by the cost of its upkeep. This custom is believed to be the origin of which term describing a fearsomely expensive but ultimately useless object?

Round Two

1. What are, and where would one find, the Eastern and Western Ghats?
2. In the Spanish Civil War, in what part of the body was George Orwell shot?
3. Which is the only miracle mentioned in all four Gospels?
4. Which two of Jane Austen's six great novels were published after her death? A point for each.

5. What type, or nationality, of whisky has a 1,500-year history but, until 2001, had not been distilled for more than a century?

6. What is the connection between the songs 'Happy Birthday' by Stevie Wonder and 'Pride (In The Name of Love)' by U2?

7. Which scientist was part of the team that produced the V1 and V2 rockets, and after World War II worked for NASA on the design and production of rockets, culminating in the Saturn V used in the Apollo programme?

8. Peter Carey's novel *The Secret Life of Ned Kelly* won the Booker Prize in 2001, but it's also notable, in the chapters supposedly written by the bushranger, for the complete and unusual absence of a particular punctuation mark. Which one?

9. In the Asterix books, what is Obelix's favourite food?

10. Buster Merryfield, who played Uncle Albert in *Only Fools And Horses*, died in 1999 aged seventy-eight. He took up acting full-time only in 1978, after retiring as what?

Bonus Round

1. Which 1988 film starred Kevin Costner and Tim Robbins in sporting roles as Crash Davis and 'Nuke' LaLoosh, and Susan Sarandon as Annie Savoy, their number one fan?

2. Which band was formed by Evan Dando and Ben Deily in Boston in 1987, their breakthrough album being *It's A Shame About Ray*?

3. Born in 1934, the actress Louise Fletcher may be best known these days for her portrayal of the cunning Kai Winn in *Star Trek: Deep Space 9*. In 1975, though, she won the Best Actress Oscar for her role in that year's winner of the Best Picture Oscar. What was the name of her character?

4. The Foundation for Environmental Education promotes, among other things, the idea that beaches should be clean and hygienic. In 1987, it instituted an award for beaches which comply with the EC Bathing Water Directive. What is this award called?
5. Which road safety feature, introduced in Britain in 1951, has since been incorporated into the Abbey Road studios logo?
6. Which film and theatre director was born in Dudley, West Midlands, in 1889, died in California in 1957, and directed, among other films, *Frankenstein* in 1931, *The Bride of Frankenstein* in 1935, and *Showboat* in 1936?

Tie-Break

In which year, so far as we know, did the Vikings first visit England?

Round Three

1. Portsmouth has traditionally been regarded as the home of the Royal Navy. For a point each, which three famous Royal Navy fighting ships are on permanent exhibition there?
2. The name of which silvery-white metallic element was long believed to have been derived from an old French phrase that referred to the effects of this element in a case of multiple monk poisoning from the 15th century?
3. Canaletto's *Chelsea from the Thames*, painted in 1751, was seven feet wide, but after completion, it was sliced in two by the artist. Why?
4. Who runs the Post Office in *Postman Pat*?

5. Sharing its name with a James Cameron film, what is the name of the boundary on the moon separating the area lit by the sun from the area that remains perpetually unlit?

6. According to Monty Python, what did the highwayman Dennis Moore demand from his victims?

7. Pink Floyd's first album, *The Piper at the Gates of Dawn*, was named after Chapter 7 of which children's classic novel?

8. Llywelyn ap Gruffydd was the last Welsh one, Edward II was the first English one. What?

9. The American Richard Drew invented Scotch Tape in 1930. For which company did he work?

10. A question about nursery rhymes. Who was the black sheep's second bag of wool for? What is Tuesday's child? And who put pussy in the well? A point for each.

Round Four

1. Which species of dung beetle was revered by the Ancient Egyptians as a symbol of resurrection?

2. In which US state is most of Yellowstone National Park?

3. What word is used to describe the ancient quarter of several north African cities and is also the longest river on the Isle of Wight?

4. Where might you find the Cassini division?

5. What is Albert Square's postal district?

6. Name the fictional families who lived at the following addresses: (i) 32 Windsor Gardens; (ii) 4 Privet Drive; (iii) 165 Eaton Place. A point for each.

7. 'A spectre is haunting Europe, the spectre of communism.' The opening words of what?

8. Which European capital city stands on the river Vistula?

9. In Scotland, why would you not wish to encounter *culicoides impunctatus*?

10. Which 13th/14th century explorer's last words, according to legend, were 'I did not tell half of what I saw, because no one would have believed me'?

The answers to Quiz Twenty-Seven begin on page 387

QUIZ TWENTY-EIGHT
RUSSELL & TARA (4)

Round One

1. In 2002 the University of Hull acquired a lawnmower to add to their collection, which already includes an armchair, an umbrella and a duffelcoat. Why?

2. Despite half a century of Cold War, Russian and American troops have directly fought against each other only once. During which 20th century conflict?

3. *Zadok The Priest* and *Crown Imperial* are famous marches written by Handel and Walton respectively for the coronations of British monarchs called George. Which two Georges, for a point each?

4. William S. Preston and Theodore Logan were a well-known fictional duo. How were they better known?

5. The chemical substance 2,4,6-trichloroanisole is responsible for what common gastronomic dysfunction?

6. What do Frederick Fowell, Richard Starkey and Charles Hatcher – all of them born in the early 1940s – have in common?

7. In 1820 a storm in Woolsthorpe, Lincolnshire, blew down a tree that had, according to legend, made a unique contribution to British history just over a century and a half earlier. What was the tree's significance?

8. Lionel Jeffries played Dick van Dyke's father in *Chitty Chitty Bang Bang*, and Crispin Glover played Michael J. Fox's father in *Back To The Future*. What was unusual about these performances?

9. Which of these revolutionaries did not have a reader's pass at the British Library: Marx, Lenin, Stalin or Trotsky?

10. Pairs of famous brothers. We will give you their first names, you give us their last name. A point for each.
(i) Jacob and Wilhelm: (ii) Philip and Donald; (iii) Jake and Elwood; (iv) Auguste and Louis; (v) Tom and Ed; (vi) Rock and Gravel.

Round Two

1. 'I distrust people that write books and people that read books. I cannot understand people who have enough time to sit down and read about other people's experiences. I find myself far too busy talking or lying in wet fields drunk.' Which actor who died in 1999 uttered these profound sentiments?

2. The South American spirit Pisco is distilled from which fruit?

3. What is the connection between fictional composer Gustav von Aschenbach and real-life composer Richard Wagner?

4. Donald Sinclair, a bad-tempered former Royal Navy Officer who died in 1981, and his wife Beatrice were the inspiration behind which sitcom couple?

5. What is the nearest star to the Earth?

6. Apart from the ones mentioned in the title, which other two animals appear in Edward Lear's poem 'The Owl and the Pussycat'?

7. 'Paperback Writer' by the Beatles, 'Famous Blue Raincoat' by Leonard Cohen' and 'Stan' by Eminem. What do these songs have in common?

8. Which regular member of the cast of *Frasier* was born in Blackpool, Lancashire?

9. What prop, borrowed from the set of *Dixon of Dock Green*, formed the basis for a new and subsequently long-running TV series?

10. The following orchestral pieces all open with a solo instrument. Which instrument in each case? A point for each.
    (i) Gershwin's *Rhapsody in Blue*.
    (ii) Debussy's *Prelude à l'après-midi d'un faun*.
    (iii) Stravinsky's *The Rite of Spring*.
    (iv) Grieg's *Piano Concerto*.

Bonus Round

It's normal for a beer round to have a connection, so it's only fair to let you know that these answers have nothing in common.

1. Which organisation has its headquarters at 25 Soho Square?
2. Which film made in 1997, and starring Ray Winstone and Kathy Burke, marked Gary Oldman's directorial debut?
3. Who was the 19th-century writer of the satirical novels *Crotchet Castle* and *Nightmare Abbey*?
4. What is the everyday name for approximately 50 species of the family Anatidae, order Anseriformes?
5. Who played Max Bialystock in Mel Brooks's original 1968 film of *The Producers*?

Tie-Break

Complete this quotation from Arnold Schwarzenegger: 'Money doesn't make you happy. I now have $50 million but I was just as happy when I had . . .'

Round Three: Overlaps

Did the lives of the following pairs of famous people overlap? (In other words, was the older one still alive when the younger one was born?) We want a Yes or No answer. Two points for each. Clue: there are five Yesses and five Nos.

1. George Stephenson and Robert Louis Stevenson?
2. George Eliot and T.S. Eliot?
3. Thomas Hardy and Oliver Hardy?
4. Ramsay Macdonald and Ronald McDonald?

5. Lord Baden-Powell and Colin Powell?
6. Henry Ford and Harrison Ford?
7. George Bernard Shaw and Sandie Shaw?
8. Eric Blair and Tony Blair?
9. Stevie Smith and Zadie Smith?
10. Tennessee Williams and Robbie Williams?

Round Four

1. In the 1960s Melanie Coe eloped with her boyfriend, Diane Ashley broke into a house in St John's Wood and Lucy Richardson posed for a painting. Why are these events still remembered?
2. Canute was king of England between 1016 and 1035. Which other two countries did he also rule?
3. They used to be called Pythagoreans until 1847 when, at their first formal gathering in Ramsgate, they coined a new name that persists to this day. There are now some four million in Britain. Who are they?
4. The song 'Good Morning to All', composed in 1893 by Patty Smith Hill and Mildred J. Hill, is today more familiarly known under the first line of its second verse. What is its modern title?
5. In which English city is St John's church, where captured Royalists were imprisoned during the Civil War, and which became a symbol of banishment?
6. Former GI George Jorgenson became the first person to do what (or at least, admit to it publicly) in New York in December 1952?
7. David Hasselhoff came to fame in the punningly-named 80s TV series *Knight Rider*, in which he played a detective with an indestructible talking car. But was his character called Michael Knight or Michael Rider?

8. They called themselves after a song that was at number one for six weeks in 1962. In 1986 they had a number one hit in collaboration with the artist who sang the original song they took their name from. Who?

9. I take a boat from Greenwich to the Royal Botanical Gardens. From there I walk the short distance to Hyde Park. From Hyde Park I walk along Liverpool Street until I reach Kings Cross. At Kings Cross I turn south along Victoria Street, take a left at the junction with Oxford Street and walk the length of Oxford Street, passing through Paddington on the way. Where am I?

10. In Cole Porter's song 'Miss Otis Regrets', why is Miss Otis unable to lunch today?

The answers to Quiz Twenty-Eight begin on page 391

QUIZ TWENTY-NINE
MARCUS (5)

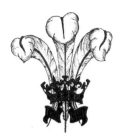

Round One

1. A guitar from Bono; several bottles of wine from Jacques Chirac; a rug from the Libyan government; earrings from the Italian government; and 'a selection of merchandise' from *The Simpsons*' production company. What is the connection?

2. Mabbott's Pearmain, Gascoyne's Scarlet and Golden Knob are varieties of what type of fruit?

3. An increasingly popular accessory for some Christians, particularly in America, is a bracelet inscribed with the letters 'W.W.J.D.' What do the letters stand for?

4. What is the most northerly town in France?

5. Which was the last century in which a woman did not sit on the British or English throne in her own right?

6. Johan Sermon of Belgium died in February 2004 aged twenty-one of a heart attack in his sleep. Michel Zanoli of the Netherlands died the previous December aged thirty-five, also of a heart attack. He had suffered mental problems and served a prison sentence for drug-smuggling. Marco Rusconi of Italy died in November 2003 aged twenty-four. He had a heart attack just after leaving a friend's birthday party. Jose Maria Jimenez of Spain died in December 2003, aged thrity-two. He had a heart attack in a Madrid psychiatric hospital while presenting a slideshow of his career. All four of these men were professional sportsmen. Which sport were all four associated with?

7. Which 19th-century composer, pianist and cleric was the father-in-law of Richard Wagner?

8. Which religious leader is known as 'Al Baba' in Arabic?

9. Geometrically, what shape are PG Tips teabags these days?

10. Marathon is now Snickers. Oil of Ulay is now Oil of Olay. What, in the name of global marketing, are these famous old products now called? A point for each. (i) Immac; (ii) Switch; (iii) Mr Dog; (iv) Ever Ready. (v) And for an extra point, Twix is now Twix everywhere as well. What was it called in continental Europe until 1991?

Round Two

1. What three-word phrase, borrowed from wrestling terminology, means 'anything goes' or 'with all restrictions removed'?

2. These days it is buried in the grounds of Sidney Sussex College, Cambridge. Once it was on a spike at Westminster Hall. What?

3. The 1985-86 season of *Dallas* was certainly unusual and possibly unique in television history. Why? You will need to be precise here to get both points.

4. George III's second son, Prince Frederick, is now remembered chiefly as an ineffectual military commander. What two things is he best remembered for doing? Clue: everyone who reads this book knows this.

5. What name is given to the scientific study of the geographical distribution of plants and animals?

6. In the 1950s Britain spent untold millions of pounds developing its own Intermediate Range Ballistic Missile, or IRBM, which took so long to design that before they had built one, it was already out of date. In 1960 the Macmillan government cancelled the programme and bought Polaris from America instead. The rocket that never flew: what was it called?

7. Which future Poet Laureate edited and wrote the *Shell Guides* for Motorists in the 1930s? Some were illustrated by his friend John Piper.

8. Which two methods of dismissal have never occurred in Test cricket (as of April 2006)? A point for each.

9. The 27th President of the United States, who served between 1909 and 1913, was also the heaviest, weighing up to 25 stones and several times getting stuck in the White House bathtub. What was his name?

10. London, Paris, Tokyo, New York. For one point, which of these cities has the highest annual rainfall? And for the other point, which of these has the lowest annual rainfall?

Bonus Round

1. The opening phrase of all suras but one in the Koran can be translated as 'In the name of Allah, most gracious, most merciful'. How is this phrase known for short?

2. This stock character in *commedia dell arte* was introduced into England soon after 1670. He was a braggart and a poltroon, and was usually dressed in a black Spanish costume. What was his name?

3. This god of the Philistines was referred to in Matthew 12:24 and elsewhere as 'the prince of the Devils'. His original name in Phoenician meant 'lord of the seat', but the Jews chose to interpret his name as 'lord of the dungheap' or 'lord of the flies', because his statue, which was constantly covered in blood, attracted flies. Milton placed him next in rank to Satan himself. What was his name?

4. He lived between 1564 and 1642. In his spare time he composed music for the lute. And he was the first person to observe the largest moons of Jupiter. Who?

5. He was the central character of two plays by Beaumarchais, and later of operas by Rossini and Mozart based on those plays. The character later gave his name to a Parisian periodical, which appeared from 1826 to 1833 and then again from 1854. What is his name?

Tie-Break

How long does it last, in minutes and seconds?

Round Three

1. Which German football club is owned by the pharmaceutical company that invented aspirin and heroin?
2. Which city of northern England was once called Monkchester, after an Anglo-Saxon religious community that was based there? Its current name is taken from a fortification built by Robert Curthose, son of William the Conqueror, on the side of a Roman fort.
3. Who, according to Sherlock Holmes, is 'the most indispensable man in the country' and can be found every evening at the Diogenes Club from a quarter to five to twenty to eight?
4. A shortage of cash forced him out of the race before polling day, but which jazz musician briefly declared himself a candidate for the US Presidency in the 1964 election?
5. Unau is another name for which modestly digited mammal?
6. A film adaptation of James Joyce's *Ulysses*, released in 1967, was the first film to be granted a certificate in the UK to contain what, precisely?
7. At 986 feet, the Eiffel Tower was the tallest structure in the world until 1930, when it was superseded by which building in New York City, 1,046 feet high?
8. The first time they did it was in Montreal in 1964. The second and last time was in Botswana in 1975. Who were they and what did they do?
9. What name connects a biblical figure and the world's largest type of frog?

10. 'The Elizabethan poet Ben Jonson has the distinction of being the only person to be interred at Westminster Abbey . . .' Finish that sentence.

Round Four

1. Ingvar Kamprad was born on a farm called Elmtaryd in the parish of Agunnaryd. Now he is one of the richest men in the world. Why?
2. What nickname was shared by the eponymous heroes of the film *Amadeus* and the TV sitcom *Citizen Smith*?
3. Habilis, rudolfensis, erectus, ergaster, heidelbergensis, neanderthalensis. What is the current version called?
4. What was the capital of Portugal between 1807 and 1821? Clue: it wasn't in Portugal.
5. How were Dr Stantz, Dr Spengler and Dr Venkman better known in the 1980s?
6. Excommunication by the Pope, the loss of Normandy and a major baronial revolt were misfortunes suffered by which medieval English monarch?
7. What was the last James Bond film in which Roger Moore played Bond?
8. Dr Georgios Papanikolaou devised which life-saving medical procedure, still much used today?
9. Which of the four major Channel Islands lies closest to the coast of France, about 10 miles, in fact?
10. Babar the elephant. What colour is his suit?

The answers to Quiz Twenty-Nine begin on page 394

QUIZ THIRTY
CHRIS & JOHN (2)

Round One

1. What is the appropriately named American space probe, launched on August 3rd 2004 on a seven-year mission to visit the innermost planet of the solar system, Mercury?
2. What in medicine was first classified into the AOB system in 1902?
3. Who is supposed to have said, 'A girl must marry for love, and keep on marrying until she finds it' – and followed her own advice?
4. Which is the only Central American country with no coast on the Caribbean Sea?
5. Threatened with demolition in the late 1960s, this New York building was saved by a campaign led by Jacqueline Kennedy Onassis and architect Philip Johnson. Since 1975 it has been listed in the National Register of Historic Places. What is it?
6. Which fruits are a hybrid between (i) a blackberry and a raspberry, and (ii) a grapefruit and a tangerine? A point for each.
7. A January King, a Spring Hero, a May Express, a Derby Day and a Christmas Drumhead are all varieties of which vegetable?
8. How many years were there, exactly, between the battles of Bannockburn and Agincourt?
9. Who is Nicolas Cage's famous uncle?
10. Using all the composite letters only once, you could 'derive' four elements each from the words 'arsenic' and 'carbon'. Two points for each list of four: full names please.

Round Two

1. What was the laconic and rather philosophical reply of the early British mountaineer George Mallory, when asked why he wanted to climb Mount Everest?
2. Originally an Australian creation, the Carpetbag steak is stuffed with what essential ingredient?

3. What (rather bizarrely and theoretically lethally) links the M1's London Gateway services, formerly known as Scratchwood, and HMS *Belfast* on the Thames?

4. Sarah Churchill, the Duchess of Marlborough, she called Mrs Freeman. And Mrs Freeman called her Mrs Morley. Who are we talking about?

5. Which species of large bird, the heaviest flying bird in the world, was hunted to extinction in Britain in the 1830s but is now being reintroduced in Salisbury Plain after the arrival in 2004 of a consignment of 28 chicks from the Russian steppes?

6. Which pop star owns the publishing rights to the majority of Buddy Holly's songs?

7. In a sailing dinghy, what would you do with a thwart?

8. Which city in the world has the most skyscrapers (here defined as buildings over thirty-five metres high)?

9. Whose last acting role, before he took up another profession in the public eye, was in the 1964 film *The Killers*?

10. What common idioms are the English equivalents of these slightly different French idioms?
    (i)   Avoir un chat dans la gorge.
    (ii) Couper les cheveux en quatre.
    (iii) Une pomme de discorde.

Bonus Round

1. Who was born in Braunau-am-Inn, Austria, the son of a minor customs official, in 1889?

2. His film credits include *Billy Liar*, *2001: A Space Odyssey* and *Barry Lyndon*. He also created two classic TV comedy characters in two very different long-running series and advertised a certain drink with more spills than thrills. Who was he?

3. Another potted biography of another versatile actor: he appeared in *Fire Down Below* (1957), *Northwest Frontier* (1960) and *Phantom of the Opera* (1962), but is probably best remembered as Inspector Clouseau's increasingly deranged boss in several *Pink Panther* films. Who is he?
4. 'Tomorrow to fresh Woods, and Pastures new.' This is the last line of a poem written on the death of Edward King, the poet's contemporary at Christ's College, Cambridge. Who was the poet?
5. Quoting the Athenian playwright Menander, immediately before crossing the river Rubicon with his loyal rebel legions, who said 'the die is cast'?
6. And what is the link?

Tie-Break

How many pubs line the route of the London Marathon?

Round Three

1. In a standard pack of playing cards, the King of Hearts is the only king lacking what?
2. Which country in the world has the most borders with other countries?
3. The two commonest species of ladybirds in Britain each have a specific number of spots. What are those numbers? (They are both less than ten.)
4. What word is defined as the reflecting power of a planet or satellite, expressed as a ratio of the light reflected by a surface to the total amount falling on the surface?
5. Who played Sam in Casablanca?
6. What is the name of the extremely well preserved castle on Anglesey, built by command of Edward I?

7. A four-pointer. Between which two cities, on which two seas, did Churchill declare in 1946 that 'an iron curtain has descended across the continent'?

8. The Denmark, the Cook, the Menai and the Singapore are all examples of what?

9. Which sometime motor racing driver, philanthropist and head of a non-profit-making food company, the recipe for whose best known product is a zealously guarded secret, has enjoyed a different and rather more public career in another field?

10. Subtitled *Travels into Several Remote Nations of the World*, how do we best know this literary work?

Round Four

1. Who is the only *Blue Peter* presenter ever to be appointed Chief Scout?

2. For a point each what, specifically, do the following collect: (i) cartophilist; (ii) deltiologist; (iii) fromologist?

3. What is the best known street in Erinsborough?

4. What are Michael Jackson's two sons called? A point for each.

5. Penguin paperbacks were first published in 1935. How much did they cost?

6. Which singer was Billy Wilder's first choice for the role of Jerry/Daphne in *Some Like It Hot*?

7. Lutetia and Lusitania were the ancient Roman names for which European city, and the greater part of which country, respectively?

8. What is the second lightest gas after hydrogen?

9. "'Beauty is truth, truth beauty.' That is all / Ye know on earth, and all ye need to know.' The words of which English poet?

10. Which London landmark has the postal address 1 Canada Square, E14?

The answers to Quiz Thirty begin on page 398

QUIZ THIRTY-ONE
DAVID (5)

Round One

1. In 2005, which country did Jacques Chirac claim was the only one in Europe whose food was worse than ours?
2. St Winifred's School Choir, of 'There's No-one Quite Like Grandma' fame, are often called one-hit wonders, but that is not quite true, as they had provided uncredited backing vocals for a number one hit two years earlier. What was it?
3. In July 1929, in the first obscenity hearing to involve works of art, 13 paintings by which novelist were seized from the Warren Gallery in London by the Metropolitan Police's so-called 'Dirty Squad'?
4. Recent research by an American university has revealed which colour to be the most prominent in the flags of the world, being visible in some degree in 74 per cent of them?
5. William Foulke, Sheffield United's goalkeeper at the beginning of the 20th century, was the first player to have what chanted at him?
6. One of the first problems for Edward Heath's new government in 1970 was the death, a month after the election, of his Chancellor of the Exchequer. What was his name?
7. In an attempt to make them more anatomically correct, what were Barbie dolls given for the first time in the year 2000?
8. Which English town lost six of its landmarks as a result of the 1987 hurricane?
9. The title character of which TV cop show has not put in an appearance on the show for more than twelve years?
10. Six times in the history of the football World Cup has the host nation won the trophy. Name the six countries, for a point each.

Round Two

1. Which national scheme was launched in the 1930s in Scotland, made compulsory in 1946 and notoriously abolished by the Secretary of State for Education in 1971?

2. Who in 1956 became the first film star in the world to appear on a postage stamp?

3. Duelling in Paraguay is legal between consenting adults, as long as both parties are registered in what way?

4. In 1975 who became the first posthumous duo ever to have a record in the UK single charts?

5. Which British comic character had unusually religious origins, given that the editor of the comic was a clergyman, one of the early writers went on to found the Samaritans, and the intended subtitle for the first strip was 'Chaplain of the Interplanet Patrol'?

6. Who is the only title character of a Disney animated feature film that does not speak?

7. All the US Presidents did it, except for James Buchanan. Six of them did it more than once. And Grover Cleveland was the only one who actually did it in the White House. What?

8. In 1991, after a quarter century of confusion, a small Buckinghamshire village changed its name to Middleton, so that it would no longer be confused with a larger place in the same county. What was its former name?

9. Which now-defunct national newspaper was the first in this country to be printed in full colour every day?

10. Who is the only actor to have won an Oscar, both of whose parents have won Oscars?

Bonus Round

1. By the time he stepped down which former Secretary-General of the United Nations had been awarded thirty-five honorary degrees or doctorates by the world's colleges and universities?
2. Dorothy Parker began her journalistic career as drama critic of *Vanity Fair* magazine, initially working as a holiday stand-in for which famous novelist?
3. The first feature film Sidney Lumet directed was the only film co-produced by Henry Fonda, who also starred in it. What was it?
4. In 1998 a man called Trevor Montague admitted he had flouted the rules of which Channel 4 quiz show by entering and taking part several times, once under the assumed name 'Steve Romana'?
5. What was the title of Pete Wingfield's only hit single? It reached number seven in summer 1975.

Tie-Break

The Comedy Of Errors is Shakespeare's shortest play. How many lines has it?

Round Three

1. Which computerised character spends most of his time trying to avoid four ghosts called Inky, Pinky, Blinky and Clyde?
2. Which notorious citizen of York was born in Stonegate, baptised at the nearby church of St Michael le Belfrey in 1570, and hanged in London just under thirty-six years later?

3. Before he found fame in TV's *The Beverley Hillbillies*, actor Buddy Ebsen had to turn down which film role when he suffered a collapsed lung from inhaling metal dust in the costume?

4. Rugby league. Who in July 2001 became the first Englishman to score 500 career tries?

5. One of the wealthiest men of his time had the rare honour of having an airport named after him in 1938. Unfortunately it was only briefly, as Houston residents objected to this honour being given to someone who was still alive. Who?

6. *Lady Chatterley's Lover* was one of two novels by D.H. Lawrence to be officially banned in Britain. What was the other one?

7. Which Tory minister was once seen on our TV screens feeding his four-year-old daughter a beefburger in an attempt to calm fears over BSE?

8. Which are the only two US states whose names contain six vowels? A point for each.

9. Which Beano strip was axed in 1990, the last one to have featured in the comic more or less continuously since the first issue?

10. Which Tim Burton film features twenty-seven beheadings, a record for major motion pictures?

Round Four

1. Whose election slogan, mainly used on bumper stickers, was 'AuH$_2$O 64'?

2. In the 19th century a woman called Mary Anning became one of the world's foremost palaeontologists, and would frequently allow visitors to her home in Lyme Regis to buy fossils she had discovered. This story is believed to be the source of which tongue twister?

3. What is the cinematic connection between Calvin Klein in the 1950s and Clint Eastwood in the 1980s?

4. This water meadow is the location for three memorials, one honouring John F. Kennedy, another honouring the men and women of the Allied Air Forces who died during World War II, and the third commemorating the site's most famous historic event, which took place in the 13th century. Where is it?

5. Andrew Motion's first official poem as Poet Laureate was written to mark which event?

6. In Scrabble which is the only letter worth five?

7. Which international athletics stadium was opened by Fatima Whitbread in April 1993?

8. Which inventor is believed to be the first person to have used the word 'Hello' as a greeting?

9. Whose life was the basis of the film *Personal Services*?

10. First printed in 1725 these British banknotes were discontinued on April 22nd 1943 and withdrawn altogether two years later. What was the face value of these notes?

The answers to Quiz Thirty-One begin on page 402

QUIZ THIRTY-TWO
RUSSELL & TARA (5)

Round One: This and That

In this round each question asks you to identify two words or names. Put the two together and you should get a common phrase, given the odd misspelling. For instance: a star of *The Odd Couple* and a character in *The Third Man*. Answer: Jack LEMMON and Harry LIME. Here are ten more. (You only need the capitalised words for the points.)

1. The man who was 71st on the 2006 *Sunday Times* Rich List, and Melanie Chisholm.
2. A former owner of the *Daily Telegraph,* and a long-time contributor to the *Today* programme's 'Thought For The Day' slot.
3. A 19th-century Yorkshire manufacturer and philanthropist, and a pop album released in 1967.
4. The band whose lead singer was David Gates, and (in London) Oxford and Cambridge.
5. A cartoon drawn by Rupert Fawcett, and Chris Evans's onetime production company.
6. Broccoli and brussels sprouts, and the eleventh and twelfth books of the Old Testament (1611 Authorised Version).
7. Dahl's Charlie and Hammett's Sam.
8. The Beatles' first ever record and an orang-utan.
9. The most-capped Cameroon footballer who played for Liverpool and West Ham, and an actor who was in *Hilary and Jackie* and *Gosford Park*, and played Neil Hamilton on TV.
10. The European mountain ash and a short-tailed bird of the swallow family.

Round Two

1. Which 20th century poet's nickname was Possum?
2. Who in 1972 wanted to marry her uncle Raymond?
3. In 1779 the 12th Earl of Derby and Sir Charles Bunbury tossed a coin to see which of them would bear a certain honour. Who won and what was the honour?
4. What is the only country in the world whose name begins with an O in English? And for a bonus point, name a European country whose name begins with O in its own language.
5. Which Chinese expression, literally meaning 'work together', is used in English to denote mindless enthusiasm?
6. Prokofiev's Piano Concerto No. 4 in B flat and Ravel's Piano Concerto in D major were both written for the pianist Paul Wittgenstein, the brother of the philosopher Ludwig. What was special about the works?
7. Rodrigo de Jerez was the first European to adopt which habit in 1492, which caused him to be imprisoned by the Inquisition for seven years?
8. There are two different provinces in Europe called Galicia. One is in one country, the other is divided between two countries. Name all three, for a point each.
9. In filming *The African Queen* the only two members of cast or crew who didn't contract diarrhoea or dysentery were Humphrey Bogart and the director John Huston. Why might this have been?
10. Former footballer and occasional hair model David Ginola's name is an anagram of two rather rude words. What are they?

Bonus Round

Elder or younger? The answer to each of the last five questions in this round is either 'elder' or 'younger'. You therefore have a 50:50 chance with each one, and a one in 32 chance of getting them all wrong.

1. Who was killed when he commanded the Roman fleet to sail in closer to observe the eruption of Vesuvius? Pliny the Elder or Pliny the Younger?
2. The original bridge that stood on the site of Blackfriars Bridge in London was built in 1760. Who was it named after? William Pitt the Elder or William Pitt the Younger?
3. Who wrote the *Blue Danube* waltz? Johann Strauss the Elder or Johann Strauss the Younger?
4. Who wrote *The Count of Monte Cristo*? Alexandre Dumas the Elder or the Younger?
5. Who said, 'I'm for a stronger death penalty'? George Bush the Elder or George Bush the Younger?

Tie-Break

Gilbert and Sullivan were both knighted. How long elapsed between Sullivan receiving his knighthood and Gilbert getting his?

Round Three: Plagiarism

1. Ireland's all-time leading goalscorer is Robbie Keane. Who did he overtake to achieve this record in 2004?
2. The 1970s kids' TV programme *Hector's House* featured a cohabiting dog and cat named Hector and Zaza. What sort of neighbour was their inquisitive neighbour Kiki?
3. Vientiane is the capital of which country?

4. 'In llama land, there's a one man band / And he'll toot his flute for you.' Which Sammy Cahn/Jimmy van Heusen song, best known in a version by Frank Sinatra, is this lyric from?

5. What in the UK officially lasted from February 19th 2001 to January 15th 2002 and made a brief celebrity of an animal called Phoenix?

6. Which law of physics states that the volume of a gas is inversely proportional to its pressure at constant temperature?

7. In the double act Hale and Pace, which one had the moustache?

8. In which 1975 film did Donald Sutherland play a character called Homer Simpson?

9. Which tongue-in-cheek British band released their first album, *Permission to Land*, in 2003 and a follow-up, *One Way Ticket to Hell . . . and Back*, in late 2005?

10. Richard the Lionheart, Henry VIII and Charles I all came to the throne under similar circumstances. What?

Round Four: Ages of Man

The answer to each question is an age. The ages are in ascending numerical order.

1. In the Eurovision-winning Brotherhood of Man song 'Save Your Kisses For Me', how old is the object of the singers' affection?

2. A. A. Milne wrote a book of children's poems called *When We Were Very Young*. How old was the reader supposed to be to read the sequel?

3. For the last fifty-odd years Charlie Brown has always been what age?

4. How old was Liesl von Trapp?

5. How old was the girl the Beatles saw Standing There?

6. What was the average age of American combatants in the Vietnam War, as Paul Hardcastle reminded us in 1985?

7. 'Emma Woodhouse, handsome, clever, and rich, with a comfortable home and happy disposition, seemed to unite some of the best blessings of existence; and had lived BLANK years in the world with very little to distress or vex her.' The opening lines of *Emma* by Jane Austen. So, how old was Emma at the beginning of the novel?

8. Billy Bragg blatantly lifted the opening couplet for his song 'A New England' from a Paul Simon song 'Leaves That Are Green'. These lines state the singer's (supposed) age at the time he sang the song. How old were they both?

9. In the Dr Hook song 'The Ballad of Lucy Jordan', covered by Marianne Faithfull and Belinda Carlisle, among others, we learned that 'At the age of BLANK she realised she'd never ride through Paris / In a sports car, with the warm wind in her hair.' What age?

10. How old was Sir Paul McCartney on June 18th, 2006?

The answers to Quiz Thirty-Two begin on page 406

QUIZ THIRTY-THREE
A.J. & CEILI (2)

Round One

1. Which Irish swimmer won three gold medals and a bronze at the Atlanta Olympics but was later banned for failing a drugs test?

2. Which cocktail – half gin or vodka, half lime juice – shares its name with a small handtool?

3. Which Royal Navy ship, later the subject of a famous painting, was mentioned in dispatches after the Battle of Trafalgar?

4. Which pop musician's CV includes founding Buggles, playing with Yes and producing, among others, Dollar, ABC, Seal, Grace Jones and Frankie Goes To Hollywood?

5. In which European countries are the sources of the rivers Danube and Elbe? A point for each.

6. In the UK a traffic signpost containing a walking pedestrian on a white background within a red circle means 'no pedestrians'. But in which direction is the pedestrian walking? From left to right or from right to left?

7. Which TV character was born in 1926, was married successively to Phyllis, Renée and Audrey, was twice elected mayor of his town, helped found its trade association Weatherfield Association of Retail Traders, or WARTS, and died in 1999 after suffering a stroke at the eighteenth birthday party of his step-grandson Nicky?

8. The emblem of St Peter is often used as a pub sign. What emblem?

9. During the reign of which British monarch was the family name changed from Saxe-Coburg-Gotha to Windsor?

10. Which US Presidents said the following? A point each.

    (i)   'Let me assert my firm belief that the only thing we have to fear is fear itself.'

    (ii) 'They say hard work never hurt anybody, but I figure why take the chance?'

    (iii) 'I know the human being and fish can coexist peacefully.'

Round Two

1. When Larry White was executed in Huntsville, Texas, in May 1997, his last request was, unusually, denied. Why?

2. Which artist said, of Sir Joshua Reynolds, 'this man was hired to depress art'? He also saw angels descending on a ladder from heaven (in Sussex) and angels and giants battling (in Kentish Town).

3. Of which metal is galena the most abundant ore?

4. In which century did the following all occur: Izaak Walton published *The Compleat Angler*; the Glencoe Massacre; the founding of the Manchu Dynasty in China; building work started on the Taj Mahal?

5. Which area of London has an academy that doesn't teach, a windmill that doesn't mill, and a fridge that doesn't cool anything down?

6. Which actor was the first to be paid $1 million for a film? And for the second point, what was the film?

7. What is the derived SI unit of pressure, equivalent to 1 Newton per square metre?

8. Which legendary francophone singer started life as Jean-Philippe Smet?

9. Which Vladimir did Jimmy Greaves consider to have had the greatest influence on his football career?

10. All the following writers were born in Dublin. But what order were they born in? Two points for the correct order: Samuel Beckett. Bob Geldof. James Joyce. Jonathan Swift. W. B. Yeats.

Bonus Round

1. What aid to the textile industry was invented by Samuel Crompton in 1779, combining the rollers of the Water Frame with the moving carriage of the Spinning Jenny?
2. Since 1986 whose birthday has been commemorated in the USA with a bank holiday on the third Monday in January?
3. Who famously said, in response to the suggestion that he was Irish, 'Being born in a stable does not make one a horse'?
4. What is the name given in electronics to a circuit which can be in either of two states, reversed by an electrical pulse? (Its alternative name is 'bistable'.)
5. What was the murder weapon wielded by Jennifer Jason Leigh in the 1992 film *Single White Female*?

Tie-Break

How long does a female turkey incubate her eggs before they hatch?

Round Three

1. When Tony Blair suggested to fellow Cabinet Ministers in 1997 that they should not accept a recommended salary increase, who said, 'You have a wife who earns money, I have one who spends it'?
2. Which agricultural term is used to describe fodder that has been preserved through controlled fermentation?

3. Mia Farrow, Goldie Hawn, Jasper Carrott and Bryan Ferry were all born in the year David Lloyd George died. Two points if you get it exactly, one point if you are a year out.

4. In Greek myth, Oedipus was the king of which city-state?

5. What was the name of the research vessel used by Jacques Cousteau for his voyages from 1951 onwards? And for the second point, which ocean-travelling documentary-maker, in a 2004 film, sailed in the SS *Belafonte*?

6. Which Royal Air Force station near London is the oldest continually occupied military airbase in the world, and was also the busiest civilian airport in Europe in the seven years after World War II?

7. Which health product was invented in Britain in the late 1770s by William Addis, even though he was in Newgate prison at the time?

8. Which European country administers the Caribbean islands of Aruba, Bonaire and Curacao?

9. Which Oscar-winning actress was born Susan Abigail Tomalin in 1946?

10. In which TV detective series did the following characters appear:
(i) Detective Andy Sipowicz; (ii) Officer Stacy Sheridan; (iii) Sergeant Phil Esterhaus; (iv) Officer Francis Poncherello?

Round Four

1. Which television soap was first televised on November 2nd, 1982?

2. If St Cletus was third and St Linus was second, who was first?

3. Of which ex-Soviet republics are these cities the capitals? A point for each.
(i) Minsk; (ii) Yerevan; (iii) Vilnius; (iv) Tashkent.

4. Which five-time Italian Prime Minister was kidnapped and murdered in 1978 by the Red Brigade?

5. Which eminent theatrical Dame played Sally Bowles in the first West End production of *Cabaret*?

6. In April 1987, when he was elected to Ashburton Town Council in Devon, Alan Hope became the first representative of which political party to be elected to public office?

7. Which other sport besides ski-ing takes place on a piste?

8. The human body normally contains around 14 milligrams of iodine. In which organ of the body does most of it accumulate?

9. If the United Kingdom is represented by Halley and Rothera, Australia by Casey and Davis, Chile by Professor Julio Escudero and Bernardo O'Higgins, and Argentina by San Martin, where am I?

10. Who was the first England player to congratulate Geoff Hurst after he scored his hat-trick goal in the 1966 football World Cup Final, as regularly seen in the opening credits to They Think It's All Over?

The answers to Quiz Thirty-Three begin on page 410

SNOWBALL
QUESTIONS

In 2002 the ownership of the Prince of Wales changed, and the new landlord, who like several people in this tale is called Chris, had a new idea to give the quiz a bit of spark. In truth the Snowball is not a new idea at all – similar wheezes have been tried with great success in pubs all over the country – but it was new to us in our tiny North London quizzing bubble, and we embraced it with an enthusiasm that has never wavered. There is something about the possibility of winning a substantial sum of money that is impossible to resist.

The Snowball is held after the main quiz, not long before closing time, when everyone is nearly as drunk as they are going to get. During round three the bar staff will have circulated through the pub, selling raffle tickets to anyone who wants them for £1 a throw. On our team Patrick almost always buys five, and as a result of this aggressive investment policy has had his ticket pulled out of the hat more often than anyone. Because he knows so much, he has won more often than anyone as well. He has therefore become the pub's pantomime villain, invariably booed when his ticket is drawn, and cheered if he gets the question wrong.

If your ticket is drawn you are called up to the quizmaster's table and whoever is running the Snowball – let's call him the Snowballer – gives you the choice of three envelopes, A, B or C. The one you choose is opened. The Snowballer instructs everyone else to be quiet and not shout out the answer, or otherwise the whole exercise will be declared void. Astoundingly, everyone obeys. The Snowballer then asks you the question in the envelope. If you answer correctly you win the proceeds of the raffle ticket sales. If you do not, the money is held over till next week. Over weeks and, occasionally, months, the sum can mount up. When it reaches £500, as it has done several times, the rules change slightly. If the person whose ticket was drawn answers incorrectly, then a second ticket is drawn. This person has two envelopes to choose from, but can only win half the total prize money. If Victim 2 answers incorrectly, a third ticket is drawn, the last envelope is opened and this time a quarter of the total prize money is at stake. £500, £250, £125: it's always worth winning, and it all comes in lovely cash.

At first I was the Snowballer. In fact I did the job for two and half years, saving up my most vicious and otherwise unusable questions for those envelopes, writing them out in longhand and then leaving them behind in the pub afterwards (so no record of any of my questions survives). Eventually I ran out of material, and was keen to take part myself, so Chris P took over at the beginning of 2005. Below are all the questions he asked that year, with the amounts at stake. The questions are, of course, much harder than normal pub quiz questions. They have to be, although Chris notes that, almost always, there is someone in the pub who knows the answer. Only very occasionally is it the person whose ticket has been chosen.

A good example is the question for February 8th. As it happens, a variant of the same question cropped up in someone else's quiz, and is elsewhere in this book. Chris & John asked 'If Eugene Cernan was the last, who was the first?' You can guess at that; indeed, most teams who got it right would never previously have been able to state that Eugene Cernan was the last man (to date) to walk on the moon. But to stand up in front of the whole pub and be asked 'Who was the last man to set foot on the moon?' That's challenging.

To make things a little tougher the answers in the back of the book have been scrambled. This will remove (or at least reduce) the temptation to look up the following answer before you have read the question. As you grapple with these, imagine yourself tired, tense, slightly befuddled with drink and agonisingly keen not to make a fool of yourself. Or get someone else to answer the questions and imagine them in that state. That's even more fun.

At the last quiz of 2004, there had been £61 in the kitty.

04.01.05 For £93:

The most recent invasion of any part of England came in July 1667, when a Dutch armada landed at which east coast port?
See answer 52.

11.01.05 For £148:

Which Dutch footballer is the only player to have won the UEFA Champions League with three different clubs?
See answer 10.

18.01.05 For £180:

Who wrote the song 'Look At Your Game Girl', which Guns 'N' Roses recorded on their 1993 album *The Spaghetti Incident*?
See answer 75.

25.01.05 For £214:

Which major scientific discovery was made in the early 1980s by Professor Sir Alec Jeffreys at the University of Leicester?
See answer 24.

01.02.05 For £252:

Apart from the Beatles, who was the only other person who appeared in all their three live action films?
See answer 44.

08.02.05 For £272:

Who was the last human, to date, to set foot on the moon?
See answer 3.

15.02.05 For £319:

Who wrote the thriller *At Risk*, which was published in July 2004?
See answer 58.

22.02.05 For £355:

Neil Jenkins of Wales holds the world record for points scored in Rugby Union internationals with 1,049. Whose record did he break?

See answer 18.

01.03.05 For £415:

In 1519, ships called the *Trinidad, San Antonio, Concepción, Vittoria* and *Santiago* made up the fleet of a famous explorer. Who was he?

See answer 36.

08.03.05 For £481:

Who is said to have ridden a horse called Aethenoth?

See answer 67.

15.03.05 For £611:

Who wrote seventeen children's books between 1977 and 1990 about an unruly Afghan puppy called 'What-A-Mess'?

See answer 6.

15.03.05 For £305:

Which religious movement was founded by an Anglican priest called John Smyth in Amsterdam in 1609?

See answer 25.

15.03.05 For £152:

Who is the only UK sportsman or woman, apart from Kelly Holmes, who won an individual medal in a track and field event at the 2004 Athens Olympics?

See answer 80.

22.03.05 For £742:

Who writes the novels whose hero is a larger-than-life oceanographer called Dirk Pitt?

See answer 57.

22.03.05 For £371:
He's the former leader of NUPE and UNISON and was President of the National Pensioners' Convention until early 2005. Who is he?
See answer 38.

22.03.05 For £185:
In which event of 1911 did a Latvian called Peter Piatkow, also known as Peter The Painter, take part, although he was never caught?
See answer 17.

22.03.05 For £92:
The Lancashire township of Marsden was renamed early in the 19th century. What is its current name?
See answer 77.

22.03.05 For £46:
Which 1960s pop singer was a host of the 1980s children's TV show *Beat The Teacher*?
See answer 4.

29.03.05 For £838:
Which city in California houses the California Institute of Technology and NASA's Jet Propulsion Laboratory?
See answer 30.

29.03.05 For £419:
Where did the United Nations Monetary and Financial Conference meet in July 1944?
See answer 54.

29.03.05 For £210:
They had a Number Seven hit in 1981 and made Number Six in the album charts the same year with *Hi Infidelity*. Which band was named after an American make of fire engine?
See answer 72.

29.03.05 For £105:
Who travelled by climbing aboard a pogo stick, which doubled as an umbrella with a duck's head called Jefferson for a handle?
See answer 16.

29.03.05 For £53:
Since it restarted in the 1945/46 season, the FA Cup has been won by the same club in consecutive years on four occasions. Tottenham have done it twice, Arsenal once. Which is the only other club to have retained the FA Cup since the war?
See answer 45.

05.04.05 For £958 (the largest sum anyone had ever competed for in the pub, so no pressure):
Daughter of the Dales, *Seasons of My Life* and *The Commonsense Book of a Countrywoman*. These were all books ghost-written in the early 1990s for a lady who was found living in the Yorkshire Dales on a farm miles from anywhere. The TV company that found her then sent her to the USA and all manner of other places. What is her name?
See answer 64.

05.04.05 For £479:
In which TV situation comedy did ex-cricketer Fred Trueman appear?
See answer 1.

05.04.05 For £240:
Which actor has as his stage name the alternative name of the site of the Battle of Otterburn between the forces of Henry Percy, Earl of Northumberland and James, Earl of Douglas in 1388?
See answer 22.

05.04.05 For £120:

In 1986, when Liverpool won the League/FA Cup double, the same team was runner-up in both competitions, in a unique losers' double. Which team?

See answer 49.

05.04.05 For £60:

In 1707, he hanged a sailor who had argued with his navigator's estimate of their position. The following day his ship, the *Association*, ran aground on the Scilly Isles with the loss of all hands. Who was he?

See answer 79.

12.04.05 For £1000:

What does John Stuart Mill have in common with Sir Douglas Haig, John Cleese, Tim Brooke-Taylor and Andrew Neil?

See answer 8.

12.04.05 For £500:

The Manchester-based American sculptor Mitzi Cunliffe designed which award, many of which are presented annually in a televised ceremony?

See answer 61.

19.04.05 For £706:

We've all heard of Q, the gizmo man in the James Bond films, but who was the literary Q?

See answer 43.

19.04.05 For £353:

He had been a test pilot since the end of the war. On 10th March 1956 he broke the world air speed record with a speed of 1,132 mph in a Fairey Delta 2 aircraft. Who is he?

See answer 7.

19.04.05 For £176:

According to the official rules of the Royal and Ancient Golf Club, what is the diameter of the hole on a golf course?
See answer 23.

19.04.05 For £88:

Mark Lawrenson, the former Liverpool player and now BBC TV pundit, was for seven months in 1988 the manager of which football club?
See answer 62.

19.04.05 For £44:

At which army camp in Dorset can you find a museum dedicated to the military tank?
See answer 37.

26.04.05 For £836:

Edward Whymper, an artist and engraver, became, in 1865, the first man to accomplish which feat?
See answer 15.

26.04.05 For £418:

One of New Zealand's highest paid sportsmen is a man called Steve Williams. What does he do?
See answer 50.

26.04.05 For £209:

Where might you find a famous piece of military hardware called Mons Meg?
See answer 70.

03.05.05 For £719:

Which vessel in World War II was commanded by Captain Hans Langsdorff?
See answer 27.

10.05.05 For £53:

Who was the mother of both Richard the Lionheart and King John?

See answer 11.

17.05.05 For £98:

Which novel and film featured the doings of a member of staff at an undertakers called Shadrack & Duxbury?

See answer 63.

24.05.05 For £140:

He appeared on stage with, among others, Perry Como, Liza Minnelli and the Rolling Stones. He made his career out of impersonating George Formby and died in April 2005, aged seventy-one. Who was he?

See answer 42.

31.05.05 For £180:

In Wagner's *Ring* cycle, if not necessarily in Norse mythology, the Valkyries were fathered by Wotan. Who was their mother?

See answer 19.

07.06.05 For £225:

In 1960 a businessman called Selim Zilkha founded what has become one of the biggest names on the UK High Street. Which chain of shops is this?

See answer 53.

14.06.05 For £273:

In which country was Roger Whittaker, who had many forgettable middle-of-the-road hits in the 1970s, born?

See answer 71.

21.06.05 For £335:

Present Indicative and *Future Indefinite* were the two volumes of autobiography written by whom?
See answer 39.

28.06.05 For £384:

The ratel is a mammal native to Africa and south Asia with another much more commonly used name. What?
See answer 20.

05.07.05 For £415:

We all know that Beatrix Potter wrote the books about Peter Rabbit, but who wrote those about the Little Grey Rabbit?
See answer 40.

12.07.05 For £40:

The song 'Woke Up This Morning' is the theme to *The Sopranos* on Channel 4. Which British band recorded it?
See answer 59.

19.07.05 For £86:

Who wrote Petula Clark's Number One hit from 1967, 'This Is My Song'?
See answer 33.

26.07.05 For £143:

In which sport or pastime might you be taking part if you performed something called an Immelmann turn?
See answer 12.

02.08.05 For £189:

Who was the pioneering plastic surgeon during World War II whose grateful patients founded the Guinea Pig Club?
See answer 73.

09.08.05 For £226:

Agatha Christie's Hercule Poirot has been played on screen by Albert Finney, Peter Ustinov and David Suchet, among others. Who played him in the BBC Radio dramatisations of the Poirot stories that were produced in the 1990s?
See answer 56.

16.08.05 For £23:

What connects F. D. Roosevelt (three times), Winston Churchill (twice), along with Gandhi, Hitler and American Women?
See answer 29.

23.08.05 For £53:

Why would an Irishman called Kevin Moran be most likely to remember May 18th 1985?
See answer 14.

30.08.05 For £19:

Although much of the modern city is Georgian, people have been living there since earliest times. It was called Noviomagnus by the Romans, and was at the other end of the Roman Road called Stane Street. Which city?
See answer 66.

06.09.05 For £63:

Who, in 1990, became the first political head of government anywhere in the world to give birth while in office?
See answer 48.

13.09.05 For £98:

'The customer is always right' was a motto coined by the founder of which department store?
See answer 32.

20.09.05 For £44:

Which European country's economy is based largely, but not exclusively, on the production of power tools and false teeth, of which it is the world's largest producer?

See answer 76.

27.09.05 For £88:

Who do we know was the MP for Birmingham East for at least the period from 1980 to 1988?

See answer 55.

4.10.05   For £125:

Professor Robert Knox probably deserved prosecution in November 1828, but got away with his crime. What was the offence?

See answer 28.

11.10.05 For £181:

There is a website called www.forgivenforlife.com run by a group of American evangelicals, on which a man called David Berkowitz explains that he has seen God and that he's sorry for all that he has done. What was he known as in 1977?

See answer 68.

18.10.05 For £215:

Twenty-odd years ago the name of Betty Callaway was very famous in a particular sporting context. Why was she so well known?

See answer 47.

25.10.05 For £254:

Which British landmark is known as Penn An Wlas in the local language?

See answer 9.

01.11.05 For £274:

Which fictional detective appeared for the first time in the book
Quiet As A Nun in 1977?
See answer 34.

08.11.05 For £305:

During World War I, many people in Britain were exhorted to
collect horse chestnuts (conkers). To what purpose were they put?
See answer 60.

15.11.05 For £367:

What is the name of the Indian Ocean island group that is
sometimes known as The Perfumed Isles?
See answer 78.

22.11.05 For £386:

Who is the current Father of the House of Commons – the MP
who has been sitting there the longest?
See answer 46.

29.11.05 For £429:

In Ernest Hemingway's *The Old Man and the Sea*, what kind of fish
did the old man Santiago catch?
See answer 5.

06.12.05 For £484:

Families in which nation begin Christmas every year with a meal
that they call Wigilia?
See answer 26.

13.12.05 For £567:

What is the significance to transport in London of the Ernest
Bevin, the John Burns and the James Newman?
See answer 69.

13.12.05 For £284:

Which creatures are affected by Isle of Wight disease?

See answer 35.

13.12.05 For £142:

Which lighthouse, one of the most exposed in the world, stands on a rock ledge 46 metres long by 16 metres wide, just four miles west of the Scilly Isles?

See answer 13.

20.12.05 For £637:

Which Hollywood superstar is the cousin of two sportsmen who have both captained their national side?

See answer 51.

20.12.05 For £318:

What are the names of George W. Bush's twin daughters?

See answer 74.

20.12.05 For £159:

Who was the first person to win a by-election under the banner of the Liberal/SDP Alliance after its formation in 1981?

See answer 21.

27.12.05 For £707:

Which one-act ballet is set in a toyshop and was presented for the first time in 1919 with choreography by Massine?

See answer 2.

27.12.05 For £353:

Empty Glass (1980) and *All The Best Cowboys Have Chinese Eyes* (1982) are both solo albums by which man who is more usually known as a member of a major rock band?

See answer 41.

27.12.05 For £176:

Who is the only player to be awarded the Footballer of the Year title by both the Football Writers' Association and the Professional Footballers' Association and who also was European Footballer of the Year?

(For the first time in the entire year, my ticket was drawn. I had invested a straight fiver every week, and yet chancers like Patrick and David had each been called up countless times. Not that I had known many of the answers. All year I had been teasing Chris that he only ever asked questions about football and World War II. And I had known the Pete Townshend question. So when he started with 'who is the only player . . .' my heart sank. If no particular sport is mentioned by name in the first few words, it's football. Still, I thought about it, which didn't last long, as I could only remember one British footballer – and I assumed he was British – who had ever won the European Footballer of the Year award. So what was there to lose? 'Have to hurry you,' said Chris, grinning evilly. 'Is it . . . Kevin Keegan?' said I.)
See answer 65.

The answers to the Snowball begin on page 417

ANSWERS

ANSWERS TO QUIZ ONE

Round One

1. On a table football set.
2. Sauerkraut.
   (Anti-German sentiment had sent sales plummeting. In the US, a hamburger became a 'liberty sandwich' and German measles 'liberty measles'. The US singer-songwriter Rufus Wainwright has written a song called 'Liberty Cabbage'.)
3. The sciatic nerve.
   (It runs from the hip, via the buttock, down the back of the leg to the foot.)
4. They are all derived from tree bark.
5. Crosswords.
6. Dorothy Parker.
7. *High Noon*.
8. Rift valley.
9. *Balamory*.
10. Constance; Fitzwilliam; Mark; Lemuel; Joe.
    (Clint Eastwood is credited as 'Joe' in both *A Fistful Of Dollars* and *The Good, The Bad And The Ugly*, and he is actually addressed as Joe by a minor character in the first of these. Also accept 'Monco', as someone calls him this in *For A Few Dollars More*.)

Round Two

1. They were all assassinated.
   (Abraham Lincoln, James A Garfield, William McKinley and John F Kennedy.)
2. Laurence Olivier and Joan Plowright.
3. A tie.
4. Toad.

5. Gin.
6. Battenburg.

   (Try as I might, I can't confirm the truth of this. But I like the question so much I'm putting it in anyway.)
7. *Twelfth Night*.
8. Houston.
9. They are all officially missing.

   (Most have been stolen and never recovered.)
10. (i) Australia and England; (ii) England and India; (iii) Australia and South Africa.

Bonus Round

1. Captain Square.

   (Played by Geoffrey Lumsden with a huge handlebar moustache. The character had been a Colonel in World War I and was therefore sometimes addressed as 'Captain Colonel Square'.)
2. Elizabeth.
3. Private Godfrey.

   (In Gents' Outfitting, for forty-five years.)
4. Philip Madoc.
5. Sergeant-major.

Tie-Break

Soft toilet paper was first sold in the UK in 1947.

Round Three

1. Italy.

   ('La corsia della vergogna')
2. Sulphuric.
3. Erik Satie.

4. **Apollo; Pythiad.**

   (Pythios, or 'python slayer', was the name under which Apollo was worshipped there. The word Pythiad is analogous to Olympiad, which is the four-year period between Olympic games and not, as is widely supposed, another name for the games themselves.)

5. **Crewcut.**

6. **Margaret Beckett.**

7. **Kent.**

   (There are another nine Hams in the British Isles, including two in Somerset. But no other Sandwich.)

8. **He cut his head off.**

   (Or so it is thought. He was the Common Hangman of London at the time, but he is known to have refused the job when originally approached. Maybe he changed his mind later. After his death in the same year, his supposed confession was published, admitting that he had been paid £30 for the task 'all in half crowns'.)

9. **Bertie the Bus; Harold the Helicopter; Terence the Tractor.**

   (Not to be confused with Trevor the Traction Engine.)

10. **They were the original forenames given to the Phoenix siblings.**

    (River died aged twenty-three in 1993. Leaf now calls himself Joaquin, Libertad is Liberty, Rainbow is Rain. It could have been so much worse: their father's original surname was Bottom.)

Round Four

1. **Kellogg's Bran Flakes.**

   (Some teams insisted it was Kellogg's Fruit 'n' Fibre. They remembered an ad featuring the actor Ross Kemp before he found his fame and lost his hair in *EastEnders*. Not the right ad, though.)

2. He was standing on the moon at the time.

(It was a six-iron, attached to a lunar sample scoop handle. Shepard could only hit the ball one-handed, because of the bulkiness of his spacesuit, but he said it went 'miles and miles'.)

3. Cowslip.

(It was believed that they grew best where cattle had inadvertently fertilised the meadows.)

4. Fear of Friday the 13th.

5. Chow.

(Also known as chow-chow.)

6. By a blue plaque.

(To be absolutely precise, the plaques only became blue in 1901, when the London County Council took over the task. The Royal Society of Arts had been sticking memorial tablets on houses since 1867, starting with the house where Byron was born.)

7. A.

8. The USSR. (Accept 'Russia'.)

9. Synchronised swimming.

10. The guillotine.

ANSWERS TO QUIZ TWO

Round One

1. **Stella McCartney.**
2. **Michael Heseltine.** (Henley-on-Thames.)
3. **Can turn into an animal (and back) at will.**
4. **Tripe.**
   (They are from the different stomachs of the cow. Blanket or flat tripe is from the rumen; honeycomb or pocket tripe is from the reticulum; and if you take it from the omasum it's book, Bible or leaf tripe. Yum.)
5. **Pangalactic Gargleblaster.**
6. *Who's Afraid Of Virginia Woolf?*
   (Elizabeth Taylor and Sandy Dennis both won, Richard Burton and George Segal both lost.)
7. **Colonel Gaddafi of Libya.**
8. **One.** (It was Robin Smith in 1995/96.)
9. **Led Zeppelin.**
   (They are the covers of *Led Zeppelin I*, *Led Zeppelin II* and *Physical Graffiti*.)
10. **Christopher Trace, Leila Williams, Anita West, Valerie Singleton, John Noakes and Peter Purves.**
   (Anita West is the difficult one here. She was the show's shortest serving presenter: May 7th to September 3rd 1962. No *Blue Peter* footage of her survives. But thirty years later she did appear in an episode of *Lovejoy*.)

Round Two

1. **The ball burst.**
   (Remarkably, it happened in 1947 as well.)
2. **Polari.**

3. **They were both owned at one time by a man called Alf Roberts.**

    (Alderman Alfred Roberts, of Grantham, Lincs, was Margaret Thatcher's father.)

4. **Lord Snooty.**

    (Who made his first appearance in the very first issue of *The Beano*, on July 30th 1938. His real name is Marmaduke, Earl of Bunkerton.)

5. **They illustrated the song with a huge picture of Jocky Wilson, the darts player.**

6. **A silverback.**

7. **The Lubyanka.**

8. **John Glenn.**

    (He cadged a lift on the space shuttle *Discovery*, thirty-six years after his first space flight.)

9. **Portugal.**

10. **Angie's Den.**

    (Named after her parents, Angie and Den. In 2005 Johnny Allen acquired the club and renamed it Scarlet, after his daughter.)

Bonus Round

1. **Singapore.**

2. **Zanzibar.**

3. **Morocco.**

4. **Bali.**

5. **Hong Kong.**

6. **Utopia and Rio.**

    (They are the destinations of the seven *Road* films, made in the 1940s and early 50s and starring Bob Hope, Bing Crosby and Dorothy Lamour.)

Tie-Break

390,127.

(That's 0.7 per cent of the population, a higher proportion than either Jews, Sikhs or Buddhists. The greatest concentration, 2.6 per cent of the local population, could be found in the Brighton & Hove area.)

Round Three

1. **Pepsi.** (From dyspepsia. One enterprising team suggested 'Cockburns'. They got one point.)
2. **Dick Francis.**
3. **No marks at all.**
   (The ceremony takes place in the third week of July on the river Thames between Sunbury and Pangbourne. Liveried swan-uppers progress slowly upstream in boats, inspecting the swans' bills and then marking those of their offspring.)
4. **A net.**
5. **Speaker of the House of Representatives.**
6. **Rugby league.** (Between 1990 and 1994.)
7. *Goldfinger.*
   (The Queen Mother declared it was the best film she had ever seen.)
8. **Waylon Jennings.**
9. **Hugo Boss.**
   (He designed the famous black uniform in 1932.)
10. **Indian, Cowboy, Construction Worker, Cop, Biker and Soldier.**
    (Almost all teams in the pub put 'Sailor', but there wasn't one, honest. Clearly a cultural stereotype at work here.)

Round Four

1. Dr Crippen was arrested.
2. The *Golden Hind*.
3. Five.
4. Ho Chi Minh.
   (He lived in London between 1913 and 1917, and worked for Escoffier at the Carlton Hotel in Haymarket.)
5. The Irish harp.
6. Hungary beat England 6-3.
   (It was the first time England had been beaten at home by continental opposition.)
7. They dined on mince, and slices of quince.
   (Which they ate with a runcible spoon.)
8. Ted Moult.
9. The Duchess of York (later Queen Elizabeth the Queen Mother) and her two daughters, Princess Elizabeth and Princess Margaret-Rose.
10. 'For those in peril on the sea.'
    (Written in 1860 after the Rev. William Whiting survived a fierce storm at sea.)

Extra Tie-Break

1,525.

ANSWERS TO QUIZ THREE

Round One

1. Iraq.
2. Disgusted of Tunbridge Wells.
3. Groundhog Day.
4. Bloodhounds.

   (They are such good trackers, they have been known to follow trails more than four days old. They can even testify in the courtroom. If evidence left at the scene of the crime is shown to the bloodhound, it can identify the person whose scent is all over it – if that person happens to be in the courtroom at the time.)

5. Turquoise.

   (He now believes that the world is controlled by a race of reptilian humanoids, whose numbers include HM The Queen, George W. Bush and Kris Kristofferson.)

6. Texas.

   (After gaining its independence from Mexico in 1836, and before becoming a state in 1845.)

7. Operation.

   (A year before the anniversary, manufacturers Hasbro gave him a new ailment, Brain Freeze, represented by an ice cream cone stuck in his head.)

8. Harvey Smith.

   (Years later he admitted in interviews that the gesture was exactly what we all thought it had been.)

9. Two.
10. (i) *Porridge*; (ii) *The Young Ones*; (iii) *The Good Life*; (iv) *One Foot in the Grave*.

Round Two

1. Tonto.
2. It was London's first nude statue.
   (It was erected in honour of the Duke of Wellington and his troops by 'their countrywomen'.)
3. Rockall.
4. Will Hay.
5. Stylophone.
6. Leicestershire, Nottinghamshire, Derbyshire.
   (Oddly enough, one place where Stilton was never traditionally produced was the town of Stilton. It takes the name because that's where it was first sold.)
7. *Sergeant Pepper's Lonely Hearts Club Band* by The Beatles.
8. The starfish.
   (One team put 'teenage boy after gallon of cider'. Nice try, but no points.)
9. The Congo.
   (The Amazon runs just south of the equator through its entire length.)
10. *La Bohème* (Puccini), *Carmen* (Bizet), *Aida* (Verdi), *Tosca* (Puccini), *Rigoletto* (Verdi).

Bonus Round

1. Charles Bronson.
2. Yul Brynner.
3. Steve McQueen.
4. James Coburn.
5. Brad Dexter.

Tie-Break

The Magnificent Seven lasts 128 minutes.

Round Three

1. Bolognese.
2. Comma.
3. **Kent** (Larkins) **and Bedfordshire** (Silas).
4. Peter Tchaikovsky.
5. The Tufty Club.
6. Beaver.
7. James Dean.
8. *Goodness Gracious Me.*
9. Pisa.
10. **Derek Ibbotson** (in 1957), **Sebastian Coe** (in 1979 and twice in 1981), **Steve Ovett** (in 1980 and 1981), **Steve Cram** (in 1985).

Round Four

1. Norman Schwarzkopf.
2. **It's fictional** (2 points). **Terry Pratchett's Ankh-Morpork** (1 point).
3. **West Germany.**
   (They are the teams England played in the 1966 World Cup.)
4. **Sir Ben Kingsley.**
   (Gandhi in Sir Richard Attenborough's film.)
5. The Bee Gees.
6. Denis Compton.
7. St Mark.
8. Switzerland.
9. They are the ones on Mount Rushmore.
10. France, Spain, Greece, Chad, Laos and Guam.
    (David actually asked for the five countries whose names only have one syllable. Then someone put Guam and he thought, fair enough, there are six. Someone else then argued that Laos could be pronounced as two syllables (which of course it

can, but not necessarily), and then someone else wanted Guam disallowed because it sounded like slightly more than one syllable, if not quite two syllables. One and a half syllables, maybe. All of which proves the old maxim: the quizmaster is always right, whether he is right or wrong.)

ANSWERS TO QUIZ FOUR

Round One

1. A sea horse.
2. In the brain.
   (You'll find it in the floor of the lateral ventricle. It's so called because in cross-section it is shaped like a sea horse.)
3. Oscar Wilde. (In *Lady Windermere's Fan*.)
4. The bullet train.
5. Portable Document Format.
6. James Boswell's.
7. England had 16 men on the field.
   (For which they were fined £10,000 – or nearly £300 per second.)
8. Abacus.
9. Five.
10. (i) 'On First Looking into Chapman's Homer'. (ii) John Keats.
    (iii) In the opening credits of *University Challenge*.

Round Two

1. Adelaide and Darwin.
2. Broadcasting Radio Caroline. (One point for 'pirate radio'.)
3. A winding hole.
4. Four times.
   (In 1397, 1398, 1406 and 1419.)
5. Casablanca.
   (In the late 1960s it was one of only a handful of places where transsexuals could go for surgery. Raskind/Richards later had the operation elsewhere.)
6. Bob Monkhouse.
7. Harold Lloyd. *Safety Last.* (Made in 1923.)

8. **Potential of hydrogen.**
   (It's equal to the common logarithm of the reciprocal of the concentration of hydrogen ions in moles per cubic decimetre of solution, in case you were wondering.)
9. **Colleges at Durham University.**
10. **'Ring of Fire'.**

Bonus Round

1. **Norris McWhirter.** (Who died a month before the anniversary.)
2. **Iffley Road, Oxford.** (One point for Oxford.)
3. **John Landy.**
4. **Chris Brasher and Christopher Chataway.**
5. **Trevor Bannister.**

Tie-Break

Gunder Hägg's 1945 record was 4 minutes 1.3 seconds.

Round Three

1. **(i) Countess; (ii) Marchioness.**
2. **Sanjay Gandhi.** (Rajiv succeeded him.)
3. **John F Kennedy and Ronald Reagan.**
   (In 1961 and 1981 respectively.)
4. **Mick Jagger.**
5. **(i) 16; (ii) 30.**
6. **An Anderson shelter was outdoors, in the garden. A Morrison shelter was indoors.**
7. **That was Nelson Mandela's prison number on Robben Island.**

8. 'In fact it belongs to me.'
   (Anything roughly along these lines should get the points.)
9. 19th. (Also accept: 1800s. It was actually 1870.)
10. (i) Mozart; (ii) Berlioz; (iii) Verdi; (iv) Fauré; (v) Britten.

Round Four

1. Linoleum.
2. Julian Barnes. Kavanagh is his wife's surname.
3. George I, II, III and IV.
4. Icebergs.
   (Larger examples are classified less entertainingly as 'small iceberg', 'medium iceberg', 'large iceberg' and 'very large iceberg'.)
5. *The Young Visiters* by Daisy Ashford.
   (Patrick only gave two points for the novel if the title was spelt absolutely correctly. One point to anyone who spelt it *Visitors*. Somehow, bloodshed was avoided.)
6. A4 paper.
7. Marlon Brando's film career.
8. Lemony Snicket.
9. Gibraltar.
   (With him was the excellently named Sir Cloudesley Shovell, who will crop up elsewhere in this book.)
10. Jelly beans.

ANSWERS TO QUIZ FIVE

Round One

1. **The Planck length.**
   (Named after Max Planck, the formulator of quantum theory. He postulated that this was the shortest possible distance between two points. Not to be confused with Planck's constant, which is something else entirely.)

2. **Don McLean; 'American Pie'.**
   ('Killing Me Softly' was written for Lori Lieberman, who had seen McLean at The Troubadour in Los Angeles and had her mind well and truly blown. She recorded it first, but Flack had the hit.)

3. **Bury.**

4. *Mary Reilly.*
   (Julia Roberts played the title role. One review said that Malkovich was miscast as Jekyll but not as Hyde.)

5. **Senegal.**

6. **John Milton.**

7. **The gorilla.**

8. **Shaft.**
   (As in 'Theme from Shaft' by Isaac Hayes. Can you dig it?)

9. **The M32.**

10. **Jake Lloyd, Hayden Christiansen, David Prowse, James Earl Jones, Sebastian Shaw.**
    (J. Lloyd played him as small boy, H. Christiansen as sulky teen and tortured young adult, D. Prowse, a.k.a. the Green Cross Man, was his body in the original trilogy, J. E. Jones was his voice, and S. Shaw was his face after he died. Also accept Bob Anderson, who isn't strictly an actor, but a master swordsman who performed the lightsabre fights in *The Empire Strikes Back* and *Return Of The Jedi*.)

Round Two

1. **Climb Everest.**
   (His son Brad was there as well: they were the first father and son team to reach the summit.)
2. **Fleetwood Mac; Bachman-Turner Overdrive.**
   (With 'The Chain' and 'You Ain't Seen Nothing Yet' respectively.)
3. **Khartoum in Sudan.**
   (It was designed by Lord Kitchener. He thought it would make it easier to defend.)
4. **Floyd Patterson.**
5. **Anna Pavlova.**
6. **Samuel Beckett;** *Quantum Leap*.
7. **Douglas Adams.**
8. **Onomatopoeia.**
9. **Chris Morris.**
   (In *The Day Today* and *Brass Eye*.)
10. **Kenneth Baker** (1990-2), **Kenneth Clarke** (1992-3), **Michael Howard** (1993-7), **Jack Straw** (1997-2001), **David Blunkett** (2001-4), **Charles Clarke** (2004-6).

Bonus Round

1. **Goodfellas.**
2. **Daily Express.**
3. **Dominoes.**
4. **The Four Seasons.**
   (Subsequently known as 'The Four Seasons with the sound of Frankie Valli,' 'The Four Seasons with Frankie Valli' and 'Frankie Valli and the Four Seasons'.)
5. **Pizza the Hutt.**

Tie-Break

Melvin Hemker grew a sunflower with 837 heads.
(That's the official record. Some websites say it was 856. What is certain is that Mr Hemker was eighty-two at the time.)

Round Three

1. **David Hasselhoff.**
2. **Earthquakes.**
   (Not to be confused with the Richter scale, which measures the magnitude of earthquakes. Although no one without the relevant degree can explain the difference, this is a regular pub quiz question.)
3. **Dylan Thomas.**
   (According to another observer, his actual last words were 'After thirty-nine years, this is all I've done.')
4. **California; Wyoming.**
   (Some teams put Alaska for the lowest, but that has 626,000 inhabitants.)
5. **A tittle.**
   (One point for 'diacritic', which is the name given to any mark above or below a letter, such as an acute accent or a cedilla. A tittle is therefore a type of diacritic.)
6. **Sinn Fein.**
   (Markiewicz was her married name; she was born Constance Gore-Booth. Her husband left for Ukraine in 1913 and never came back. She was later elected to the first Dail Eireann and served as Minister for Labour.)
7. **Edward V and Edward VIII, neither of whom were crowned at all.**
8. **Morgan Spurlock.**
9. **Eddie Van Halen.**
10. **Agatha Christie.**

Round Four

1. Tap dancing.
2. Iceland and Finland.

   (We define 'Nordic' here as being a member of the Nordic council. Estonia would like to join but haven't as yet. The Faroe Islands and Greenland are autonomous territories, not nations.)
3. They all have a Friday the 13th.
4. Earth, Wind & Fire.
5. The Haka.

   (As sung by New Zealand rugby union teams whenever they get the opportunity.)
6. Fish.
7. Syria.
8. The compact disc.

   (It was reputedly the favourite recording of the then-President of Sony, and its length, 74 minutes, determined the capacity of the first CDs.)
9. In the periodic table of elements.

   (Tantalum, atomic number 73, is named after the Greek mythological king Tantalus. Niobium, atomic number 41, is directly above it in the table.)
10. **Bryan Robson, Steve Bruce, Eric Cantona, Roy Keane** (all Manchester United), **Tony Adams, Patrick Vieira** (both Arsenal), **Tim Sherwood** (Blackburn Rovers), **John Terry** (Chelsea).

ANSWERS TO QUIZ SIX

Round One

1. **Tom Cruise.**

   (The International Dyslexia Association remained unimpressed. 'There is not a lot of science to support the claims that the teachings of Scientology founder L. Ron Hubbard are appropriate to overcoming dyslexia,' said its executive director.)

2. **Tonsils.**

   (The palatine tonsils are the ones we usually just call 'the tonsils'. Pharyngeal tonsils are more familiarly known as the adenoids.)

3. *Play School.*

   (It has a square window, a round window and an arched window.)

4. **The discus.**

   (The men's record, as of January 1st 2006, was 74.08 m; the women's was 76.80 m. But the men's discus is heavier: 2 kg as opposed to 1 kg.)

5. **Don.**

   (There are yet more in France, India and Canada.)

6. **Whistler's mother.**

   (Anna McNeill Whistler. 'Arrangement In Grey And Black' was painted in 1871 and is now owned by the Musée d'Orsay in Paris. Whistler clearly had a thing about Cheyne Walk: he also lived at no. 21 and no. 101 and died at no. 74.)

7. **Darren Gough.**

8. **Barristers.**

   (Alternative theories have them mourning for Charles II, who died in 1685, or Queen Anne, 1714.)

9. **St. Trinian's.**

10. **(i) Father and son; (ii) brothers; (iii) uncle and niece.**

Round Two

1. Sir Roger Moore.
2. Sir Isaac Newton.
   (Another version of the story is that he asked for the window to be closed because of the draught.)
3. **On any Euro banknote.**
   (They are the initials of the European central bank in various languages.)
4. **Wombat.**
   (The Northern Hairy-nosed is now critically endangered.)
5. **Velázquez.**
   (Its true title is 'Venus At Her Toilet'. Rokeby Park was the house in which it hung for most of the 19th century. It's the only surviving nude painted by Velázquez, and one of only two in all 17th-century Spanish art. The Spanish Inquisition probably dealt with the rest.)
6. **90°; 360°.**
7. **The Black Death.**
   (Carried by rats. Within four years a third of Europe was dead.)
8. **Kidney and bacon.**
9. **Sat Down And Wept.**
10. **Prunella Scales; Maggie Smith; Diana Rigg.**
    (Diana Rigg's first name is Enid.)

Bonus Round

1. *West Side Story* (1961) and *The Sound of Music* (1965).
2. *Platoon* (1986) and *Born On The Fourth Of July* (1989).
3. *From Here To Eternity* (1953) and *A Man For All Seasons* (1966).
4. *One Flew Over The Cuckoo's Nest* (1975) and *Amadeus* (1984).
5. *Schindler's List* (1993) and *Saving Private Ryan* (1998).

(This was a low-scoring round. I thought it would sort the sheep from the goats but none of our regular film buffs turned up that week, which just left the goats. Note the clarification on Oscar years. All questions about the Oscars are complicated by the need to remind everyone that the 1950 Oscars were awarded in spring 1951, and so on.)

Tie-Break

Twenty-five US Presidents had been lawyers.

Round Three

1. **These were the survival rates on the Titanic.**
   (Overall, 32 per cent of those on the ship survived. Male adult survival rate was 20 per cent, female adult 74 per cent, children 52 per cent. Women and children really did go first.)
2. **They were all women.**
   (Respectively, Ruth Wakefield in 1950, Josephine Cochrane in 1886, Marion Donovan in 1950, Mary Anderson in 1903, Melitta Benz in 1908, Emily Canham also in 1908, and Sarah Guppy in 1811.)
3. **Lazarus.**
4. **M*A*S*H.**
5. **'Rasputin' by Boney M.**
6. **Irrational.**
7. **Endymion.**
8. **French wine appellations.**
   (Chateauneuf du Pape, Moulin à Vent, Entre-Deux-Mers and Côte Rotie.)
9. **Plasma.**
10. **(i) New Zealand; (ii) South Africa; (iii) Sri Lanka.**

Round Four

1. **Frank Butcher; Martin Fowler.**
   (In 1998 and 2002 respectively.)

2. **Phasers on stun.**
   (Civil liberties groups 'slammed' Mr Arundale, insisting that the weapons, if they existed, 'could kill people with weak hearts.')

3. **Aspirin.**
   ($CH_3COOC_6H_4COOH$.)

4. **Cayman Islands.**
   (Columbus gave them their original name when he sailed past in 1503. Sir Francis Drake renamed them when he landed in 1586.)

5. **Pursued by a bear.**

6. **Kiwi fruit.**
   (In Chinese it is known as the Macaque peach or, less frequently, as the hairy pear.)

7. **Red Rum.**
   (His trainer Ginger McGrath took Red Rum for a therapeutic swim in the sea off Southport before each Grand National. He – horse, not trainer – is now buried under the finishing line at Aintree.)

8. **New.**

9. **September 30th.**
   (The last day of September. There are variants, but this is the most popular version.)

10. **Mrs Merton.**

ANSWERS TO QUIZ SEVEN

Round One

1. Chemistry.
2. Seal.

   (The first two are antarctic seals, while Northern Fur lives in the north Pacific ocean.)

3. He reads the Harry Potter books on audiotape.

   (He also claims the world record for creating the most character voices on an audiobook: 134 on *Harry Potter and the Order of the Phoenix*.)

4. Larry Holmes.

   (George Foreman, an almost exact contemporary, had an even longer career but never fought Tyson.)

5. *Brave New World*.

   (By Aldous Huxley. AF 632 was equivalent to AD 2540: the starting date for their calendar was the date on which Henry Ford introduced the Model T.)

6. Your sense of smell.

7. Been out first ball in cricket.

   (The club raises money to provide sports facilities for the vision-impaired.)

8. Miss Scarlett.

   (In the board game Cluedo. In Spain Professor Plum becomes Dr Mandarino.)

9. Buster.

   (He never appeared in the original strip, but Reg Smythe created him and drew him for several years. When Buster was passed on to another illustrator, the relation to Andy Capp was quietly forgotten. According to Wikipedia, 'Andy Capp is not to be mistaken with the German curler Andy Kapp'.)

10. (i) George Harrison; (ii) Michael Palin; (iii) Alan Ball.

Round Two

1. 'Rebel Rebel'.
2. Tintin.
3. Beriberi.
   (Tulp only described it. Two hundred years passed before Dutch physicians established that the disease was caused by a deficiency of thiamine, vitamin B1, in the diet.)
4. Yo-yo.
   (When asked what it is good for, Figaro says, 'It is a noble toy, which dispels the fatigue of thinking.')
5. Lord Haw-Haw.
   (He was actually American, but inherited the title from a previous broadcaster who had had a pronounced upper-class drawl.)
6. Yum-Yum.
7. The The.
8. Ha-ha. (Accept 'haw-haw'.)
9. Mau Mau.
10. Laa Laa. (In *Teletubbies*.)

Bonus Round

1. Gladys Pugh. (In *Hi De Hi*, in the 57th of the series' 58 episodes.)
2. Miss Pugh. (Grizelda.)
3. Dangerous Dan McGrew.
   (From Robert Service's poem, 'The Shooting of Dan McGrew'.)
4. Rev. Cuthbert Dibble. (He receives 9 minutes in the handicap.)
5. Grub Street.
   (The link was Trumpton. The town's firemen were Pugh, Pugh, Barney McGrew, Cuthbert, Dibble, Grubb.)

Tie-Break

In a standard game of Cluedo there are 324 possible outcomes.

(The gift and 50th anniversary editions add a seventh weapon, which increases the number to 378.)

Round Three

1. **Details of his budget speech.**

   (He was Chancellor of the Exchequer. On his way to deliver his budget speech, he answered questions from a lobby correspondent – off the record, he believed. The news was in the papers before he could announce it in the House.)

2. **Vermont and Connecticut.**

   (In addition, there are only two that end with a Y and only one that ends with a G.)

3. **Black.**

4. **They were married to each other.**

   (Joe di Maggio in 'Mrs Robinson' and Marilyn Monroe in 'Candle in the Wind'.)

5. **Monkey.**

   (Strictly Hanuman is half-human, half-monkey, and Thoth is sometimes depicted with the head of an ibis. But you get the drift.)

6. **Kentucky and New Jersey; Wyoming.**

7. **Terylene.**

   (Invented in the UK in 1940; first yarn made from it in 1944; manufacture started in 1949.)

8. **Lincolnshire.**

   (New York is between Scrub Hill and Sandy Bank on the B1183.)

9. **Learie Constantine.**

10. **Blamire, Foggy, Seymour, Truly.**

(Cyril Blamire, 1973-75, played by Michael Bates. Walter 'Foggy' Dewhurst, 1976-85 and 1990-97, played by Brian Wilde. Seymour Utterthwaite, 1986-90, played by Michael Aldridge. Herbert 'Truly' Truelove, 1998 to date, played by Frank Thornton.)

Round Four

1. **From the Hollywood sign.**

(Built in 1923, it had originally read 'Hollywoodland'. It had only been meant to last a year and a half. In an unrelated incident, the actress Peg Entwistle leapt to her death in 1932 from the letter 'H'.)

2. **St Alban.**

(In the earliest verson of the story, dating from the 6th century AD, he was a Roman living in Britain, possibly in St Albans, and was executed for sheltering a fugitive Christian.)

3. **November.** (The 20th.)

4. **Sleeping Beauty.**

(Made in 1959. Princess Aurora's willowy body shape was inspired by that of Audrey Hepburn. Prince Philip, who rescues her, may be the only Disney hero specifically named after a member of the British Royal family.)

5. **Sumo wrestling.**

6. **Roulette.**

(Another story holds that, like almost everything else, the game was brought to Europe from China by Dominican monks.)

7. *Miami Vice.*

(She and Sonny Crockett even got married. But after five episodes she was killed off.)

8. *The Bedford Incident.*

(It was Poitier's first film in which there was no reference to his colour.)

9. Istanbul.

10. James A Garfield.

(He died 80 days after he was shot in 1881, from a massive heart attack following blood poisoning and bronchial pneumonia. Several doctors had stuck unsterilised fingers into the wound to look for the bullet; one doctor had punctured the President's liver while doing so. At the autopsy, examiners agreed that Garfield would have survived if the doctors had just left him alone. The man who had shot him argued at his trial that he was not responsible for his death, but was found guilty and hanged anyway.)

ANSWERS TO QUIZ EIGHT

Round One

1. Henri Paul.
2. Hong Kong.

   (John Lanchester used the phrase as the title for his 2002 novel about the former British colony. Fragrant trees were once abundant on Hong Kong Island.)

3. Spinach.
4. Duff Beer. (In *The Simpsons*.)
5. Charlie Chaplin.
6. 18.

   (The spots on opposite sides of a die always add up to 7. Therefore 7+7+4=18.)

7. Catalan.
8. Spike.

   (Occasionally billed as Killer or Butch, but only Spike gets the two points.)

9. 1980s.

   (To be precise, 1982. It was the first new brand since 1886 to use the Coca-Cola trademark.)

10. (i) Jean Sibelius; (ii) Maurice Ravel (accept Joseph-Maurice); (iii) Joaquin Rodrigo; (iv) Gabriel Fauré; (v) Joseph Haydn (accept Franz-Joseph); (vi) Modest Mussorgsky.

Round Two

1. Buster Crabbe.

   (He also played Billy the Kid and Tarzan.)

2. Jeffrey Archer.

3. **The Rams.**

(They were the Cleveland Rams between 1937 and 1946, and then the Los Angeles Rams until 1995.)

4. **The Scorpions.**

(The film features some of the oldest high school kids in screen history. John Travolta was twenty-four at the time, Olivia Newton-John thirty and Stockard Channing, who played Rizzo, thirty-four.)

5. **John Scales.**

6. **Lion.**

(The song is also known as 'Wimoweh' and 'The Lion Sleeps Tonight'.)

7. *Twins.*

8. **Virgin.**

9. **Goat Island.**

10. **'Aquarius'.**

(From *Hair*. You may wish to mention the astrological link in this round beforehand. Or you may not.)

Bonus Round

1. **George Bernard Shaw.**

2. **Lulu.**

3. **'A brotherhood of man'.**

4. **Buck's Fizz.**

(Mr McGarry was barman at Buck's Club in London. A Mimosa contains champagne and orange juice but no grenadine.)

5. **The Mexican wave.**

(Its origins are much disputed. Others claim to have started it at an American football game in Seattle two weeks later. Its first appearance in world football was at the Mexico World Cup of 1986; hence the name.)

(Link: The five British winners of the Eurovision song contest. Sandie Shaw in 1967, Lulu in 1969 with three other countries, Brotherhood of Man in 1976, Bucks Fizz in 1981, Katrina and the Waves in 1997.)

Tie-Break

3.7 million Americans believe they have been abducted by aliens.

Round Three

1. **Albert Einstein.**

   (The inferior parietal region of his brain, the part believed to be related to mathematical reasoning, was later found to be 15 per cent wider on both sides than normal.)

2. **'Baker Street'.**

   (By Gerry Rafferty. In the 1990s an extraordinary urban myth went round that *Blockbusters* host Bob Holness had played that saxophone figure. This had been invented by the NME's Stuart Maconie in an obviously fake 'Did You Know?'-type column. Among his other revelations were that Neil Tennant was a qualified rugby official, David Bowie had invented Connect 4 and Billy Bragg could breathe underwater.)

3. **Bruce Willis.**

   (According to unconfirmed reports – i.e. gossip – Willis tried to enlist in the military to fight the second Gulf War, but was rejected as too old.)

4. **The Harry Potter books.**

   (Accept any one. They are George Weasley, Neville Longbottom, Sirius Black and Albus Dumbledore.)

5. **Syphilis.**

6. **Croydon.**

   (Original meaning: 'valley where wild saffron grows'. May no longer be literally true.)
7. **Bikini.**
8. **Bob Monkhouse.**
9. **It was under the sea at the time.**
10. **Deuteronomy, Ecclesiastes, Song of Solomon, Lamentations.**

    (If you went for the Roman Catholic Vulgate, the question would be more complicated. First and Second Books of Paralipomenon, Canticle of Canticles, Wisdom of Solomon . . .)

Round Four

1. **Twelve.**
2. **'Back to the howling old owl in the woods, hunting the horny back toad.'**

   (You'd need it word perfect for the two points. I thought this was ridiculous, but a surprising number of teams had at least one member who knew the John/Taupin oeuvre down to the last syllable.)
3. **Maidstone.**

   (Disraeli was MP for Maidstone. Golding was a teacher at the grammar school, whose alumni include Dr Beeching and the TV presenter James Burke. Maidstone United went bust and left the league in 1992.)
4. **Psalms.**

   (117 has two verses; 119 has 176.)
5. **Antonio Salieri.**
6. **National Provincial Bank** (established 1833) **and the Westminster Bank** (established 1836).
7. **Acute and chronic.**
8. **BUD.**

9. Cabernet Sauvignon and Merlot.
   Bonus: Malbec, Petit Verdot and Cabernet Franc.
10. Aston Villa, Boston United, Charlton Athletic, Hull City, Leyton Orient, Oxford United, Port Vale, Sheffield Wednesday.

ANSWERS TO QUIZ NINE

Round One

1. Prime Minister's Question Time.
2. The jawbone of an ass.
3. New Zealand.
4. Austria.

   (After the Anschluss, the Austrian players played for Germany, who lost 4-2 to Switzerland in a replay in the first round.)

5. His blood group.

   (You could have it in Gothic lettering or Latin lettering: your choice.)

6. Lyon.
7. Dustin Hoffman. (*Tootsie.*)
8. He was a plasterer.

   (And more recently has been a law student at Loughborough.)

9. William I.

   (a.k.a the Conqueror. He founded the abbey himself.)

10. Captain Kirk and Lieutenant Uhura.

Round Two

1. Harry Carpenter.
2. Alexandra Palace.

   (The first structure had been called The People's Palace.)

3. Glasgow.

   (It was opened in 1896 and is informally known as 'the Clockwork Orange'.)

4. Seymour Skinner.

   (Principal of Springfield Elementary School in *The Simpsons*. Nickname: Spanky.)

5. **The Boomtown Rats.**
   (Their original name was Nightlife Thugs.)
6. **Slovenia.**
   (She has recorded the fastest 100m times for any female athlete aged 30, 31, 32, 33, 34, 35, 36, 37, 38, 39 and 40.)
7. **They were all born twins.**
   (Presley's brother Jesse was stillborn.)
8. **Sack.**
9. **Indiana.**
10. **'Mother's Little Helper'.** (By the Rolling Stones.)

Bonus Round

1. **Focus.**
2. **Granada.**
3. **Cortina d'Ampezzo.** (Accept 'Cortina'.)
4. **Zephyr.**
5. **T.**
   (The link was Ford Motors. You could also ask the name of the pilot of Fireball XL5, or the Mediterranean island on which Gracie Fields lived, or several thousand others.)

Tie-Break

Twenty-six Popes have been assassinated.

Round Three

1. **Greenstick.**
2. **Promenade des Anglais.**
   (Reverend Lewis Way, who lived in Nice during the winter, decided in 1822 that the road had to be built and persuaded fellow Brits to stump up the money. A little disappointingly, they decided not to call it 'Lewis Way'.)

3. A roc.

(Not only could it lift an elephant, it could carry it back to its mountain nest and eat it.)

4. Nicole Farhi.

5. A semi-house-trained polecat.

(Tebbit was not remotely upset by this jibe. When later elevated to the House of Lords, he had a polecat incorporated into his new coat of arms.)

6. A gutter.

7. Brookside Close.

8. The Jabberwocky.

(From Lewis Carroll's *Alice Through The Looking Glass*, first published in 1871.)

9. Sir Henry Irving. (In 1895.)

10. Dundee.

Round Four

1. Humphrey Bogart and Kathleen Hepburn. (In *The African Queen*.)

2. The official ball at the football World Cup.

3. Gary Barlow.

('Forever Love' in July 1996. Robbie Williams's first number 1 was 'Millennium' in September 1998.)

4. Nottingham.

5. Burial at sea.

(According to one website, 'sea burials are not particularly encouraged and there are complex guidelines.' For instance, the corpse should not be embalmed, 'as this is a preservative, which is detrimental to the marine environment.')

6. December 26th. (St Stephen's Day.)

7. Peruvian.

(After going to university in California, he represented the US in the Davis Cup in 1958-9, but remained a Peruvian citizen throughout.)

8. *East Of Eden.*

9. **A Battlefield.** (Love was, in each of these cases.)

10. **Electric light.**

ANSWERS TO QUIZ TEN

Round One

1. The Daleks.
2. Viv Richards.
3. Tom Hanks; *The Ladykillers*.
4. A shark preserved in formaldehyde in a tank.
   (Anything along these lines should get the point. 'Pickled shark', for instance, is fine).
   And the artist was Damien Hirst.
5. She was part of the conspiracy to assassinate President Lincoln.
6. Terminus.
   (He was a very old and important deity, whose festival in February was called the Terminalia.)
7. Cleopatra. (In *Antony And Cleopatra*.) **Antony had just died.**
8. Occam's razor.
   (William of Occam, 1285-1349, was probably born in Ockham in Surrey.)
9. A bagpipe or bagpipes.
10. Showjumping; running (3000m cross country); shooting (air pistol); fencing (épée); swimming (200 m freestyle).

Round Two

1. Black with a vertical white cross.
   (It's the emblem of St Piran. The white cross symbolises tin, the black background symbolises the ground from which it was dug.)
2. Mebyon Kernow.
   (Established in 1951.)
3. The Minack open-air theatre.
   (Near Porthcurno.)

4. Fish heads and tails protruding through the crust.
   (Usually pilchards.)
5. The A30 (2 points). Hounslow (1 point).
   (It's the junction with the A4 at Henley's roundabout.
   Astoundingly, a couple of teams got this.)
6. John O'Groats; New York.
7. Sir Humphry Davy.
   (Often misspelled Humphrey. He also discovered the pain-
   relieving effects of nitrous oxide, or laughing gas, to which he
   became addicted.)
8. The Eden Project and the restoration of the Lost Gardens of
   Heligan.
9. Helston.
10. Sir John Betjeman.
    (He lived in Highgate as a child and went to Highgate Junior
    School.)

Bonus Round

1. Paul McCartney.
2. Shirley Conran.
   (It was the rallying cry of her *Superwoman* books.)
3. Steve McQueen.
4. Flora Macdonald.
   (Betty Burke was the disguise affected by Prince Charles
   Edward, a.k.a. Bonnie Prince Charlie or 'the Young Pretender',
   in his escape after the failure of the Forty-Five Rebellion. At
   one point, according to Boswell, while crossing the rivulet, the
   Prince lifted his skirts 'a great deal too high'. But no one
   noticed and he got away with it.)
5. Galliano.
   (It contains star anise and vanilla, and is also an ingredient in a
   variant of the Screaming Orgasm.)

(The link was fashion designers: Stella McCartney, Jasper Conran, Alexander McQueen, Julien Macdonald, John Galliano.)

Tie-Break

Between the mutiny on the Bounty and the storming of the Bastille, there were 77 days.
(Bounty: April 28th 1789. Bastille: July 14th 1789.)

Round Three

1. **The £2 coin; Sir Isaac Newton.**
   (In a letter to Robert Hooke, he wrote, 'If I have seen further, it is by . . .' Some teams put 'an Oasis album'. Patrick argued that this was not an everyday object, as he had never seen one. More pertinently, Noel Gallagher called his album *Standing On The Shoulder Of Giants*, for dim-witted reasons entirely of his own.)

2. **The Oval.**
   (Wanderers beat Royal Engineers 1-0; England beat Ireland 7-0.)

3. **Prince Charles.**
   (Arthur and George are his last two Christian names, and one of his many titles is the Earl of Carrick.)

4. **Tammany Hall.**

5. **The Grand Canal in Venice.**

6. **Vespa.**
   (When he saw the prototype in 1945, Enrico Piaggio said, 'It looks like a wasp.')

7. **Brian Clough Way.**
   ('I certainly wouldn't say I'm the best manager in the League, but I'm in the top one.')

8. **Rudyard Kipling.**
   (His parents courted there.)

9. **Craven A cigarettes.**
   (Another slogan was 'Made especially to prevent sore throats'.)
10. **C. G. Jung.**

Round Four

1. **The USA.**
   (They won the gold the last time rugby was an Olympic sport, in 1924, beating France 17-3 in the final.)
2. **Jane Seymour.**
   (Number three. She was rewarded for giving birth to his only son, Edward VI.)
3. **Midnight Cowboy.**
   (The rating was later downgraded after some judicious minor editing.)
4. **French Guiana.**
5. **A lime tree.**
   (It was 290 years old, and has since been replaced by an offshoot specially grown for the purpose.)
6. **Prototype tanks.**
7. **Above the lip.**
   (It's the vertical groove between lip and nose. John Major has an unusually long one. The ancient Greeks believed that the philtrum was one of the most erogenous spots on the human body, but they may have been wrong.)
8. **Suttee.**
   (The self-immolation of a widow on her husband's funeral pyre.)
9. **A mackerel sky.**
10. **(i) After Eisenhower's grandson. (ii) Shangri-La.**
    (When he grew up, non-camp David married Richard M. Nixon's younger daughter Julie.)

ANSWERS TO QUIZ ELEVEN

Round One

1. **Leave the country if Labour were elected.**
   (Phil Collins threatened to come back if the Conservatives won the 2005 election.)
2. **Anne Boleyn.**
3. **Gay/lesbian marriages.**
4. **Liger.**
   (As opposed to tigon or tiglon, the offspring of a male tiger and a female lion. More often encountered in quizzes than in the wild, one suspects.)
5. **André Agassi.**
   (Wimbledon is grass, US Open is hardcourt, French is clay, and Australian is 'Rebound Ace', a combination of polyurethane and fibreglass that apparently gets a bit sticky in high temperatures.)
6. **Led Zeppelin.**
   (John Bonham, John Paul Jones, Jimmy Page, Robert Plant.)
7. **Peckham.**
   (*Only Fools And Horses* is the TV series. 'Pecheham' was mentioned in the Domesday Book. The 'Rye' in Peckham Rye comes from the Old English for 'stream'.)
8. **Etch-a-Sketch.**
   (It still sells and has barely changed in the intervening years.)
9. **Philip Larkin.**
10. **(i) *The Mail on Sunday*. (ii) Abbey National. (iii) Zanussi. (iv) Kia-Ora. (v) Renault Clio.**

Round Two

1. **Go into space.**
   (She died in the Challenger space shuttle disaster. Twenty-seven schools have since been named after her.)

2. **Peter O'Toole and Richard Burton.**
   (Seven times each. O'Toole won a Lifetime Achievement Award in 2003 but he was reluctant to accept it, as he still felt he was good enough to win the real thing.)

3. **Brasilia.**
   (It has a 'North Wing' and a 'South Wing', and its central area, the fuselage, is known as the 'Pilot Plan'.)

4. **Clement Attlee.**
   (He was also the first to have a majority in Parliament.)

5. **John Daly.**

6. *Jane Eyre.*

7. **Phil Collins.**
   (Who insists that the presence of the paint pot on the piano was mere coincidence. The song was 'In The Air Tonight'.)

8. *Dogtanian and the Three Muskehounds.*
   (Spaniards talk much faster than almost everyone else, and the American voiceover artists followed their lead, giving the show a breakneck pace. It still only lasted one season.)

9. **Kenilworth.**

10. (i) **AC Milan.** (Originally Diavoli Rossineri, the red and black devils.)

    (ii) **Juventus.** (The Old Lady. They have also been known as Gobbi, the hunchbacks.)

    (iii) **Fiorentina.** (The violets.)

    (iv) **Inter Milan.** (The black and blues. Also known as Biscioni, the adders.)

    (v) **The Italian national team.** (The blues.)

Bonus Round

1. **Nelson** Piquet.
2. Robert **Winston**.
3. The **Eden** Project in Cornwall.
4. **Henry Cooper.**
5. **Diana** Ross.

   (The link is Norwegian football commentator Bjorn Lillelien, who celebrated Norway's 2-1 victory over England in September 1981 with the following speech: 'Lord Nelson! Lord Beaverbrook! Sir Winston Churchill! Sir Anthony Eden! Clement Attlee! Henry Cooper! Lady Diana! Maggie Thatcher! Your boys took one hell of a beating! Your boys took one hell of a beating!')

Tie-Break

In 1789, the life expectancy at birth for American men was 34 years 6 months.

(Washington, when he became President, was 56 years 347 days old.)

Round Three

1. Andy García.
2. Richard Cromwell.

   (He was Lord Protector for eight months between 1658 and 1659, during which he celebrated his 32nd birthday. He resigned after a demand from the Rump Parliament and lived another half century in obscurity.)
3. Kylie Minogue.

4. (i) W. G. Grace; (ii) Ian Botham; (iii) Michael Vaughan.
   (Kevin Pietersen was the 626th person to play for England, and so on. Most players now wear these numbers on their shirts and caps.)
5. Because 'pajero' is Spanish for 'wanker'.
   (In the late 1970s, the American computer company Wang could not understand why its British branch was so reluctant to use its latest slogan, 'Wang Cares'.)
6. Terry Pratchett.
7. Robert Maxwell.
8. Carlos the Jackal (2 points). A copy of Frederick Forsyth's *The Day Of The Jackal* was once found among his belongings (1 point).
9. Erwin Schrödinger.
   (It is not known whether or not Schrödinger owned a cat, which itself illustrates the incompleteness of the history of quantum mechanics.)
10. (i) Shakespear's Sister; (ii) Tears For Fears; (iii) Orchestral Manoeuvres In The Dark (OMD); (iv) The Righteous Brothers; (v) Chas and Dave.

Round Four

1. *The Sopranos*.
   (A third working title was *Red Sauce*. Had someone been watching *The Royle Family*?)
2. Putting towels on sun loungers.
   (Reported with glee by all British newspapers in August 2005. Mr Hocker added that the practice also annoys many Germans, including him.)
3. Aldous Huxley.
   (Thirteen writers are credited, but not the author of *Brave New World*. He had previously co-written screenplays for several films in the 1940s, including *Jane Eyre* and *Pride And Prejudice*.)

4. **The Bank of England.**

    (This was in Walbrook, on a site that dated to the founding of Londinium by the Romans. The Bank moved to Threadneedle Street in 1734.)

5. **Bob Mortimer.**

6. **Charing Cross.**

7. **The chances of being hit by something from space.**

    (Such as an asteroid or a comet. The scale also takes into account the likely impact of that collision, from no impact at all to global catastrophe.)

8. **Chevy Chase.**

    (The second of the three was born Cornelius Crane Chase, and nicknamed Chevy by his grandmother.)

9. **The Duke of Wellington.**

10. **King Kong.**

    (And again in 2005. The lead female character in the 1976 version, played by Jessica Lange, was inexplicably called 'Dwan'.)

ANSWERS TO QUIZ TWELVE

Round One

1. **Alfred Hitchcock.**
   (In cameo appearances in his films: *Spellbound*, *The Paradine Case* and *Strangers On A Train*.)
2. **Cheese.**
3. **Elvis Presley.**
4. **(i) The gay villains in *Diamonds Are Forever*; (ii) The ancient hecklers in *The Muppet Show*; (iii) Ben & Jerry.**
   (There is a jewellers in west London called Wint & Kidd; and an Australian band and a Danish record label called Statler & Waldorf.)
5. **Daughter.**
   (She played *Elizabeth R* and he played Henry VIII in different BBC historical dramas, both broadcast for the first time that year.)
6. **Shaw, shore, Sure, Shure.**
   (This question would probably not work in Scotland, America, South Africa or any place in the world where the four words are not pronounced in exactly the same way. Good question for north London, though.)
7. **Gilbert and George.**
8. **Siblings in the group.**
   (The Gallagher brothers, the Greenwood brothers, the Appleton sisters and, for a time at least, the Finn Brothers.)
9. **Wimbledon.**
   (Men's Doubles. He was partnered by Wing-Commander Louis Greig and they were knocked out in straight sets by the 1909 champions A. W. Gore and H. R. 'Roger' Bassett.)
10. **Richard II** (1397), **Henry IV** (1406), **Henry V** (1420).

Round Two

1. **Laika the dog.**

   (Known as 'Muttnik' to the American press and 'Curly' to animal rights activists. 'Laika' is Russian for 'barker'. She died a few hours after the launch from stress and overheating.)

2. **Lara Croft.** (From *Tomb Raider*.)

3. **Income tax.**

   (It started at 2d in the pound – 0.833 per cent – on incomes over £60 a year, and increased to a maximum of 2s – 10 per cent – on incomes over £200.)

4. **Rod Stewart.**

5. **Harlem.**

   (In 1938 a young songwriter called Billy Strayhorn met Ellington and made a good impression. Several weeks later, having heard nothing more, Strayhorn phoned the bandleader's office and found out that the band was playing in Harlem that evening. On a whim he decided to travel up from Pittsburgh and see them. On the way, he wrote a song using the travel instructions the office had given him: Take the A-Train.)

6. **All have starred opposite apes in movies.**

   (*Bedtime For Bonzo, Every Which Way But Loose, Mookie.*)

7. **Margaret Thatcher.**

8. **St Valentine.**

9. **Marathon running.**

   (According to legend, he was the messenger who ran from Marathon to Athens with news of the Greeks' victory over the Persians. But this may never have happened. According to Herodotus, Pheidippides may have been a professional long-distance runner who ran from Athens to Sparta on another occasion for another reason entirely . . .)

10. (i) John Rambo; (ii) Thomas Magnum; (iii) Bernard Quatermass; (iv) Quincy Magoo; (v) Henry Jekyll; (vi) Abraham van Helsing.

Bonus Round

1. **'I wandered lonely as a cloud'** (William Wordsworth, 'Daffodils').
2. **'In Xanadu did Kubla Khan'** (Samuel Taylor Coleridge, 'Kubla Khan').
3. **'Season of mists and mellow fruitfulness'** (John Keats, 'To Autumn').
4. **'O my love is like a red, red rose'** (Robert Burns, 'Red, Red Rose').
5. **'Let us go then, you and I'** (T. S. Eliot, 'The Love Song of J. Alfred Prufrock').

Tie-Break

The largest earthworm ever found measured twenty-two feet from tip to tail.

Round Three

1. **Palindromic surnames.**
2. *Hawaii Five-0*.
   (In that year Hawaii became the 50th state of the USA. *Five-0* was the longest running cop show, running 12 full seasons from 1968 to 1980, until *Law And Order* overtook it two decades later. Book him Danno, murder one.)
3. **Organist.**
4. **White.**
   (Mr White, Colonel White and Mrs White.)
5. **Rupert Murdoch.**

6. **Royal mistress.**

   (While pregnant with his fourth child, she fell ill and died of 'flux of the stomach'. She was probably poisoned.)

7. **Gore Vidal.**

8. **'Eleanor Rigby'.**

   (Paul McCartney sang lead vocal, John Lennon and George Harrison sang backing vocals, but the only instruments were a double string quartet of session musicians.)

9. **Sodom and Gomorrah.**

10. **A speeding bullet; a locomotive; to leap tall buildings with a single bound.**

Round Four

1. **Damien Hurst.**

2. **Twenty.** (On a dartboard.)

3. **The Mona Lisa.**

   (Stolen from the Louvre by Vincenzo Peruggia. He walked out of the door with it hidden under his coat.)

4. **James Bond.**

5. **The Dalai Lama.**

6. **Sir Alec Douglas-Home.**

   (The six in between all went to grammar schools.)

7. **Dudley Moore was Derek, Peter Cook was Clive.**

8. *All's Well That Ends Well, (The) Winter's Tale.*

9. **The Artful Dodger.**

   (In *Oliver*. Davy Jones played the role in London and on Broadway, where he was nominated for a Tony award.)

10. **Money.**

    (As in 'Money', 'Money Money' and 'Money Money Money'.)

ANSWERS TO QUIZ THIRTEEN

Round One

1. **The transporter.**
   (Apparently even time travel is more feasible.)
2. **Liverpool.**
3. **Kamikaze.**
4. **(i) Chitty Chitty Bang Bang; (ii) Inspector Morse.**
5. **Macduff.**
6. **Elephant.**
7. **Seven.**
8. **150.**
9. **United States and Great Britain.**
10. **N – Caracas. E – Brasilia. S – Montevideo. W – Quito.**
    (Montevideo is only just south of Buenos Aires, which itself is only just south of Santiago.)

Round Two

1. **Twenty-three.**
2. **New College.**
   (Originally established for the education of priests, as there was a shortage of well-educated clergymen after the Black Death. The original St Mary's is now known as Oriel.)
3. **The curvature of the earth.**
4. **He shot Ronald Reagan.**
5. **Self-destruct.**
   ('As usual, should any of your IM Force be caught or killed, the Secretary will disavow any knowledge of your actions. This tape will self-destruct in five seconds. Good luck, Jim.')

6. **The American Civil War.**
   (When she married William Martin she was twenty-one and
   he was eighty-one. He died four years later. Two months after
   that, she married his grandson.)
7. **Macgregor.**
8. **(i) Joel and Ethan; (ii) Peter and Bobby; (iii) Larry and Andy.**
9. **Less.**
   (Around 10 per cent less, in fact, and it's falling by an average
   of 0.3 per cent a year. Scientists are calling it 'global dimming'.)
10. *The General Belgrano.*

Bonus Round

1. **Eric Morecambe.**
   (Fifty-eight. Tommy Cooper was sixty-three.)
2. **Sir Bobby Moore.**
   (Fifty-one. St Thomas More was fifty-seven.)
3. **Gandhi.**
   (Seventy-eight. Weissmuller was seventy-nine.)
4. **Mama Cass.**
   (A close one. She was thirty-two years ten months ten days.
   Karen Carpenter was thirty-two years eleven months two days.)
5. **Sid Vicious.**
   (Twenty-one. Red Rum was thirty.)

Tie-Break

The median age of the British population (as of 2005) is
thirty-nine years, three months and eighteen days.

Round Three

1. **Thomas à Becket.**
2. **Henri Matisse.**

3. **Baikal.**

   (It has as much water as all of North America's Great Lakes combined.)

4. **Trinidad.**

   (Born in 1932, 1939 and 1969 respectively.)

5. **'Dancing Queen'.**

6. **Kings of France called Charles.**

7. **(i) Sard. (ii) Surd.**

8. **Powys.**

9. **Spleen.**

10. **Billy Bob Thornton.**

Round Four

1. **Canada, Cyprus, Cameroon.**

2. **Into orbit.**

   (They were the first space tourists.)

3. **(i) Charles Darwin; (ii) Jacob Bronowski.**

4. **Hawaii.**

   (The flag is one of the oldest flags in the world in continuous use. It officially predates a majority of the states of the Union.)

5. **Husband to Joan Collins.**

   (Maxwell Reed 1952-57, Anthony Newley 1963-71, Ronald Kass 1972-83, Peter Holm 1985-87, Percy Gibson 2002 to date. She divorced Reed after he attempted to sell her to an Arab sheik.)

6. **Ten.**

   (There are 10 for the 100 metres hurdles too.)

7. **Jordan.**

   (A.k.a. Katie Price. She polled 713 votes.)

8. **Smoke it.** (It's a peace pipe.)

9. **Top Shop.**

10. **The Krankies.**

ANSWERS TO QUIZ FOURTEEN

Round One

1. Emily.
2. Michelangelo.

   (Michelangelo's full name was Michelangelo di Lodovico Buonarotti Simoni.)
3. A bow and arrow.

   (In Hereford you can shoot a Welsh person at any time of day, but only on a Sunday, with a longbow, in Cathedral Close.)
4. Malta.

   (It's also the smallest by population.)
5. She was the voice of the speaking clock.

   (According to BT, the speaking clock is 'about the size of a small suitcase'.)
6. Queen Elizabeth II.
7. Rhône (2 points). They are the numbers of the French *départements* of those names (1 point).

   (The list is broadly alphabetical. 75 used to be Seine, but is now assigned to Paris.)
8. Wordsworth.
9. Fifteen.
10. George Mainwaring, Arthur Wilson, Jack Jones, James (or Jock) Frazer, Joe Walker, Charles Godfrey, Frank Pike.

Round Two

1. F. W. de Klerk.
2. Cakewalk.
3. **Number 42.** (They are the Kumars.)
4. Wild boar.
5. Knights of the Round Table.
6. *Sale of the Century*.
7. Gregory; John.
   (There have been 23 Johns).
8. Blue.
   (Note that we have used the words 'slightly stained', as opposed to many newspapers and websites, who preferred 'encrusted'.)
9. Shane Richie.
   (Anyway, it's *Ritchie* Blackmore, and *Ritchie* Neville.)
10. Scottish country dances.
    (The first two are jigs, the second two reels.)

Bonus Round

1. Sulu.
2. Dr Benjamin Spock.
3. Anton Chekhov.
4. Kirk Stevens.
5. Bones.
   (A few people have a 207th, an extra rib. The link was the original series of *Star Trek*.)

Tie-Break

In May 2004, there were 441 nuclear reactors in operation worldwide.

Round Three

1. Uranus.
2. Boscastle.
   (After the 2004 floods, according to *Private Eye*, the RAF airlifted 55 residents out of the village, and someone else airlifted 35 BBC employees in.)
3. Shane MacGowan.
   (Of the Pogues. His former girlfriend Victoria Clarke suggested that one factor in the ruination of his teeth may be that he had once eaten a copy of the Beach Boys' *Greatest Hits Vol. 3* LP while under the influence of LSD.)
4. White.
5. Blackberry.
   (Admittedly, only his chum Stalin called him this. Everyone else called him 'The Poison Dwarf' or 'The Bloody Dwarf'.)
6. Jasper Carrott.
7. Barbados.
   (When the island was first visited by the Portuguese, they saw the trees and called them 'Los Barbados', or the bearded ones. The 'Los' was later dropped.)
8. Parallel Olympics.
9. Otis.
10. Malleus, stapes and incus. Or hammer, stirrup and anvil.
    (They are the auditory ossicles.)

Round Four

1. Pepsi.
2. Albert Einstein.
3. Truckle.
4. Blair.
   (Eric Blair a.k.a George Orwell, Sir Ian Blair, Lionel Blair and, of course, Blair.)

5. **The Royal Mint.**

   (He became Master of the Mint in 1699.)

6. **Macadamia nuts.**

   (Or actually their shells.)

7. **Texas.**

8. **Branches of McDonald's.**

9. **Three Day Event.**

   (For the horses. They must also be of the same nationality as the rider.)

10. **Captain Brastrap and Reverend Worthywinkle.**

    (Serjeant Buzfuz is a lawyer in *The Pickwick Papers*. Luke Honeythunder turns up in *Edwin Drood*, Dick Swiveller in *The Old Curiosity Shop*, and Mrs Todgers is a boarding house proprietor in *Martin Chuzzlewit*.)

ANSWERS TO QUIZ FIFTEEN

Round One

1. Lord Kitchener.
2. The tongue.
3. Aghanistan and Azerbaijan.
4. Goalposts.
   (The Mexican goal collapsed under the weight of several players falling into the net.)
5. The Bates Motel. (In *Psycho*.)
6. Exeter.
7. Hercule Poirot.
8. Jim Broadbent.
9. The Birdman of Alcatraz.
10. (i) Netherlands; (ii) Spain; (iii) Sweden; (iv) Thailand.
   (Both Norway and Denmark are ruled by Schleswig-Holstein-Sonderburg-Glücksbergs. Korea used to be ruled by the House of Yi.)

Round Two

1. Idi Amin.
2. France and Spain.
3. Bill Bailey.
4. Michael Jackson was the best man each time.
   (Other guests at the Geller event included Sir David Frost, Nigel Mansell, Barry Gibb of the Bee Gees, Dave Stewart of the Eurythmics and David Blaine.)
5. Charles Hawtrey.
6. Catherine Parr.
   (She then married again and died in childbirth in 1548, aged thirty-six.)

7. Bedford.
8. Kiwi.
9. *King Lear.*
   (George III was believed to be insane at the time, and the play was therefore deemed inappropriate.)
10. Mark Haddon; Asperger's Syndrome; Sherlock Holmes; 'Silver Blaze'.

Bonus Round

1. **Anthony** Newley.
2. **Norma** Major.
3. **Jim** Clark. **(In 1962-5.)**
4. **Barbara** Castle.
   (She made it compulsory for cars to be fitted with seatbelts. Compulsory wearing of them came later.)
5. **Denise** Lewis.
6. **The Royle Family.**

Tie-Break

Anthony Blunt was Surveyor of the King's (later Queen's) Pictures for 27 years.
(He was appointed in 1945 and retained the post until 1972. Along the way he was knighted in 1956, revealed as a spy in 1964 and shopped to a baying public by Margaret Thatcher in 1979. His knighthood was then revoked, along with his honorary fellowship of Trinity College, Cambridge.)

Round Three

1. Not paying your television licence.
2. Corby trouser press.
3. Duck-billed platypus.

4. *Only When I Laugh*.
   (Played by James Bolam, Peter Bowles and Christopher Strauli. The series ran between 1979 and 1982. Richard Wilson, later of *One Foot In The Grave*, had a regular supporting role.)
5. *Chicago*.
   (Renée Zellweger and Catherine Zeta Jones.)
6. 'The Haywain'.
   (When exhibited under its original title at the Royal Academy in 1821, it failed to find a buyer.)
7. Liechtenstein and Uzbekistan.
   (The first is bordered by Austria and Switzerland, the second by Afghanistan, Kazakhstan, Kyrgyzstan, Tajikistan and Turkmenistan. Some teams got this right.)
8. Fred Astaire and Ginger Rogers.
   (It was the only film they made in colour. Songs include 'They Can't Take That Away From Me'.)
9. Galileo.
   (Not long after the 350th anniversary of his death. One newspaper headline read: 'Galileo Acquitted: Earth Actually Round, Says Pope'.)
10. Steve Davis, Terry Griffiths, Tony Meo, Dennis Taylor, Willie Thorne.
    ('Poor Willie Thorne / his hair's all gorn.')

Round Four

1. Telephone call.
   (March 10th 1876. Bell's words were 'Mr Watson, come here, I want you.')
2. Hungary.
3. Cock robin.
   ('I, said the sparrow, / With my bow and arrow, / I killed Cock Robin.')

4. It was the day they switched from driving on the left to driving on the right.
5. Kenny Everett.
6. Robert Runcie.
7. San Marino.
   (It was founded in AD 301 by a Christian stonemason named Marinus, from the island of Rab. He was fleeing the religious persecution of Emperor Diocletian.)
8. Whoopee cushion.
   (Bronx cheer is an American slang term for fart. Raspberry is in fact cockney rhyming slang: raspberry tart.)
9. Jumble.
10. He said them in German. She didn't speak German.

ANSWERS TO QUIZ SIXTEEN

Round One

1. Philip Larkin.
2. Garon.

   (Some people believe not only that Elvis is still alive, but that he has assumed the identity of his stillborn brother and is living under the name 'Jesse Garon Presley'. Someone really should look him up in the phone book.)

3. Jacques Tati.

   (Well, nearly top-class: he was chosen mainly for the 3rds.)

4. Franz Beckenbauer.

   (Mario Zagallo of Brazil is the only other man to win the World Cup both as a player, in 1958 and 1962, and as a manager, in 1970. But he didn't win as captain.)

5. Seville.
6. Castaways on *Desert Island Discs*.
7. British Columbia.
8. Plymouth Brethren.
9. Palladium.
10. Turquoise and beige.

    (With turquoise they appeared to confirm David Icke's pronouncements on the subject. But not with beige.)

Round Two

1. Temple.
2. Bryan Gould.
3. Joe Frazier and Muhammad Ali; Muhammad Ali's.

   (Laila Ali, twenty-three, beat Jacquelyn Frazier-Lyde, thirty-nine, in eight rounds on a majority decision.)

4. Denmark & Sweden.

   (It's the longest combined road and rail bridge in Europe.)

5. **Naseby.**

   (It's not far from Market Harborough.)

6. **Ruth Ellis.**

   (The last woman to be hanged in Britain.)

7. **Lacrosse.**

   (It's not a French game, as many assume; it was invented by North American Indians, who called it baggataway. Some form of the game was played by at least forty-eight tribes in southern Canada and part of the United States. The game had religious significance and matches often lasted two or three days.)

8. **Portugal.**

   (It's now called Western European Time, or WET.)

9. **Porton Down.**

10. **Ray Davies.** (Of the Kinks.)

Bonus Round

1. 1982.
2. 1992.
3. 1982; Milk.
4. 1994.
5. 1990.

Tie-Break

Asked in a 2002 survey which was Britain's highest mountain, 14 per cent of respondents answered 'Mount Everest'.

(One in ten thought that Cheddar Gorge was the name of Britain's first cheese museum.)

Round Three

1. Britain.
2. Helios.
   (It was over 110 feet tall, took 12 years to build, and was destroyed in an earthquake in 226 BC. The statue snapped at the knees and fell over onto the land. The remains lay on the ground for more than 800 years.)
3. Richard Whiteley.
4. Glasses.
5. Belvedere.
   (Landmarks of Belvedere in Kent include a Methodist chapel, a Sikh temple and a high technology sludge incinerator.)
6. Rudolf Hess.
7. Puerto Rico and the southern tip of Florida.
8. Death.
9. Leicester City. (Four times.)
10. George, Paul, Ringo, John.

Round Four

1. Joseph Pulitzer.
2. Abélard & Heloïse.
3. Bootlegging.
4. Jimi Hendrix.
5. Vienna (capital of Austria) and Bratislava (capital of Slovakia)
   (Tallinn and Helsinki are also about 60 km apart, but separated by sea.)
6. Five per cent.
7. Jimmy Young (1955), The Righteous Brothers (1990), Robson and Jerome (1995), Gareth Gates (2002).
8. Sudan.

9. The Queen Mother.
10. £1,000.

('Oh we've let down those poor children!' she shrieked, as they were ushered offstage.)

ANSWERS TO QUIZ SEVENTEEN

Round One

1. **Star Trek.**
   (She was a Vulcan elder in the episode 'Amok Time', during which Spock nearly got married. Slightly less catchily, his putative wife's name was T'Pring.)
2. **The owl.**
   (The Greek goddess of wisdom, strategy, crafts, war, skills, industry and justice. She was not born, but sprang fully formed from the head of Zeus.)
3. **Colour blindness.**
4. **Llareggub.**
   (In *Under Milk Wood* by Dylan Thomas. In print it appeared as 'Llaregyb', to avoid offence.)
5. **Snoopy.**
6. **The Berlin Philharmonic Orchestra.**
7. **The Old Bailey, or Central Criminal Court.**
8. **The Dalai Lama.**
   (In recognition of his commitment to the non-violent liberation of his homeland.)
9. **Squash.**
   (Ross Norman of New Zealand beat him in the final of the 1986 World Open in Toulouse. Jahangir was then unbeaten for another nine months.)
10. *What's New, Pussycat.*

Round Two

1. **Captain Marvel.**
   (Shazam was the name of the wizard who gave him his superpowers.)
2. **Chess Records.**
3. **A horse.**
   (They are descended from a small thoroughbred and a Shetland pony, and named after the family who 'developed' them. They are only 7 hands, or 2 feet 3 inches, high.)
4. **Edinburgh.**
   (On Princes Street. It has been there since 1838.)
5. **Derek Redmond.** (In the 400 metres.)
6. **Beef Wellington.**
7. **Stella Artois.**
   (The horn remains part of its trademark.)
8. **A youth hostel.**
9. **A parselmouth.**
10. **He never had the Latin.**
    (In 1964 Wisty formed the World Domination League, among whose demands were 'the bodily removal from this planet of C. P. Snow and Alan Freeman and their replacement with fine trees'.)

Bonus Round

1. **Michael Foot.**
2. **The Base.** (Also accept 'The Foundation'.)
3. **Billy Crystal.**
4. **Meat.**
5. **'Lucille'.**
   (You picked a fine time to leave me, and so on.)
6. **They are all types of ball.**

Tie-Break

1,186 different cover versions of 'Yesterday' were recorded in the song's first seven years.

(It still holds the record for the most cover versions of any song ever written – over 3,000, according to *The Guinness Book of Records*.)

Round Three

1. Jupiter.
2. Martha Gellhorn.
3. It has a button in its ear.
4. Nanook.
5. They all played for England in the 1966 World Cup, but not in the final.
6. Marriage.
7. The Pink Panther.
8. Ernest Bevin.
   (32 unions in all. He served as General Secretary from 1921 to 1940, when he joined Churchill's wartime government as Minister for Labour.)
9. Dollar.
10. Captain Mainwaring.

Round Four

1. *Oliver!* (2 points). 1968 (1 point).
2. The depth of the Marianas Trench.
   (Its nadir, known as Challenger Deep, is 36,201 feet deep. Everest is 29,028 feet high.)
3. Jim.
   (The sisters are Andrea, Caroline and Sharon.)
4. Josiah Wedgwood.

5. Denis Healey.
6. Thermoman.
7. Aphids.
8. Richard Branson.
9. Chalky.
   (Rick Stein is the uncle of Radio 1 and nightclub DJ Judge Jules.)
10. Joss Stone.

ANSWERS TO QUIZ EIGHTEEN

Round One

1. **Travis.**
2. **Tomato.**
   (The heaviest tomato ever weighed 7lb 12oz and was grown by Gordon Graham of Edmond, Oklahoma in 1986.)
3. **James James Morrison Morrison Weatherby George Dupree.**
   (From the poem 'Disobedience' by A. A. Milne. "'Mother,' he said, said he: "You must never go down to the end of the town if you don't go down with me.'")
4. **Cain.** (He killed Abel.)
5. **Audie Murphy.**
   (It was the highest grossing film in Universal's forty-three-year history, and remained so until 1975 when surpassed by *Jaws*.)
6. **A bishop (in chess).**
7. **(i) Green; (ii) red.**
8. **First Briton to die in an air crash.**
   (Not long after he had become the first man to fly across the Channel and back non-stop. He was thirty-three.)
9. **Eleven.**
   (*David Copperfield, Oliver Twist, Nicholas Nickleby, Little Dorrit, Pickwick, Dombey and Son, Martin Chuzzlewit, Edwin Drood, Our Mutual Friend, Barnaby Rudge*.)
10. **Because both towns have reverted to their pre-revolutionary names.**
    (Sverdlovsk became Ekaterinberg in 1991 and Gorki became Nizhny-Novgorod in 1990.)

Round Two

1. **Julio Iglesias.**
   (It was his first recording. Dana won with 'All Kinds Of Everything' and Mary Hopkin was second with 'Knock Knock Who's There'.)

2. **Siegfried Sassoon.**
   (He lived till 1967. Brooke died of blood-poisoning in 1915, Rosenberg in the trenches in 1918, and Owen a week before the armistice.)

3. **The United States ambassador to the United Nations.**
   (The Italian ambassador to the Vatican does not qualify, as technically the Vatican City is another country.)

4. **Silver, Tonto and the Lone Ranger** ('Kemo Sabe').

5. **Car number plate.**
   (Which naturally was A1. Two years earlier the Earl had been convicted of bigamy, but sentenced to only three months in prison, on account of the 'extreme torture' he had suffered in his first marriage. Nothing to do with being an Earl, then.)

6. **Thailand.**
   (It exists, and it is not far from the town of Kanchanaduri.)

7. **They all died in the bath.**
   (Marat was stabbed, Morrison died of a drugs overdose, and François was electrocuted while changing a lightbulb.)

8. **Miss Joan Hunter Dunn.**
   (From *New Bats in Old Belfries*, originally published in 1945.)

9. **Burt Bacharach.**

10. *Othello, Antony and Cleopatra, Twelfth Night, The Tempest.*

Bonus Round

1. The Flat**iron** Building.
2. The Mad Hatter's **Hat**.
3. —**ship**.

4. Racing Cars.

(They reached number 14.)

5. Dog.

(*Portrait of the Artist as a Young Dog*, published 1940, was a collection of largely autobiographical short stories.)

6. Boot.

(They are the playing pieces in Monopoly.)

Tie-Break

According to *Maxim*'s poll, 98 per cent of women would rather date someone who liked cats than someone who didn't.

Round Three

1. Brandenburg.

2. Snails.

(Americans tend to call them *escargots*, possibly to avoid the terrifying word 'snails'.)

3. René Magritte.

4. Thomas Hardy.

(His ashes were buried beside Dickens in Westminster Abbey. Gosse himself was dead in four months, and only Shaw lasted more than ten years.)

5. Mount Everest.

(Named after Sir George Everest, surveyor-general of India. The Chinese still use its original name, Qomolangma Feng.)

6. All take place at Christmas.

7. Anonymous.

(They are all Victorian erotica. *The Autobiography of a Flea* was recounted by a very philosophical flea who witnessed the ravishment of two innocent French girls; *The Whippingham Papers* is almost self-explanatory.)

8. The cat flea.

(They are more common on dogs than the dog flea. Cats are also sometimes troubled by the rabbit flea and the hedgehog flea.)

9. Clark Gable and Marilyn Monroe.

(Gable died shortly afterwards from a heart attack, just before his fifth wife gave birth to his only son. Monroe was sacked from her next film for persistent lateness and committed suicide.)

10. Great.

(The Great Fire of London, the Great Exhibition, the Great Train Robbery.)

Round Four

1. Austria and Estonia.

2. Spaghetti western.

(This first one was *A Fistful of Dollars*. In Japan they called them 'macaroni westerns'.)

3. Edward Elgar, Gustav Holst, Frederick Delius.

(They died on February 23rd, May 25th and June 10th respectively.)

4. Newfoundland.

(Which includes the Labrador coast. It was Britain's first ever colony, and only voted to unite with the rest of Canada in 1949.)

5. Most letters: Russian. Fewest letters: Hebrew.

(Russian 33, Arabic 28, English 26, Greek 24, Hebrew 23. The smallest in the world seems to be Rotokas, used in the Solomon Islands, with 11 letters. The largest is Khmer, with 74 letters.)

6. Nepotism.

(Pope Callixtus III, of the Borgia family, made two of his 'nephews' Cardinals; one of whom, Rodrigo, later became Pope himself, Alexander VI. He then made his mistress's brother a Cardinal, who went on to become Pope Paul III, and made two of his teenage 'nephews' Cardinals.)

7. Five.

(The term actually dates back to World War I, when French newspapers described Adolphe Pegoud as an ace after he became the first pilot to shoot down five German aircraft.)

8. The Salvation Army.

(The name was adopted in 1878.)

9. Emperor Hirohito.

(He renounced his divinity in 1946.)

10. *Charlie's Angels*.

(In the original TV series. Jill Munroe, played by Farrah Fawcett; Kelly Garrett, Jaclyn Smith; Sabrina Duncan, Kate Jackson; Kris Munroe, Cheryl Ladd; Tiffany Welles, Shelley Hack; Julie Rogers, Tanya Roberts.)

ANSWERS TO QUIZ NINETEEN

Round One

1. **The assassination of President Kennedy.**
2. **Princess Eugenie.**
3. **Took part in the University Boat Race.**
   (Moynihan for Oxford, the other two for Cambridge.
   Snowdon and Moynihan were coxes.)
4. **Both founded by Sir Stamford Raffles.**
5. **Condoleezza Rice.** (The term is 'con dolcezza'.)
6. **(i) A flutist (or flautist); (ii) a lutanist (or lutenist).**
   (Flutist – 1603 – is a much older established word than
   flautist – 1860. Pepys coined 'fluter' in 1666. Some flute
   players prefer 'flute player'. Lute players have also been known
   as 'luters' and, in the US, 'lutists'. A luthier makes the damn
   things.)
7. **Kaiser Wilhelm II.**
8. **Animals killed in war.**
   (The sculpture depicts two mules, a horse and a dog.)
9. **They have all won the FA Cup.**
   (In 1879, 1881 and 1880 respectively. The Old Etonians won
   again in 1882, and lost in the finals of 1875, 1876, 1881 and
   1883.)
10. **(i) Geoffrey Chaucer; (ii) John Milton; (iii) Samuel Pepys.**

Round Two

1. **Inert or noble gases.** (Helium, neon, krypton, xenon.)
2. **Prime Ministers.** (The last four in order.)
3. **Played Jesus Christ on film or TV.**
4. **Created by Beachcomber.** (J. B. Morton.)
5. **US states.** (Florida, Colorado, Nevada, Montana.)

6. **All Bond girls.**
   (Respectively played by Daniela Bianchi in *From Russia With Love*, Barbara Bach in *The Spy Who Loved Me*, Fiona Fullerton in *A View To A Kill*, and Izabella Scorupco in *Goldeneye*.)
7. **Awarded city status in those years.**
8. **Identities of the kings in old French packs of playing cards.**
9. **Wrote books in prison.**
10. **British Olympic gold medallists in 4x100m relay in Athens 2004.**
    (Jason Gardener, Darren Campbell, Marlon Devenish, Mark Lewis-Francis.)

Bonus Round

1. Havergal **Brian.**
2. Father **Dougal** McGuire.
3. Because **Dylan** Thomas drank there.
4. **Florence.**
5. **Zebedee.** (Matthew 4:21)

Tie-Break

One-way streets were first established in London in 1617.

Round Three

1. **Nigel Planer.**
2. *The Medusa*; Géricault.
3. **Ride in the Grand National.**
   (She was also the first woman to finish the Grand National, two years later.)
4. **Abraham Lincoln.** (He invented a lifting device for ships.)
5. *The Woman In White.* (By Wilkie Collins.)

6. **AZERTYUIOP.**

    (A racehorse of this name was Champion Chaser in 2004/5.)

7. **He took Britain's first driving test.**

    (He passed it too. Driving tests had been introduced in France a mere forty-two years earlier.)

8. **The London Eye.**

    (135m compared with the Arch's 133m. Take the Eye off its mounting on the south bank of the Thames, and it is said that you could roll it under the Arch, should you feel so inclined. But as they stand, with mounting included, the Eye is slightly higher.)

9. **Richard Whiteley's, in the first ever *Countdown*.**

    (He is said to be the most-seen face on British TV of all time, after Carole Hersee, the girl on the test card.)

10. **FRS: Fellow of the Royal Society. FRCS: Fellow of the Royal College of Surgeons. FRICS: Fellow of the Royal Institution of Chartered Surveyors.**

Round Four

1. **Harland & Woolf shipyard, Belfast.**
2. **Typefaces or fonts.**
3. **Lord Elgin.**

    (Specifically the 7th Earl of Elgin and 11th Earl of Kincardine.)

4. **Casablanca.**
5. **Paul Gauguin.**
6. **Eleanor of Aquitaine.**

    (She also led her own troops on the Second Crusade, dressed as an Amazonian warrior.)

7. **A pipe which sounds when it is not played.**
8. **George IV.**

    (Brummel is remembered for saying one thing about and one thing to the then-Prince of Wales – the other one being 'Shut the door, Wales.')

9. **Maine.**

(The border is with New Hampshire.)

10. **They have all been subjects of films that won a Best Picture Oscar.**

(In order: *A Man For All Seasons* in 1966, *Amadeus* in 1984, *The Life Of Emile Zola* in 1937, *Gandhi* in 1982, *Patton* in 1970 and *Lawrence of Arabia* in 1962.)

ANSWERS TO QUIZ TWENTY

Round One

1. **Ellen MacArthur.**
2. **Starbucks.**
   (Starbuck is the 'right-minded' first mate of the *Pequod*.)
3. **Status Quo.**
   (By September 2005, Quo had notched up 61 and Queen were second with 52.)
4. **Prince William** (2 points); **Aston Villa** (1 point).
5. **Carlsberg.**
   (The swastika was widely used in the Victorian era and afterwards as a good luck sign. Rudyard Kipling had it on his coat of arms. American volunteers flying with the French air force during World War I used it as their symbol. Coca-Cola made a lucky swastika fob watch in 1925 . . .)
6. **Smallpox.**
7. **Viv Anderson; Paul Ince.**
   (Anderson was the 936th player to appear for England, since when roughly one in four new caps has been black. Jack Leslie, a prolific striker for Plymouth Argyle in the 1920s, was called up but later told he wouldn't be needed. Apparently they hadn't realised that he was 'a man of colour'.)
8. **Batman.**
9. **Star Trek: Voyager.**
10. **(i) Michael Vaughan; (ii) Marcus Trescothick; (iii) Steve Harmison; (iv) Duncan Fletcher; (v) Andrew Strauss.**
    (Andrew Flintoff was granted the freedom of Preston, and Ashley Giles was made an honorary citizen of Droitwich Spa.)

Round Two

1. An ASBO.
2. Anthony Hopkins in *Silence Of The Lambs*.
   (It's the shortest ever performance to win the Oscar. Hopkins described his voice for Hannibal Lecter as 'a combination of Truman Capote and Katharine Hepburn'.)
3. Mauritius.
4. Sir Oswald Mosley.
5. 'SOS' by Abba.
6. (i) Rain, or being rained on; (ii) the Pope (or the Roman Catholic church); (iv) the Dutch.
   (Ombrophobia is an alternative term for (i). The fear of peanut butter sticking to the roof of your mouth is arachibutyrophobia.)
7. The *Blue Peter* garden.
   ('It was malicious vandalism,' said Simon Groom. 'He should contribute to the *Blue Peter* appeal.')
8. Naomi Campbell.
   (*Baby Woman* sold more than 1 million copies worldwide, most of them in Japan.)
9. (i) 37.5 per cent; (ii) 40 per cent; (iii) 7.5 per cent.
10. (i) Douglas Adams; (ii) William Golding; (iii) Charles Dickens; (iv) F. Scott Fitzgerald.

Bonus Round

1. Hunter S. Thompson.
   (The cannon was fired from the top of a 153-foot tower, designed by Thompson, in the shape of a double-thumbed fist clutching a peyote button. 'Mr Tambourine Man' was played.)
2. Amazon.
3. Saracens.

4. Cobra.

(Inverted commas round 'Indian' because the Cobra we drink is brewed in the UK.)

5. Wolf.

(The link was the TV show *Gladiators*.)

Tie-Break

In the largest game of musical chairs of all time, 8,238 people took part. (It took them three and a half hours.)

Round Three

1. Moses.

2. Kazakhstan.

(Baron Cohen, in character as Borat, urged them on: 'Sue the Jew!')

3. Albert Einstein.

(Israel made him the offer in 1952. He refused.)

4. Cilla Black.

5. Andrew Lloyd Webber.

6. Smoke detector.

(The discovery of americium was informally announced on a US radio quiz show, *Quiz Kids*, in November 1945. One of the kids asked a visiting scientist from the Metallurgical Laboratory in Chicago whether they had discovered any new elements during the war and he said, well, actually we have . . .)

7. Barnardo's.

8. The Dalai Lama.

9. Phil Collins.

10. (i) Leeds United; (ii) Leicester City; (iii) Blackpool; (iv) Manchester United; (v) Fulham.

Round Four

1. **Prince Edward, Princess Anne, Duke of York, Duchess of York.**
2. **Stephen.**
   (The only English monarch from the family Blois. His son and heir died a year before he did; otherwise the next king would have been Eustace I.)
3. **Flash.**
4. **Super Mario; Bob Hoskins.**
   (As Mario and Luigi are known as 'the Mario Bros', Mario's full name is Mario Mario.)
5. **Paul Boateng.**
6. **Sachin Tendulkar.**
   (Wasim Akram was the previous record holder with 356. No Englishman has played more than Alec Stewart's 170.)
7. **She was pregnant with eight babies.** (But none survived.)
8. **(i) The armpit; (ii) the big toe.**
9. *Crazy For You.*
   ('Someone To Watch Over Me' originally came from *Oh Kay!* (1926). 'Nice Work If You Can Get it' was from the 1937 film *A Damsel In Distress*. Both were collaborations with P. G. Wodehouse.)
10. **Bere Regis, Bognor Regis, Grafton Regis, Houghton Regis, Lyme Regis, Melcombe Regis, Rowley Regis, Wyke Regis.**
    (Respectively in Dorset, West Sussex, Northants, Bedfordshire, Dorset again, Dorset yet again, West Midlands and, naturally, Dorset.)

ANSWERS TO QUIZ TWENTY-ONE

Round One

1. **France.**
   (You do need Presidential permission, but hundreds have managed to get it since the 1950s.)
2. **Red, blue and yellow.**
3. **A giraffe.**
4. **Ramsay Macdonald.** (In 1924.)
5. **Iron.**
   (There's some nickel in there as well, and current theories add traces of sulphur, oxygen and hydrogen.)
6. **Holland-Dozier-Holland.**
   (They wrote all these songs, and many others, in a golden spell between 1964 and 1966.)
7. **Phoenicia.**
8. **Penalties.**
   (Aldershot won 11-10. The European record is 34 in a Turkish FA Cup between Genclerbirligi and Galatasaray. Only one penalty was missed: the last one. Genclerbirligi won 17-16.)
9. **Avon and Severn.**
10. (i) *The Autograph Man*; (ii) *Vile Bodies*; (iii) *The Tesseract*; (iv) *Oliver Twist*.

Round Two

1. **Harvey Smith.**
2. **Maggie Smith.**
3. **Smithson.**
   (First name, James. Institution, the Smithsonian.)
4. **Dodie Smith.**
5. **Smithfield.**
6. **C. Aubrey Smith.**

7. Joseph Smith.

8. Mel Smith.

9. *Alias Smith And Jones.*

   (Between 1972 and 1975, Roger Davis was married to Jaclyn Smith, of *Charlie's Angels*.)

10. Johnny Marr.

    (Must specify 'lead' because Craig Gannon also played guitar for the Smiths in the last phase of their existence.)

Bonus Round

1. 1950 (in Brazil).

2. 1978 (in Argentina).

3. 1962 (in Chile).

4. 1990 (in Italy).

5. 1938 (in France).

Tie-Break

To reach Stratford at 9:17 a.m., Terence would have had to catch a train at Marylebone at 3:35 a.m.

(This would include three changes and a taxi ride from one end of Birmingham to the other. He decided to drive instead.)

Round Three

1. July 4th.

   (Adams and Jefferson died on the same day – July 4th, 1826 – and Monroe exactly five years later.)

2. A light year.

(The distance travelled through empty space in a year by any electromagnetic radiation. It's a unit much loved by science fiction writers, but astronomers tend to prefer the parsec.)

3. 'See God.'

4. Hammer.

(He made the grave error of surviving his boss by more than 30 years. In 1957 Khruschev called him 'a saboteur of peace' and made him ambassador to Outer Mongolia.)

5. (i) Yes. (ii) No.

(All centipedes start life with 12 legs, then grow more later. The highest number recorded is over 200. But no millipede has more than 750.)

6. Smersh. It was the only one that really existed.

(And was an abbreviation of a phrase that meant 'Death to Spies' in Russian.)

7. Zero.

8. Ford Madox. (Brown and Ford.)

9. A distance.

(In flat racing a distance is also anything over 12 lengths.)

10. Penguins.

(Specifically chinstrap penguins.)

Round Four

1. The Fat Controller.

(In the Thomas the Tank Engine books.)

2. B&Q.

3. Michael Foot.

4. Brussels.

(198 miles. Paris is next – 212 – followed by Amsterdam on 220. Dublin is 290 miles away.)

5. February.

('With every paper I delivered.' In 'American Pie'.)

6. **Winston Churchill.**

   (His American mother Jennie Jerome claimed Iroquois blood, but genealogists have yet to verify it.)

7. **Ganymede.**

   (It's larger than Pluto or Mercury.)

8. *Inspector Morse.*

9. **Dr Dolittle.**

10. **Streaked.**

    (He was also the man who streaked on Fred Talbot's weather map on *This Morning* in 1995. At the 2006 Winter Olympics he ran across the men's bronze medal curling match between USA and UK wearing a rubber chicken on his penis.)

ANSWERS TO QUIZ TWENTY-TWO

Round One

1. **Contraception.**
   (The crocodile dung had to be mixed with honey, soda and an unnamed gummy substance and introduced into the vagina. So recommends an Egyptian papyrus from about 1850 BC.)
2. **John Profumo, John Stonehouse, Jonathan Aitken.**
   (In 1963, 1976 and 1997 respectively.)
3. **Umbro.**
4. **Swedish.**
5. **Because of the abolition of the right of hereditary peers to sit in the Lords.**
   (Except for those on a select register, and he isn't one of them.)
6. **Tesco.**
   (It was also the title of Jack Cohen's autobiography.)
7. **Bertie Bassett.**
8. **The Tower of London.**
   (The royal menagerie was situated there between 1235 and 1835: the ravens are its remnants.)
9. **Sudoku.**
10. **Bobby Charlton, Gary Lineker, Jimmy Greaves.**
    (With 49, 48 and 44 respectively. Owen had 35 in April 2006.)

Round Two

1. **A Victoria Cross.**
   (And the first living recipient since 1969.)
2. **Clifton** (2 points). **Postman Pat** (1 point).

3. *Hallowe'en.*

(The budget was so small the actors had to wear their own clothes. Jamie Lee Curtis went to J. C. Penney for Laurie Strode's wardrobe, and spent less than $100 on the entire set.)

4. **(i) First rollercoaster with 360° loop; (ii) first rollercoaster with a sheer vertical drop.**

5. **Petra.**

6. **Hanging.**

(In practice it was rarely exercised. Many miscreants agreed to join the Army or Navy instead, or in later years to be transported to Australia. It is still illegal to impersonate a Chelsea Pensioner at any time.)

7. **Alphabetti Spaghetti.**

(Heinz claimed they had brought it back because of 'parental demand'.)

8. **Jay; Montgomery.**

(Mr Burns's first name is actually Charles but he is generally known as 'C. Montgomery Burns'.)

9. **Strike.**

(In ten-pin bowling. A strike is knocking over all the pins with a single ball. A double is two consecutive strikes, a turkey is three, and so on.)

10. *The Mousetrap.*

Bonus Round

1. **Queens.**

2. **Pawnbroker.**

(No one knows for sure what 'the weasel' was – it may have been slang for a tailor's iron – but you needed to 'pop' it, i.e. pawn it, to pay for all that drinking 'in and out the Eagle'.)

3. **Rook.**

4. The Bishop of Durham.
5. A King's College.
6. Knight.
   (They are all chess pieces.)

Tie-Break

The number of possible valid solutions to a standard 9x9 Sudoku grid is **6,670,903,752,021,072,936,960.**
(Or 6.67×10^{21}.)

Round Three

1. The contraceptive pill.
2. Rachel Stevens.
3. Sicily; Sardinia; Cyprus.
4. Charlton.
   (This was revealed to the world at his marriage to Cassandra in 1989.)
5. (i) Stalin; (ii) Churchill; (iii) Gorbachev.
   (Franklin Delano Roosevelt is the only person of any nationality to have won three times.)
6. Henry.
7. Robert Schumann.
8. Mr Fantastic, the Invisible Woman, the Thing and the Human Torch.
   (The make-up of the group has occasionally changed in the comic strip, but these are the core four.)
9. The pitch.
   (It's owned by the fans.)

10. (i) Gwyneth Paltrow; (ii) Catherine Zeta-Jones; (iii) Kate Moss; (iv) Jordan (Katie Price); (v) Sadie Frost.

(In 2003 Tom, Ali & Pete proffered the following question: 'The alleged actress and Primrose Hill resident Sadie Frost is rarely out of the headlines. Name any film in which she appeared.' Although there was no limit on how many films you could name, very few points were scored.)

Round Four

1. Revoke.
2. *Close Encounters of the Third Kind.*
3. Women's 800m.
4. Fifty-two white and thirty-six black.
5. All written by the Bee Gees.
6. Ian Hislop.
7. Illinois.
8. Gross domestic product.
9. 7-Up.

(It initially contained lithium citrate, a mood-stabilising drug, but this was removed in the 1950s.)

10. (i) *Grange Hill*; (ii) *Man About The House*; (iii) *Happy Days*; (iv) *Man About The House*; (v) *Happy Days*.

ANSWERS TO QUIZ TWENTY-THREE

Round One

1. Hudson, East and Harlem.
2. Absolved of your sins.
   (With or without the help of pancakes.)
3. **Community Chest** (in Monopoly).
4. The first was Marie Curie again. The second was her daughter (Irène Joliot-Curie).
5. Alternative titles of Gilbert and Sullivan operettas.
   (*HMS Pinafore*, *The Pirates of Penzance*, *The Gondoliers* and *The Mikado* respectively.)
6. Newcastle-upon-Tyne and Sheffield.
7. **Brazil** (Portuguese), **Guyana** (English), **Suriname** (Dutch), **French Guiana** (French).
8. Fathers in the ice-cream business.
9. Wolfgang *Amadeus* Mozart.
10. It was a draw: 10 each.
    (Hairies: Salisbury, Balfour, Campbell-Bannerman, Lloyd George, Bonar Law, Ramsey Macdonald, Chamberlain, Attlee, Eden, Macmillan.
    Smoothies: Asquith, Baldwin, Churchill, Douglas-Home, Wilson, Heath, Callaghan, Thatcher, Major, Blair.
    But only the Marquess of Salisbury had a full beard.)

Round Two

1. 100 billion.
   ('Walked out this morning / Don't believe what I saw / 100 billion bottles / Washed up on the shore.')
2. El Al.

3. Dance.

('Sur le pont d'Avignon / on y danse, on y danse.' Only four of the original twenty-two arches survive: presumably the dancing took care of the rest.)

4. The (tiered) wedding cake.

(The spire consists of four octagonal arcades of diminishing size, capped with an obelisk and a ball and vane on top. Mr Rich, an 18th-century Fleet Street pastry cook, made a name for himself with his wedding cakes modelled on the spire.)

5. James Dean.

(He drove his car into another car; the others all crashed into trees.)

6. *The Joy of Sex* by Dr Alex Comfort.

7. Dragons.

(In the *Harry Potter* books.)

8. The (4th) Earl of Sandwich.

(He was not only corrupt but staggeringly incompetent. Captain Cook named the Sandwich Islands, now Hawaii, in his honour.)

9. Leonid Brezhnev.

(The awards, all from the USSR, were of course pure sycophancy. It is unlikely that Brezhnev wrote a single word of the books himself.)

10. Harmony.

(Each word is the first half of a well-known phrase. 'Manifest Destiny' encapsulates US foreign policy of the past 100 years, while the other three are song titles: 'Bittersweet Symphony' by The Verve, 'Bohemian Rhapsody' by Queen, 'Unchained Melody' by virtually everyone. Destiny, Symphony, Rhapsody, Melody and Harmony were the pilots in *Captain Scarlet*.)

Bonus Round

1. Ray Clemence.
2. Nigel Martyn.
3. Gary Bailey.
4. Alex Stepney.
5. Shoreditch and Bow.

(Oranges and lemons,
Say the bells of St Clement's.
You owe me five farthings,
Say the bells of St Martin's.
When will you pay me,
Say the bells of Old Bailey.
When I grow rich,
Say the bells of Shoreditch.
When will that be?
Say the bells of Stepney.
I'm sure I don't know,
Says the great bell at Bow . . .)

Tie-Break

In 1998 John Evans balanced 62 identical books on his head.
(Strangely enough they were all *The Guinness Book of Records*. He
also balanced 96 milk crates on his head in 2001, 235 pints of beer
in 2002, 101 house bricks in 1997, 428 cans of Coke in 1999 and
548 footballs in 1998. See his website, www.headbalancer.com.)

Round Three

1. *2001:A Space Odyssey.*
2. **A cookery book.**

(He recommends the swordfish caught off Byzantium,
especially the joint cut right from the tail.)

3. **Beards** (2 points). **Pogonophobic** (1 point).
4. **In Beatles songs.**
5. **The distance to the horizon in miles.**
6. **Great-great-great grandson.**

   (A long-lived bunch. Louis XIV reigned for 72 years, was succeeded by his great-grandson Louis XV, who reigned for a further 59 years, to be succeeded by his grandson Louis XVI, who notched up only a feeble 18 years before getting his head chopped off.)
7. **Tiramisu.**
8. **Live pigeon shooting.**

   (He killed twenty-one. Maurice Fauré of France was runner-up with twenty.)
9. **Fawlty Towers.**

   (He played the corpse in 'The Kipper and the Corpse'.)
10. **Elvis Presley. People wanted their envelopes sent back with 'Return to Sender' stamped on them.**

   (517 million Elvis stamps were sold.)

Round Four

1. **Sherpa Tenzing, of Mount Everest.**
2. **Each has the other's name in reverse.** (John Barry and Barry John.)
3. **Jurassic Park.**
4. **32 FDR, 35 JFK, 36 LBJ.**

   (American Presidents who were known by their initials.)
5. **The Bad; Lee van Cleef.**
6. **Widnes.**

   (There is a plaque at the station commemorating the event, although a new school of thought suggests he was waiting at Ditton Junction instead.)
7. **Kublai Khan.**

8. Greenland.

(It is a self-governed Danish territory. About 81 per cent of its surface is covered by ice.)

9. *His Dark Materials.*

(By Philip Pullman. In order, *Northern Lights*, *The Subtle Knife*, *The Amber Spyglass*.)

10. The Henrys.

(247 years 3 months, as opposed to the Edwards' 142 years 9 months. The latter were badly let down by V and VIII, each of whom ruled for less than a year.)

ANSWERS TO QUIZ TWENTY-FOUR

Round One

1. **London Bridge.**
2. *Alien.*
3. **Lightning.**
   (*Fulgur* is Latin for lightning.)
4. **South America.**
   (New Zealand is second, Australia third.)
5. **(i) The study of eggs** (specifically birds' eggs); **(ii) the study of ears.**
   (Orology is the scientific study of mountains.)
6. **Syrah.**
   (The Rhone valley is where the grape originally comes from.
   This is oenology.)
7. **On the cover of *Abbey Road* by the Beatles.**
   (Some people decided that LMW stood for 'Linda McCartney
   Widow', which proved that Paul was dead. As it happens, the
   car belonged to someone living in the block of flats next to
   the studio.)
8. **W. C. Fields.** (Attributed.)
9. **The Tweenies.**
10. In order: I. Smith. 2. Brown. 3. Jones. 4. Williams. 5. Taylor.

Round Two

1. **Neil Armstrong.**
   (Cernan was the last man, so far, to walk on the moon.)
2. **It snowed.**
3. **Shopping.**
   (Or maybe just walking around wishing you were somewhere
   else. They are all shopping centres.)

4. They do not tell a tale.
5. Alexander Pope.

   ('To err is human, not to, animal.' Robert Frost.)
6. Assassinate Queen Victoria.
7. (i) *coup de grâce*; (ii) *coup de foudre*.

   (Literally: blow of mercy, and lightning flash.)
8. Eros.

   (The statue at Piccadilly Circus in London. Cups were originally supplied so you could drink the water. They didn't last long.)
9. *Hamlet.*
10. All are or were left-handed.

Bonus Round

In order: 1. 'at the end of the day'; 2. 'at this moment in time'; 3. 'like' (as a form of punctuation or 'filler'); 4. 'with all due respect'; 5. 'to be honest'.

(The campaign received several emails saying 'Get a life'. They couldn't decide whether these were nominations for the survey or just abuse.)

Tie-Break

12 per cent of snake species are venomous.

Round Three

1. Charles Frost.

   (Who wasn't actually fictitious at all. He was an account executive at Ogilvy & Mather, AmEx's advertising agency, and informally known as 'Chuck'.)
2. Show jumping, cross country and dressage.
3. Sikhism.

4. **Harold Wilson and Ian Smith. Rhodesia's UDI.**

   (The negotiations were not successful. Smith described Wilson's terms as 'repugnant'.)

5. **Georgi Markov is killed.**

   (He was a Bulgarian journalist. An agent of the Bulgarian security service stabbed him, using a specially adapted umbrella which injected a poison-filled pellet into Markov's leg.)

6. **Repechage.**

7. **On your fingernail.**

   (It's the white crescent-shaped area at the base of some fingernails.)

8. **Airstrip One.**

9. **The daffodil.**

10. **None.** (It's a race for three-year-olds only.)

Round Four

1. **'For valour'** (2 points); **Captured Russian guns from the Crimea** (1 point).

2. **Paparazzo.**

3. *The Wind In The Willows.*

   (Respectively Mole, Toad and Ratty, who is a water rat.)

4. **Jack Dempsey.**

5. **The French Foreign Legion.**

6. **Ice cream.**

7. **Lizzie Borden.**

   (In reality her stepmother received nineteen whacks and her father a further ten, but they don't scan so well.)

8. **The Lake District.**

   (The Yorkshire Dales come second.)

9. **(i) Sherlock Holmes; (ii) Hercule Poirot; (iii) Simon Templar.**

10. **None.**

    (He only ever went to the Caribbean, to mainland South America on the third voyage and Central America on the last.)

ANSWERS TO QUIZ TWENTY-FIVE

Round One

1. Colin Cowdrey.
2. 'What shall we do with the drunken sailor?'
   (There are quite a few other answers, including 'Shave his belly with a rusty razor' and, controversially, 'Put him in bed with the captain's daughter'.)
3. Shelter.
4. Sir Alec Guinness.
   (In *Kind Hearts and Coronets*, 1949.)
5. Tony the Tiger.
   (Who may be the only cat in history who appears to thrive on a vegetarian diet.)
6. 'Country House' and 'Roll With It'.
7. Stabbing Monica Seles.
   (With a steak knife. He was a big fan of Steffi Graf.)
8. John Nash.
9. Ouija board.
10. (i)   'Why, that's very nearly an armful.'
    (ii) 'Yes you did, you invaded Poland.'
    (iii) 'I didn't expect a kind of Spanish Inquisition.'
    (From *The Blood Donor*, *Fawlty Towers* and *Monty Python* respectively.)

Round Two

1. Tony Jacklin and Raymond Floyd.
2. Tom Stoppard.
   (It was published in 1966.)

3. **Hermann Goering.**

    (He ended World War I as an ace, with twenty-two confirmed kills. But he was not popular: he was the only member of the squadron never invited to their post-war reunions.)

4. **Doolally.**

    (The camp was at Deolali.)

5. **The banging of the Rank gong.**

6. **The Furby.**

7. **James Stewart.**

    (He had won it in the 1940 awards, handed out spring 1941.)

8. **@.**

9. *Sex Lives of the Potato Men.*

    (*Times* critic James Christopher called it 'a sump of untreated dung'.)

10. **Stephen Fry.**

    (The film was *IQ*. The TV show was *QI*.)

Bonus Round

1. **Leeds.**

2. **Poole.**

3. **Cromer.**

4. **Dundee.**

5. **Tring.**

6. **Chester.**

7. **Slough.**

8. **Putney.**

9. **Gretna.**

10. **Bangor.**

    (All are from *The Book of Nonsense*, 1846. Number 2 starts 'There was a Young Lady . . .' Number 4 starts 'There was a Young Man . . .' The other eight start 'There was an Old Person . . .')

Tie-Break

There are 77 different species of mosquito in Florida.

(More than in any other US state.)

Round Three

1. **Lenny Henry.**
2. **Teacher.**

   (In a primary school.)
3. **Cleo Laine.**
4. **The Dashing White Sergeant.**
5. **The Lovin' Spoonful.**
6. **John Constable.**
7. **Screaming Jay Hawkins.**
8. **Dr Zhivago.**

   (Matheson played the role in the 2002 TV version, with Keira Knightley as Lara.)
9. **Jack Straw.**
10. **Columbus, Ohio.**

    (There is an underlying connection to this round: *Carry On* films.)

Round Four

1. **Coronation chicken.**
2. **Duchess of Bedford.**

   (Her husband was the 7th Duke.)
3. **A pair of boots.**

   (The player was Ernie Payne. Someone had stolen his boots, indeed all his kit; Tottenham gave him several pairs to try on; none fitted; so they gave him 10s to buy another pair. The club were hauled up before the London FA, found guilty of misconduct, and ordered to shut down for two weeks. The club turned professional two years later.)

4. Dates of end of rationing.
5. Abu Hamsa.
6. (i) Only dismissal ever for obstructing the field; (ii) handling the ball.
7. Alton Towers.
8. *The Day of the Triffids* by John Wyndham.
   (He preferred the term 'logical fantasy' for his works.)
9. Arkansas.
10. Dean Martin.

ANSWERS TO QUIZ TWENTY-SIX

Round One

1. Malaysia.
2. Rocky Marciano.
   (He is the only champion of any weight class to retire undefeated and without any draws.)
3. Mansion House.
4. *The Taming of the Shrew.*
5. Sir Michael Caine.
6. William Ewart Gladstone.
   (The fourth time he became Prime Minister, he was eighty-two years old.)
7. (i) Manchester; (ii) Exeter; (iii) Guildford.
8. Groucho Marx.
   (Chico after 'chicks', Harpo after 'harp', Zeppo after 'zeppelins', although the last is much disputed. Groucho may have been named after his grumpy disposition, after a comic character of the day, or after his habit of keeping all his money in a 'grouch-bag' for safe keeping.)
9. St Elmo's Fire.
10. Asuncion.
    (The capital and chief port of Paraguay.)

Round Two

1. Sean Penn.
   (At the time he was shooting *Shanghai Surprise*, a different sort of crime.)
2. The Thirty Years War.
3. The red kite.
4. 'Mark twain'.
5. The World of Beatrix Potter.

6. John Noakes.
7. Mir.

   (It was occupied in all for 4,594 days and made 89,067 orbits.)
8. Michael Vaughan.

   (166 in the Old Trafford Test.)
9. Monet.

   (813,000 people attended in 12 weeks.)
10. Gwyneth Paltrow.

Bonus Round

1. Jeremy Clarkson: a jet ski.
2. George Clooney: an anchored yacht.
3. Billy Connolly: a banjo.
4. Robin Cook: a chess computer.
5. Nick Hornby: an iPod.
6. Jan Morris: a hot water bottle.
7. Graham Norton: a mirror.
8. Gordon Ramsay; a fresh vanilla pod.

Tie-Break

The longest rally in table-tennis history lasted 2 hours 12 minutes.

(It was the opening point of the match. Ehrlich was known as 'the king of the chisellers', defensive players who never played an aggressive shot but just ground down opponents, and audiences. After eighty-five minutes the umpire's neck locked and a replacement had to be called in. At one point Ehrlich had a snack of bread and Polish sausage. He eventually won the point, and the rules of the sport were changed to ensure it could never happen again.)

Round Three

1. Bip.
2. *International Times*.
   (The event was billed as a 'Pop/Op/Costume/Masque/Fantasy-Loon/Blowout/Drag Ball'.)
3. David Bowie.
   (Whose real name is David Jones. Duncan Jones started life as Zowie Bowie. 'Kung Fu lesbian advert sparks viewer protests', reported the *Daily Telegraph*.)
4. The planet Pluto.
5. Roscoe Tanner.
   (He lost in 1979 to Bjorn Borg in five sets.)
6. Judi Dench, *Shakespeare in Love*.
   (Beatrice Straight won the 1976 award for her role in *Network*, which was also just under eight minutes long. If a tie-break is required, Straight spoke 260 words, as compared with Dench's 446.)
7. Geiger counter.
8. Bastion.
9. Six.
10. Sacramento, Tallahassee, Albany, Austin; Maine.

Round Four

1. Joyce Grenfell and Les Dawson.
2. William Shakespeare.
   (The National Portrait Gallery have concluded that it is a portrait of someone else who was twenty-four years old in 1588.)
3. Costa Rica.
4. Bill Gates.
   (In his teenage years he apparently allowed his obsession with computers to 'compromise his bathing routine'. Now it's payback time.)

5. **Forward Not Back.**

   (Worse was to follow when it emerged that the phrase had previously appeared as a joke in The Simpsons. A cartoon Bill Clinton had been heard to say, 'My fellow Americans. We must move forward, not backward, upward not forward, and always twirling, twirling, twirling towards freedom.')

6. **Russell Crowe.**

7. **Justin Timberlake and Janet Jackson.**

8. **Batista.**

   (First name Fulgencio.)

9. **Panorama.**

10. **Doctor Who.**

ANSWERS TO QUIZ TWENTY-SEVEN

Round One

1. **30.**
   (It's the value in old pennies of pre-decimal coinage.)
2. **Art Deco.**
3. **Mongolia.** (Ulan Bator.)
4. **Whitby.**
   (The specific issue argued over was the dating of Easter. King Oswy of Northumbria presided, while a local priest named Wilfrid argued that his Easter was that of St Peter the apostle, the holder of the keys to heaven. This clinched it for the King. 'Otherwise,' he said, 'when I come to the gates of heaven, there may be no one to open them.')
5. **The Maquis.**
6. **'Smelly Cat'; Ursula.**
   (Ursula first appeared in the sitcom *Mad About You* as a waitress. Phoebe wasn't originally going to have a twin, but the show's writers wanted to explain why Lisa Kudrow was in two shows, sometimes on the same evening.)
7. **Four.**
   (It was one of the noisiest aircraft in civil aviation history: only Concorde was consistently louder.)
8. **1840s.**
   (China ceded Hong Kong, 1841. Ether, 1842. *Rain, Steam and Speed* and *The Three Musketeers*, both 1844. The February Revolution, which brought about the abdication of King Louis Philippe and creation of the short-lived Second Republic, 1848.)
9. **Ms Dynamite.**
10. **White elephant.**
    (The current king of Thailand owns ten.)

Round Two

1. They are mountain ranges in India.
2. The throat or neck.
3. Feeding of the five thousand with five loaves and two fishes.
4. *Persuasion* and *Northanger Abbey*.
5. Welsh Whisky.
6. Both are about Dr Martin Luther King.
7. Wernher von Braun.
   (He called his autobiography *I Aim At The Stars*. The American comedian Mort Sahl suggested a subtitle: *(But Sometimes I Hit London)*.)
8. The comma.
9. Roast wild boar.
10. A bank manager.
    (He worked for NatWest for nearly forty years.)

Bonus Round

1. *Bull* Durham.
2. **Lemon**heads.
3. **Nurse** Ratched. (In *One Flew Over The Cuckoo's Nest*.)
4. **Blue** Flag.
5. **Zebra** crossing.
6. James **Whale**.
   (The link is that they are all types of shark.)

Tie-Break

As far as we know, the Vikings first visited England in AD 787.
(According to the Anglo-Saxon Chronicle, a group of men from Norway landed at Portland in Dorset. A royal official mistook them for merchants and asked them to pay a trading tax on their goods, so they killed him. The Vikings had arrived.)

Round Three

1. HMS *Victory*; HMS *Warrior* (the first British ironclad); and *Mary Rose*.
2. **Antimony.**
   (Supposedly from 'anti-moine', meaning 'hostile to monks'. Antimony had also been called stibium, hence its symbol Sb. The story goes that a prior saw his pigs grow fat on food containing stibium, so he fed the same food to fasting monks, and they all died. Tragically, this etymology may be complete fantasy.)
3. **He couldn't sell it.**
   (One half is now on display in Norfolk, the other in Cuba's national art museum.)
4. **Mrs Goggins.**
5. **The terminator.**
6. **Lupins.**
7. *The Wind in the Willows.*
8. **Prince of Wales.**
9. **3M.**
   (Five years earlier he had invented masking tape.)
10. **The dame; full of grace; little Johnny Green.**
    (Little Tommy Stout pulled her out.)

Round Four

1. **The scarab beetle.**
   (Egyptians believed that all scarabs were male and therefore managed to conceal within themselves the secret of eternal life. See *The Mummy* and *The Mummy Returns*.)
2. **Wyoming.**
   (It also edges into Montana and Idaho.)
3. **Medina.**
   (It's also the second holiest city of Islam, where you can find Mohammed's tomb.)

4. **Between Saturn's rings.**

   (This is the black gap, around 2,980 miles wide, roughly in the middle of the visible rings. The Huygens gap is next door. Not to be confused with Cassini's Division, who are an Indian rock group.)

5. **E20.**

6. **(i) The Browns** (in the Paddington Bear stories); **(ii) the Dursleys** (in *Harry Potter*); **(iii) the Bellamys** (in *Upstairs Downstairs*).

7. *The Communist Manifesto.*

8. **Warsaw.**

9. **It's a midge.**

   (The Highland biting midge, to be precise. Up to 20 per cent of summer working days in outdoor jobs in the Highlands are lost to midge attacks. They are at their most active at dawn and dusk, and on overcast days.)

10. **Marco Polo.**

ANSWERS TO QUIZ TWENTY-EIGHT

Round One

1. **They all belonged to Philip Larkin.**
   (He ran over a hedgehog with the lawnmower and it inspired his poem 'The Mower'.)
2. **World War I.**
   (In Archangel in 1918. Despite the Armistice, they carried on fighting until the Americans withdrew in early 1920.)
3. **George II; George VI.** (In 1727 and 1937.)
4. **Bill & Ted.**
   (*Bill & Ted's Excellent Adventure, Bill & Ted's Bogus Journey.*)
5. **Corked wine.**
   (The smell of which has been said to evoke mouldy newspaper, wet dog or damp basement.)
6. **They all changed their names to Starr.**
   (In order: Freddie, Ringo and Edwin.)
7. **It was the apple tree that inspired Newton's theory of gravity.**
   (Not the oak in which Charles II hid: that was in Boscobel House in Shropshire.)
8. **Each was younger than the actor who played his son.**
9. **Stalin.**
10. **(i) Grimm; (ii) Everly; (iii) Blues; (iv) Lumière; (v) Chemical; (vi) Slag** (from *Wacky Races*).

Round Two

1. **Oliver Reed.**
2. **Grapes.**
   (It is particularly popular in Chile and Peru.)

3. **They both died in Venice.**
   (Von Aschenbach was the main character in *Death in Venice*.)
4. **Basil and Sybil Fawlty.** (They ran the Gleneagles Hotel in Torquay.)
5. **The Sun.**
   (Amazing how many teams put Proxima Centauri.)
6. **Pig and turkey.**
   (The pig provides the ring, the turkey officiates at the marriage.)
7. **Written in the form of a letter to somebody.**
8. **John Mahoney.**
   (Jane Leeves was born in Ilford.)
9. **A police box.**
   (Became the TARDIS in *Doctor Who*.)
10. **(i) Clarinet; (ii) flute; (iii) bassoon; (iv) timpani or kettle drum.**

Bonus Round

1. **The Football Association (F.A.).**
2. *Nil by Mouth.*
3. **Thomas Love Peacock.**
4. **Duck.**
5. **Zero Mostel.**
   (And of course the connection was NOTHING.)

Tie-Break

'Money doesn't make you happy,' says Arnold Schwarzenegger. 'I now have $50 million but I was just as happy when I had $48 million.'

Round Three: Overlaps

1. **No.** (George d 1848, Robert b 1850.)
2. **No.** (George d 1880, Thomas Stearnes b 1888.)

3. **Yes.** (Thomas d 1928, Oliver b 1892.)

4. **No.** (Ramsay d 1937, Ronald b 1963. Ronald's birth date = his first appearance in an advert.)

5. **Yes.** (Baden d 1941, Colin b 1937.)

6. **Yes.** (Henry d 1947, Harrison b 1942.)

7. **Yes.** (George Bernard d 1950, Sandie b 1947.)

8. **No.** (Eric, a.k.a. George Orwell, d 1950, Tony b 1953.)

9. **No.** (Stevie d 1971, Zadie b 1975.)

10. **Yes.** (Tennessee d 1983, Robbie b 1974.)

Round Four

1. **They inspired Beatles songs.**
   ('She's Leaving Home', 'She Came In Through The Bathroom Window' and 'Lucy in the Sky with Diamonds'.)

2. **Denmark and Norway.**

3. **Vegetarians.**
   (Pythagoras and his followers abstained from meat in the 6th century for nutritional and ethical reasons.)

4. **'Happy Birthday to You'.**
   (They were schoolteachers, and the song was originally intended as a classroom greeting at the beginning of the school day.)

5. **Coventry.**
   (As in being 'sent to Coventry'. The city was fiercely pro-Parliament, and the residents were unusually hostile to Royalists.)

6. **Change sex.**
   (After surgery, he re-emerged as Christine Jorgenson.)

7. **Michael Knight.**

8. **The Young Ones.**
   (Their hit with Cliff Richard was *Living Doll*.)

9. **Sydney, Australia.**

10. **Because she is dead.**
    (Lynched after murdering a man who did her wrong.)

ANSWERS TO QUIZ TWENTY-NINE

Round One

1. **Gifts received by Tony Blair.**
   (And declared by him, all in 2003. He kept none of them. He can keep gifts of up to £140 in value. Anything more expensive, he must pay the difference.)

2. **Apples.**
   (Around 2,000 varieties are grown in Britain; only a tiny minority ever reach the shops. Golden Knob comes from Somerset, the other two from Kent.)

3. **What Would Jesus Do?**

4. **Dunkirk/Dunkerque.**

5. **15th century (1400s).**

6. **Cycling.**

7. **Franz Liszt.**

8. **The Pope.**

9. **Tetrahedra.**
   (Accept 'regular pyramids', but not 'pyramids', which geometrically isn't a precise enough term.)

10. **(i) Veet; (ii) Maestro; (iii) Cesar; (iv) Energizer; (v) Raider.**
    (Switch is gradually being phased out and will be gone by June 2007. In Germany the Raider/Twix name change was greeted with widespread contempt. The slogan used – 'Raider is now called Twix . . . nothing else changes' – has become shorthand for any pathetic corporate attempt to make a product look cool and modern by changing its name.)

Round Two

1. No holds barred.
2. Oliver Cromwell's head.
   (It stayed on the spike for 24 years.)
3. It was all a dream (gets you 1 point). Specifically, it was Pam Ewing's dream (gets you both points).
4. He had 10,000 men. He marched them up to the top of the hill (1 point) and he marched them down again (1 point).
5. Biogeography.
6. Blue Streak.
7. John Betjeman.
8. Hit the ball twice and timed out.
9. William Taft.
   (His tendency to fall asleep at random moments is now believed to have been a symptom of obstructive sleep apnoea, which itself was a consequence of his enormous girth. Taft was also the last US President to have a moustache.)
10. Highest: Tokyo. Lowest: London.
    (Tokyo 156 cm, New York 108 cm, Paris 64 cm, London 58 cm.)

Bonus Round

1. Bismillah.
2. Scaramouche.
3. Beelzebub.
4. Galileo.
   (He discovered Io, Europa and Callisto on January 7th, 1610, and Ganymede four nights later.)
5. Figaro.

Tie-Break

It lasts 5 minutes, 57 seconds.

(As timed on my CD player from Queen's *Greatest Hits*, so no arguments please. In 2005 the Iranian authorities finally allowed an album of Queen's songs to be released in their country, partly because they approved of the repeated use of the word 'Bismillah' in 'Bohemian Rhapsody'.)

Round Three

1. **Bayer Leverkusen.**

   (Not Bayern Munich. Heroin was originally sold as cough medicine. It was also once a Bayer trademark. For some reason the company let it lapse.)

2. **Newcastle-upon-Tyne.**

3. **His brother Mycroft.**

4. **Dizzy Gillespie.**

   (It was originally a gimmick to raise funds for Martin Luther King, but his fans were so keen on the idea, he decided to run with it. If elected, he had promised that the White House would be renamed the Blues House.)

5. **Two-toed sloth.**

6. **The word 'fuck'.**

   (The film was not approved for general release in Ireland until September 2000.)

7. **The Chrysler Building.**

   (The Empire State Building overtook it a year later. The Chrysler remains the tallest brick building in the world.)

8. **Elizabeth Taylor and Richard Burton got married.**

9. **Goliath.**

   (The Goliath frog lives in West Africa, can grow up to two feet long and can leap up to ten feet in a single bound. Unfortunately, after two or three of these jumps it is usually exhausted.)

10. **Standing up.**

   (He couldn't afford the price of a normal 6ft by 2 ft plot, so bought a 2ft by 2ft one instead.)

Round Four

1. **He founded IKEA.**
2. **Wolfie.**
3. **Sapiens.**

   (They are all species of the genus Homo. The first six are no longer with us.)

4. **Rio de Janeiro in Brazil.**
5. *Ghostbusters.*

   (Played by Dan Aykroyd, Harold Ramis and Bill Murray respectively.)

6. **King John.**
7. *A View to a Kill.*

   (Known in Hong Kong as *The Indestructible Iron Man Fights Against the Electronic Gang.*)

8. **The smear test.**

   (Also known as the Pap test.)

9. **Alderney.**
10. **Green.**

ANSWERS TO QUIZ THIRTY

Round One

1. MESSENGER.

   (Which is an acronym for **Me**rcury **S**urface, **S**pace **En**vironment, **Ge**ochemistry and **R**anging. No extra points for knowing this.)

2. Blood.

3. Zsa Zsa Gabor.

4. El Salvador.

5. Grand Central Station.

   (Real name: Grand Central Terminal. It is the largest train station in the world by number of platforms: forty-four.)

6. (i) Loganberry; (ii) ugli fruit.

7. Cabbage.

8. 101.

   (Bannockburn was on June 24th 1314, Agincourt on October 25th 1415. Even one year out gets no points.)

9. Francis Ford Coppola.

10. (i) Argon (Ar), selenium (Se), nickel (Ni), carbon (C). (ii) Calcium (Ca), rubidium (Rb), oxygen (O), nitrogen (N).

Round Two

1. 'Because it is there.'

2. Oysters.

3. Belfast's guns, now silent, have a 12.5-mile range, and to illustrate this, they are all trained on London Gateway services, which they could take out with a single volley.

   (Amazing but true.)

4. Queen Anne.

(She and Sarah Churchill were friends and confidantes, and these were their pet names for each other.)

5. Great bustard.

6. Paul McCartney.

(Holly's real surname was Holley, but it was misspelled on a contract he had to sign, so for professional purposes he became Holly. But 'Holley' was engraved on his headstone.)

7. Sit on it.

8. Hong Kong.

9. Ronald Reagan.

10. (i) A frog in the throat; (iii) to split hairs; (iii) a bone of contention.

(Literally, a cat in the throat, cut hairs in four, an apple of contention.)

Bonus Round

1. Adolf Hitler.

2. Leonard Rossiter.

(*Rising Damp* and *The Fall and Rise of Reginald Perrin*. And the Cinzano ads, during which he invariably spilled his drink over Joan Collins.)

3. Herbert Lom.

4. John Milton.

(The poem was 'Lycidas'.)

5. Julius Caesar.

(Usually quoted in Latin – *'alea iacta est'* – but according to Plutarch, Caesar actually said it in the original Greek.)

6. The real names of the five Marx brothers.

(Adolf – well, Adolph – was Harpo, Leonard was Chico, Herbert became Zeppo, Milton became Gummo and Julius was Groucho.)

Tie-Break

The route of the London Marathon is lined by 76 pubs.
(At last count).

Round Three

1. **A moustache.**
2. **China.**
   (It is either 13 or 14: the border with Pakistan falls in the disputed Kashmir province, which is claimed by India.)
3. **Two and seven.**
   (The 2-spot *adalia bipunctata*, and the 7-spot *coccinella septempunctata*. Around 40 ladybird species currently reside in the UK.)
4. **Albedo.**
   (Snow-covered ice has an albedo of about 80 per cent, dry sandy desert 37 per cent, a tropical rainforest 13 per cent.)
5. **Dooley Wilson.**
   ('Play it. Play "As Time Goes By".' Unfortunately he couldn't play the piano: he was a drummer. So someone else played piano behind a curtain, Wilson watched and copied his hand movements, sang the song and had a top twenty hit with it in 1977, twenty-four years after his death.)
6. **Beaumaris.**
   (Work began in 1295, and 400 masons and 2,000 labourers built it in three years.)
7. **'From Stettin on the Baltic to Trieste on the Adriatic . . .'**
8. **Straits (of water).**
9. **Paul Newman.**
10. *Gulliver's Travels.*

Round Four

1. Peter Duncan.
2. (i) cigarette cards; (ii) postcards; (iii) cheese labels.
   (If you specifically collected camembert cheese labels, you
   would be a tyrosemiophilist.)
3. Ramsay Street (in *Neighbours*).
4. Prince Michael and Prince Michael II.
   (Alternatively, Michael Joseph Jackson Jr and Michael Joseph
   Jackson III. The younger is also sometimes called 'Blanket',
   which doesn't bear thinking about.)
5. 6d.
6. Frank Sinatra.
   (And he wanted Mitzi Gaynor for Sugar.)
7. Lutetia: Paris. Lusitania: Portugal.
   (Lutetia was sometimes known as Lutetia Parisiorum. Lusitania
   also included the present-day Spanish provinces of Salamanca
   and Cáceres.)
8. Helium.
9. John Keats.
10. Canary Wharf.

ANSWERS TO QUIZ THIRTY-ONE

Round One

1. **Finland.**
   (It was the day before the IOC picked London for the 2012 Olympics. Chirac also said that 'the only thing the British have done for Europe's agriculture is mad cow disease.')
2. **'Matchstalk Men and Matchstalk Cats and Dogs'** (by Brian and Michael).
3. **D. H. Lawrence.**
   (The magistrate dismissed the charges on condition that the exhibition closed.)
4. **Red.**
   (White was narrowly second on 71 per cent, with blue third on 50 per cent.)
5. **'Who ate all the pies?'**
   (The Vegetarian Society adopted a variation, 'Who ate all the peas?', as a slogan. For some reason it didn't quite catch on.)
6. **Iain Macleod.**
7. **Belly buttons.**
8. **Sevenoaks.**
   (The trees lined the boundary of the Vines cricket ground. But the town wasn't named after those trees, which were only planted in 1902.)
9. **Taggart.**
   (Mark McManus died in 1994.)
10. **Uruguay** (1930), **Italy** (1934), **England** (1966), **West Germany** (1974), **Argentina** (1978), **France** (1998).

Round Two

1. Free school milk.
2. Grace Kelly.
3. As blood donors.
4. Laurel and Hardy.
   (With 'Trail of the Lonesome Pine'. The second posthumous duo were 2Pac & Notorious BIG, whose 'Runnin'' reached number 15 in July 1998, just a year after Notorious's demise.)
5. Dan Dare.
   (Chad Varah provided scriptwriting assistance, and Dan Dare 'Chaplain of the Future' became 'Pilot of the Future' sometime before issue 1.)
6. Dumbo.
7. Get married.
8. Milton Keynes.
   (Middleton was actually its original name, hundreds of years before.)
9. *Today*.
   (Launched March 1986, closed November 1995.)
10. Liza Minnelli.

Bonus Round

1. U Thant.
   (U is an honorific in Burmese, roughly equivalent to 'Mister'. Thant was his only name.)
2. P. G. Wodehouse.
3. *12 Angry Men*.
4. *Fifteen-to-One*.
   (Montague has subsequently published a quiz compendium, *The A-Z of Almost Everything*.)
5. 'Eighteen with a Bullet'.
   (The link is British cinema classifications: U, PG, 12, 15, 18.)

Tie-Break

The Comedy Of Errors, the shortest of Shakespeare's plays, has 1,770 lines.

(*Hamlet* has the most lines: 3,924.)

Round Three

1. Pac-Man.
2. Guy Fawkes.
3. The Tin Man in *The Wizard of Oz*.
   (He had actually recorded all his songs and been filming for a week, when he had his near-fatal allergic reaction to the dust.)
4. Martin Offiah.
   (Brian Bevan and Billy Boston, who reached 500 before him, are respectively Australian and Welsh.)
5. Howard Hughes.
   (Houston later renamed its other airport after George Bush Sr, also very much alive at the time.)
6. *The Rainbow*.
7. John Selwyn Gummer.
   (The daughter, Cordelia, is now in her twenties.)
8. Louisiana and South Carolina.
9. Lord Snooty.
   (He was revived briefly in 2005, going hip-hop as 'Snoot Doggy-Dogg'.)
10. *Sleepy Hollow*. (Tag-line: 'Heads will roll.')

Round Four

1. Barry Goldwater.
2. 'She sells seashells by the seashore.'

3. **Aliases used by Marty McFly in the *Back to the Future* films.**
(In the French version he is Pierre Cardin rather than Calvin Klein. Clint Eastwood was asked permission for his name to be used, and said yes.)

4. **Runnymede.**

5. **The wedding of Prince Edward and Sophie Rhys Jones.**

6. **K.**

7. **Bedford.**

8. **Thomas Alva Edison.**
(He suggested it as the way people should greet each other on the telephone. Alexander Graham Bell had preferred 'Ahoy'. Edison was also the first person, in an 1877 letter, to spell the word with an 'e'. 'Hullo' had previously been a slang term to express surprise, developed from 'Halloo', a call to hounds.)

9. **Cynthia Payne.**

10. **£1,000.**

ANSWERS TO QUIZ THIRTY-TWO

Round One: This and That

1. Sir Alan SUGAR and Sporty SPICE.
2. Conrad BLACK and Rabbi Lionel BLUE.
3. Titus SALT and *Sergeant PEPPER*.
4. BREAD and CIRCUSES.
5. FRED and GINGER.
6. CABBAGES and KINGS.
7. Charlie BUCKET and Sam SPADE.
   (From Roald Dahl's *Charlie and the Chocolate Factory*, and
   Dashiell Hammett's *The Maltese Falcon*.)
8. BONNIE and CLYDE.
   (The Beatles' first record was 'My Bonnie', backing Tony
   Sheridan. Clyde was the orang-utan who played opposite
   Clint Eastwood in *Every Which Way But Loose*.)
9. Rigobert SONG and Charles DANCE.
10. ROWAN and MARTIN.

Round Two

1. T. S. Eliot.
   (Hence *Old Possum's Book of Practical Cats*. The nickname was
   given to him by Ezra Pound.)
2. Claire.
   (In the profoundly disturbing song by Gilbert O'Sullivan,
   whose real name was Raymond. 'Nothing means more to me
   than hearing you say / "I'm going to marry you, will you marry
   me, Uncle Ray?"')

3. **Derby. To have a flat race for three-year-old fillies named after him.**

(Sir Charles's horse Diomed won the race the following year, collecting prize money of £1,065 15s.)

4. **Oman** (2 points). **Austria** (Österreich. 1 point).

5. **Gung ho.**

6. **They were written for the left hand only.**

(Wittgenstein had lost his right arm in World War I. He refused to play the Prokofiev concerto on the grounds that he didn't like it. A phrase about beggars and choosers springs to mind.)

7. **Smoking.**

(On his return to Spain, de Jerez frightened the locals who were amazed to see smoke coming out of his mouth and nose. The Inquisition duly decided he was possessed by the devil and imprisoned him for seven years. By the time he was released, the habit had caught on and everyone was smoking.)

8. **Spain; Poland and Ukraine.**

9. **They didn't drink any water.** (They drank whisky instead.)

10. **Dildo vagina.**

(Every team got this right, so Russell didn't have to read out the answer, to his considerable relief.)

Bonus Round

1. **Elder.**

(Pliny the Younger, his nephew, wrote an account of his death.)

2. **Elder.**

(Pitt the Younger was aged one at the time. But already Foreign Secretary.)

3. **Younger.**

4. **Elder.**

5. **Elder.**

Tie-Break

Gilbert received his knighthood twenty-four years after Sullivan got his.
(Sullivan 1883, Gilbert 1907. Sullivan was a favourite of Queen Victoria, hence getting his gong earlier. Poor old WS had to wait until she was dead. Nonetheless, he was the first playwright ever to be knighted for his plays alone.)

Round Three: Plagiarism

1. Niall Quinn.
2. Frog.
3. Laos.
4. 'Come Fly With Me'.
5. Foot and mouth epidemic.
6. Boyle's Law.
7. Gareth Hale.
8. *The Day of the Locust*.
9. The Darkness.
10. **Their elder brothers predeceased them before they could inherit.** (Henry, Arthur, Henry.)
    (So why plagiarism? Nothing to do with stealing other people's work, and a lot to do with the ten Plagues of Egypt. In order: the Nile turning to blood; frogs; lice (or fleas); flies; death of livestock by pestilence; boils; hail (intermixed with fire); locusts; darkness; and death of the firstborn.)

Round Four: Ages of Man

1. Three.
2. **Six.** (*Now We Are Six*.)
3. Eight.
4. **Sixteen.** ('I am sixteen, going on seventeen.')

5. Seventeen. ('She was just seventeen, you know what I mean.')

6. Nineteen.

7. Twenty. (The BLANK stands for 'nearly twenty-one years'.)

8. Twenty-two. ('I was twenty one-years when I wrote this song / I'm twenty-two now, but I won't be for long.')

9. Thirty-seven.

10. Sixty-four.

ANSWERS TO QUIZ THIRTY-THREE

Round One

1. **Michelle Smith.**
   (Later de Bruin. Her random drugs test was found to be contaminated with alcohol: she never tested positive for a banned substance.)
2. **A gimlet.**
3. **HMS** *Fighting Temeraire*.
4. **Trevor Horn.**
5. **Germany; Czech Republic.**
6. **From left to right.**
7. **Alf Roberts.**
8. **The Cross Keys.**
   (it's also the emblem of St Servatius, St Hippolytus, St Geneviève, St Petronilla, St Osyth, St Martha and St Germanus of Paris.)
9. **George V.** (In 1917.)
10. **(i) Franklin D. Roosevelt** (in his first inaugural address, March 4th 1933); **(ii) Ronald Reagan; (iii) George W. Bush** (before he was elected).

Round Two

1. **He wanted a cigarette, but the prison was non-smoking.**
2. **William Blake.**
3. **Lead.**
4. **17th century (1600s).**
   (Taj Mahal started 1632; Manchu dynasty founded 1636, took over China 1644; *The Compleat Angler* published 1653; Glencoe 1692.)
5. **Brixton.**
   (The Brixton Academy, the Windmill and the Fridge are all

music venues of one kind or another.)
6. **Elizabeth Taylor;** *Cleopatra.*
7. **Pascal.**
8. **Johnny Hallyday.**

    (He has sold more than 100 million records in France alone, and had thirty-three number ones.)
9. **Vladimir Smirnoff.**

    (Bring back *Saint And Greavsie.*)
10. **Jonathan Swift** (1667), **W. B. Yeats** (1865), **James Joyce** (1882), **Samuel Beckett** (1906), **Bob Geldof** (1951).

Bonus Round

1. The Spinning Mule.
2. Dr Martin Luther King.
3. The Duke of Wellington.
4. Flip-flop.
5. A stiletto heel.

    (The connection is footwear.)

Tie-Break

A female turkey incubates her eggs for twenty-eight days before they hatch.

(Same as a duck. For a pigeon it's 18 days, for a chicken it's 21 and ostriches take 42 days.)

Round Three

1. John Prescott.
2. Silage.

3. 1945.

4. Thebes.

5. Calypso; Steve Zissou.

(Bill Murray played the character in *The Life Aquatic with Steve Zissou*, which was dedicated to Jacques Cousteau. Harry Belafonte first came to fame singing calypso songs.)

6. RAF Northolt.

7. The (modern) toothbrush.

(Early toothbrushes had been used in China since the 1490s, but in Britain most people had cleaned their teeth with rags. In Newgate for provoking a riot, Addis experimented with small bones from the meat he had been served and bristles he acquired from his prison guard. After his release he went into business and swiftly made his fortune.)

8. The Netherlands.

9. Susan Sarandon.

10. (i) *NYPD Blue* (Dennis Franz 1993-2005); (ii) *T. J. Hooker* (Heather Locklear 1982-7); (iii) *Hill Street Blues* (Michael Conrad 1981-7); (iv) *CHiPs* (Erik Estrada 1977-83).

Round Four

1. Brookside. (On Channel 4's first night.)

2. St Peter. (They were the first three Popes.)

3. (i) Belarus; (ii) Armenia; (iii) Lithuania; (iv) Uzbekistan.

4. Aldo Moro.

5. Judi Dench.

6. The Official Monster Raving Loony Party.

(He was elected unopposed, and later became the town's mayor.)

7. Fencing.

(But accept snowboarding if they really push it.)

8. Thyroid gland.

9. **Antarctica.**

   (They are all the names of research stations.)

10. **Alan Ball.**

    (It is now.)

ANSWERS
TO THE
SNOWBALL

1. **Dad's Army.**
   (He played E. C. Egan, a ringer brought into a cricket match.)
2. *La Boutique Fantastique.*
   (Music by Respighi, based on Rossini's miniatures.)
3. **Eugene Cernan.**
   (In Apollo 17 in December 1972.)
4. **Paul Jones.**
   (Once singer with Manfred Mann, now Radio 2 DJ. Five envelopes opened; none answered correctly.)
5. **A marlin.**
6. **Frank Muir.**
   (The prize fund was now over £500, so a second question was asked for half the amount.)
7. **Peter Twiss.**
8. **They have all have been Rector of St Andrews University.**
   (Along with Learie Constantine, Rudyard Kipling, C. P. Snow, J. M. Barrie and, er, Nicholas Parsons.)
9. **Land's End** (in Cornish).
10. **Clarence Seedorf.**
    (Ajax in 1995, Real Madrid in 1998 and AC Milan in 2003.)
11. **Eleanor of Aquitaine.**
    (The pub was a bit quieter tonight.)
12. **Aerobatics.**
    (Accept 'flying model aircraft' as well.)
13. **Bishop Rock lighthouse.**
    (Built in 1858. Sir Cloudesley Shovell's squadron had been lost nearby.)
14. **He became the first man to be sent off in a Cup Final.**
    (CORRECT! It was Katherine Montague's second quiz at the Prince of Wales. She now turns up every week, for some strange reason.)
15. **Climb the Matterhorn.**
    (Some years later he published a book called *How to Use the Aneroid Barometer*.)

16. Dr Snuggles. (Only one envelope left.)

17. The siege of Sidney Street.

(On to the fourth envelope, for an eighth of the total fund.)

18. Michael Lynagh.

(Of Australia. Since then, Diego Dominguez of Italy and Andrew Mehrtens of NZ have also beaten Lynagh's total of 911 points.)

19. Erda.

20. The honey badger.

21. Bill Pitt.

(He won Croydon North West on October 22nd 1981.)

22. Chevy Chase.

(This question also turns up elsewhere in this book in a far friendlier form, and several people in the pub knew the answer straight away. But not the person answering the question.)

23. 4.25 inches (108 mm).

24. DNA (or genetic) fingerprinting.

25. The Baptists. (A third raffle ticket was drawn.)

26. Poland.

(Still no winner. The £500 threshold again approached.)

27. *The Admiral Graf Spee.*

(CORRECT! The third winner in four weeks, but this time the whole lot went. Tom S. is a member of a team who have been regulars since mid-2004 and have started setting the quiz regularly as well. If there is a second *Prince of Wales (Highgate) Quiz Book* they will be in it. His win was the most substantial yet.)

28. He bought bodies from Burke and Hare.

29. All have been *Time* magazine's Man (or Person) of the Year.

(Another one that crops up in a different form elsewhere in this book.)

30. Pasadena.

31. Aardvark. (Not, as many people put, aardwolf.)

32. **Selfridges**
   (CORRECT! Won by Peter of the Woans. Would he take his hat off to celebrate? He would not.)

33. **Charlie Chaplin.**

34. **Jemima Shore** (in the books by Antonia Fraser).

35. **Bees.**

36. **Ferdinand Magellan.**

37. **Bovington.**
   (No winners, and the prize fund was mounting up again. The following week more than £100 worth of tickets would be sold.)

38. **Rodney Bickerstaffe.** (On to the third envelope.)

39. **Noel Coward.**

40. **Alison Uttley.**
   (CORRECT! Patrick's daughter is eight years old and he scooped the jackpot, to no one's considerable surprise.)

41. **Pete Townshend, of The Who.**

42. **Alan Randall.**

43. **Sir Arthur Quiller-Couch.**

44. **Victor Spinetti.**

45. **Newcastle Utd.** (They won it in 1951 and 1952.)

46. **Rt Hon. Alan Williams MP**
   (He has served Swansea West for Labour since 1964.)

47. **She was Torvill and Dean's trainer.**

48. **Benazir Bhutto.** (She was Prime Minister of Pakistan.)

49. **Everton.**

50. **He's Tiger Woods' caddy.**

51. **Russell Crowe.**
   (His cousins are Martin and Jeff Crowe, New Zealand cricketers.)

52. **Felixstowe.**
   (They were successfully fought off and withdrew the same night.)

53. **Mothercare.**

54. Bretton Woods, New Hampshire.

(This was the foundation of the International Monetary Fund and the World Bank. On to the third envelope.)

55. Rt Hon. James Hacker MP.

(In *Yes, Minister* and *Yes, Prime Minister*.)

56. John Moffat.

(CORRECT! It was David Burnage's second win of the year, and he was the only person in the pub who knew it.)

57. Clive Cussler.

(In *Raise the Titanic* and other books. This week, as an experiment, Chris brought along five envelopes and was prepared to open each one to get a winner.)

58. Dame Stella Rimington.

(Who apparently lives just around the corner from the pub.)

59. Alabama 3.

60. They are used in the making of the explosive cordite.

61. The BAFTA.

(CORRECT! David Burnage knew it, and won £500. This was the second highest win yet: someone else had picked up £544 in January 2003. It still left £608 in the kitty for the following week.)

62. Oxford United.

(He also briefly managed Peterborough United in 1989/90.)

63. *Billy Liar*. (By Keith Waterhouse.)

64. Hannah Hauxwell.

65. Kevin Keegan.

66. Chichester.

67. Lady Godiva.

68. Son of Sam.

69. They are the names of the Woolwich Ferries.

(We were over £500 again, so Chris pulled out another raffle ticket, for half of the kitty.)

70. Edinburgh Castle.

(CORRECT! A semi-regular called Noel, from a team of hardened quizzers, knew this, which Chris later admitted was 'the easy one'. It left £627 in the kitty.)

71. Kenya.

72. REO Speedwagon.

(The hit was 'Keep On Lovin' You'. 'REO' stands for the truck company's founder Ransom Eli Olds, who also founded Oldsmobile.)

73. Sir Archibald MacIndoe.

74. Barbara and Jenna.

 75 Charles Manson.

(It's the 'hidden track' at the end.)

76. Liechtenstein.

77. Nelson.

(One more envelope to go, for a sixteenth of the total.)

78. The Comoros Islands.

79. Sir Cloudesley Shovell.

(He swam ashore, only to be murdered for a ring he wore. He is the man after whom pubs called The Ship and Shovell are named. As none of the five questions had been answered corectly, we knew that the following week the prize fund would exceed £1000 for the first time. After long discussion, we agreed that the prize should be capped at £1000, and any money left over should go into the next winner's pot. As it happens more than a hundred tickets were sold the following week, and the full prize fund was £1108.)

80. Kelly Sotherton.

(Bronze in the Heptathlon.)

ACKNOWLEDGEMENTS

I would like to thank Russell Taylor, Chris Pollikett and David Burnage for their encouragement, suggestions, editorial judgement and, of course, questions; all the other contributors, Tom Bannatyne, Darrien Bold, Ali Goodyear, Peter Hall, Andrew 'A.J.' Leonard, Chris Millington, Matt Odwell, John Osmond, Simon O'Hagan, Patrick Routley, Pete Smith, Tara Spring, Ceili Williams for their very excellent quizzes, patience and willingness to be photographed without obvious disguise; present and former members of our team at the Prince of Wales, Stephen Arkell, George Clark, Richard Corden, Alan Doggett-Jones, David Jaques, Sally Ann Fitt, Terence Russoff; Karen Taylor and Sophie Baker for taking the photos and Suzette Field for photoshopping them; Mitchell Symons and Kate Saunders for wise counsel; Patrick Walsh for agenting beyond the call of percentage; Richard Atkinson for buying it and Nick Davies for taking it on; everyone who has worked in and/or run the Prince of Wales, including Tanja, Charlie, Fergus, Blake and now Jonathan and Sarah; Chris and Fiona Ely, who now own the pub and let me put its name to this book; and to the blond(e)s at home, Paula, Martha and James, for everything as usual.